John Rutherford Shortland

The Persecutions Of Annam: a history of Christianity in Cochin China and Tonking

John Rutherford Shortland

The Persecutions Of Annam: a history of Christianity in Cochin China and Tonking

ISBN/EAN: 9783741163883

Manufactured in Europe, USA, Canada, Australia, Japa

Cover: Foto ©Lupo / pixelio.de

Manufactured and distributed by brebook publishing software (www.brebook.com)

John Rutherford Shortland

The Persecutions Of Annam: a history of Christianity in Cochin China and Tonking

LONDON:
ROBSON AND SONS, PRINTERS, PANCRAS ROAD, N.W.

TO

THE VERY REV. JOHN HENRY NEWMAN, D.D.
FATHER SUPERIOR OF THE ORATORY, BIRMINGHAM.

MY DEAR DR. NEWMAN,

The privilege you have allowed me of dedicating this book to you is one that I highly value. In many ways I owe you more than I owe to any one else, and an expression of grateful feeling is to me most pleasant. It was my most happy lot to be at Oxford when you were there, and you did for me what you were doing for so many others— removed the veil of prejudice which quite shut out from view the Church of all nations, and made me capable of seeing her as she really is. It was you, too, who in later years brought her before me in all her beauty and dignity, and taught me to recognise in her the great Teacher of God in the world.

This book is a record of the way in which that holy teaching is carried on in distant heathen lands, of the virtues, the successes, the sufferings of her missionaries. In dedicating it to you I do not simply satisfy my feelings, but I know that I am greatly benefitting myself by placing it under the sanction of your name.

With many thanks for long-continued kindnesses,

I am, my dear Dr. Newman,
Gratefully and affectionately yours,
JOHN R. CANON SHORTLAND.

PREFACE.

THE missionary work of the Catholic Church, grand and important as it is, is very little known. It is carried on in a great variety of countries in all quarters of the globe, and accounts of the proceedings of the missionaries are annually published and disseminated in the *Annals of the Propagation of the Faith*. But, mixed up as these details are, it requires no little time and labour to draw out a connected history of what is done in any one place or country. And yet, when the labour is undertaken it meets with ample reward; and as we contemplate the virtues of these missionaries, their love of souls, their patience, their faith, their activity and endurance, the wish arises to bring them out of their obscurity, and to place them in the view of others who may profit by their example.

The country that I have chosen, in order to furnish examples of this kind, is one that for centuries has been shut out from European intercourse, and into the interior of which the only strangers who have penetrated have been the Catholic missionaries, who have done so at the risk of their lives. The work that they have accomplished has been very extensive, and has been going on for as much as two hundred and fifty years; and it has cost them an amount of privation and suffering that will strike with wonder such as have learnt nothing of it before. It has, however, in our own times been talked of, and occasionally news has been brought of havoc and destruction which, while it has shocked the hearers, has been very imperfectly understood.

All that has been here narrated rests on the authority of the missionaries themselves. The chief sources of information have been the *Annals of the Propagation of the Faith* and the *Lettres Edifiantes*, which preceded them. Use also has been made of some special accounts drawn up by particular missionaries, FF. Borri, Alexander of Rhodes, and Tissanier, respecting the earlier times, and of some lives of the more eminent missionaries that have been published. A great portion of what has been told, as will be seen, is simply a translation of original letters, of which the names of the writers are given, and in the translations, although some freedom has been allowed, great care has been taken not to infringe on the sense of the authors.

Besides the making known the wonderful and instructive events which have passed in these remote countries, and which have drawn so little attention, a further object of the present publication is to excite a sympathy for that great Association for the Propagation of the Faith which has been and is the instrument of providing funds for the missionaries. It is a work in which all ought to have sympathy, and the expression of sympathy which is asked is so easy, that none could refuse it who have any sympathy at all. One halfpenny a week, with a daily short prayer, is the full demand. More may be given by those who please, but this is enough. And yet how small is the number of those who hear the request that have been led to do even this!

One country, and one country alone, France, seems to have really recognised and carried out this high duty. She gives, and she gives freely, her sons and her alms. And so here, as in other missionary records, the prominent actors are French bishops and French priests.

In France large sums are collected in the various dioceses; in France there is created in the minds of the young an enthusiasm for missionary work which urges them to leave homes and friends and the comforts of life, that they may go away to hard labour and much suffering and the prospect of an early death; in France there is the school where these missionaries are trained and formed, where they hear read the records of their predecessors, where they see around them their relics, the instruments of their torture, the chains they have worn, prompting them, stimulating them, bracing them with the resolution that makes them confessors and martyrs in their turn.

If our own missionary work is mostly to be done in

England, if we are ourselves (as we are) recipients of missionary bounty, the more reason is there that the small pecuniary aid which is individually asked should be more generally extended. And certainly when one contemplates the grand objects on which this money is bestowed, the vast result which these contributions produce, the disasters which they remedy, the sorrows which they remove, the multiplicity of good which they effect, it can be given with a satisfaction and a pleasure that brings its reward at once; and many a one will not be content with the donation of the small trifle that is asked, but will give with a liberality more suited to the object itself.

I might add a third purpose which has really been in my mind. The missionary work of the Church is one of the great proofs of her own mission. The Catholic Church, the Church of all nations, must be doing, must show herself able to do what her name indicates. I confine myself to a single country; there is a long list of others that might be produced. Is it not a glorious work that is here seen to be done? Do not these men look like successors of the Apostles? Have they not a true love of Christ? Have they not a true love of souls? How grand and noble are some of the figures!—the Bishop of Adran or Monsignor Borie. How simple and earnest, how detached from the world, how full of faith are others!—the humble priest F. Royer, or the self-denying Monsignor Piguel, or that holy Bishop Guérard, whose letters portray his piety and his zeal. How touchingly beautiful is devotion like that of M. Venard, inflamed with a love of suffering for Christ, that never wavers in its constancy, or is appalled by the sight of danger! And then look at the Christians that have grown up in these countries—the crown of the missionary labours; see their warm piety, their intelligent faith, their dauntless courage; see the immensity of the woes they have borne in proof of their fidelity. Thousands and hundreds of thousands have been converted to the faith; and hundreds and thousands have died rather than be false to it.

CONTENTS.

CHAP.		PAGE
I.	INTRODUCTORY	1
II.	FIRST MISSIONARY WORK AND EARLIEST PERSECUTIONS	5
III.	THE BISHOP OF ADRAN	28
IV.	MISSIONARY WORK	66
V.	FIRST MISSIONARY WORK IN TONKING	72
VI.	M. LA PAVEC	90
VII.	M. GUÉRARD	106
VIII.	DISAPPOINTMENTS IN THE REIGN OF GIA-LAONG	132
IX.	MINH-MENH'S PERSECUTION	151
X.	THE DUNGEONS OF HUÈ	207
XI.	BISHOP RETORT	263
XII.	THE SPANISH DOMINICANS	314
XIII.	COCHIN CHINA DURING THE PERSECUTION	327
XIV.	PERSECUTION IN TONKING	367
XV.	A RETROSPECT OF THE PERSECUTION	420
XVI.	CONCLUSION	425

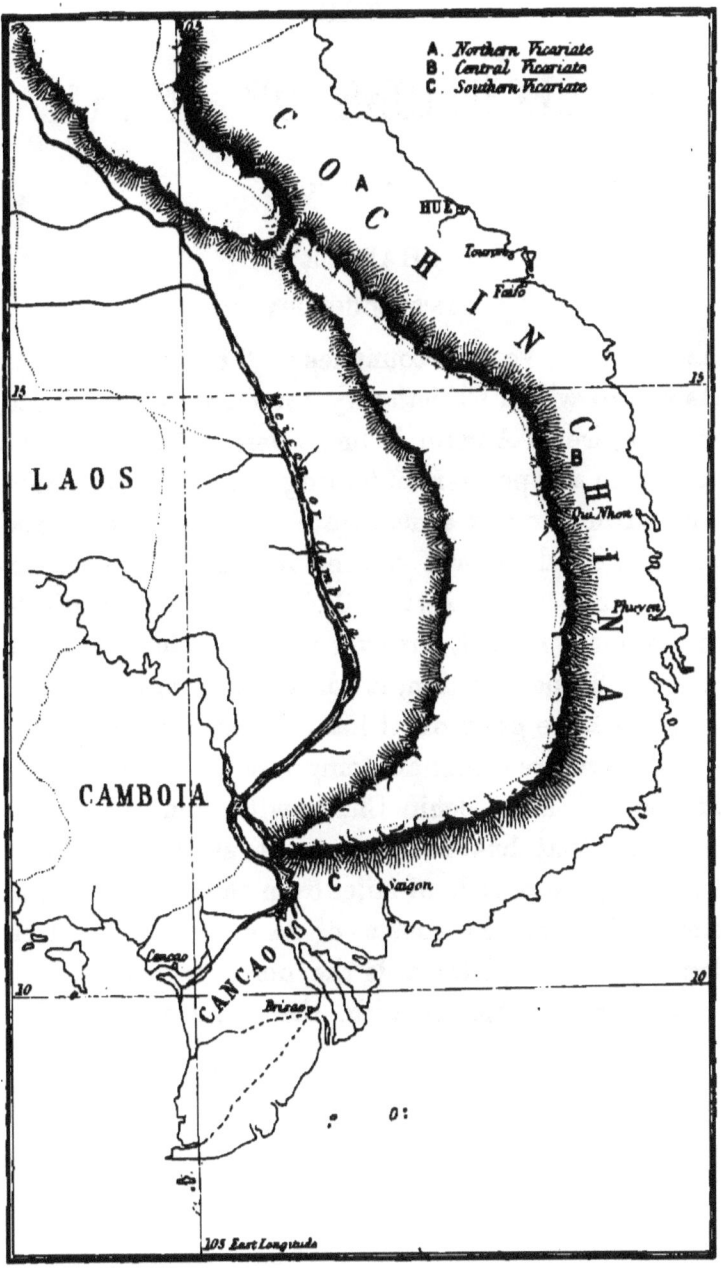

THE PERSECUTIONS OF ANNAM.

CHAPTER I.

INTRODUCTORY.

AMONGST the various countries on the extreme east of Asia into which Christianity has forced an entrance, the empire of Annam is one where it has secured a most firm and permanent footing. But it has not done this without many a desperate struggle. Again and again the rulers have treated it with a savage violence, and have exerted their utmost strength to exterminate it; but, however violent or however prolonged the persecution, it has always survived, and, as years have gone on, it has still multiplied.

The empire of Annam comprises the two countries of Tonking and Cochin China, with some adjoining territory that has been annexed, stretching down for several hundreds of miles from the south of China along the eastern coasts of Asia; in the portion forming Tonking, towards the north, spreading into some considerable breadth, then in Cochin China tapering away into a narrowness of even less than a hundred miles, till in the extreme south, where it has been increased by conquests from Camboia, the width is again enlarged.

Cochin China and Tonking from a very remote period have formed a single kingdom, and for some centuries the supreme title was maintained in regular succession in the old regal line. But, though the title was retained, the authority was eventually lost. Both in Tonking and in Cochin China this had been usurped by ambitious ministers, and so completely that it passed on from father to son in as secure and regular a manner as if they had been the real kings. Such was the state of things when the missionaries first entered the country. To them Cochin China and Tonking were two separate kingdoms; for though the old Voua, as he was called, slumbered on in Tonking, occupied his palace, and retained certain emblems of his ancestral dignity, the whole power rested with the two Chouas, who ruled with an equal independence, as if they did not in name acknowledge a superior. But towards the end of the last century a series of revolutions occurred, which resulted in the establishment of the present line of rulers, and in the concentration in their hands of the authority over both countries.

The present rulers are descendants of the Chouas or kings of Cochin China. In the year 1765 the king, Vu-Vuong, died, and out of affection for a favourite concubine he put aside the legitimate heir, and set up in his place a young boy unfitted to govern.

This was the cause of dissatisfaction and of civil disturbances. There sprang up war between the brothers, and this gave opportunity for the entrance on the scene of a new claimant, who was able to use the occasion for his own advantage. He was a bold adventurer, named Nhac, who, at the head of a hardy body of followers, the famous Taysons, came down from the mountains, and, seeming at first to side with one of the brothers, soon made his way to the front, and seized the kingdom for himself. All fell before him, and he became the acknowledged ruler, assuming the title of emperor.

But he did not stop here. He fell upon Tonking also, and with an ease and rapidity quite unexpected reduced it even more completely than he had conquered Cochin China; for in Cochin China resistance was not quite at an end. In the wars, the two brothers who had contended for the government had both perished, but there survived a son of the elder brother; and he, although with a scanty following, and in a corner of the kingdom, still asserted his rights. Gradually he gathered strength, and pushed his way on further and further, till Nhac, aroused by these successes, came down upon him with renewed vigour, and appeared to have crushed him. The unfortunate young prince was driven out altogether, and for a time his situation was most forlorn and desperate. From the beginning he had had one friend, who had stood by him and proved most useful to him. He had given him shelter when he had no home; he had consoled him, advised him, and sustained his courage. He had helped to rally around him the followers to whom he had owed his first successes, and now in his fresh sorrows his friendship proved no less valuable. This friend was a Christian, a Christian bishop, the Bishop of Adran, a name long renowned in this country, the name of one with whom the fortunes of this young prince were long and intimately connected. But more of him by and by.

CHAPTER II.

FIRST MISSIONARY WORK AND EARLIEST PERSECUTIONS.

It was not long after the Chouas of Cochin China set up for themselves that Christianity made its way into the country. Portuguese traders had before brought some slight knowledge of it, but it was not till the Jesuit father, Francis Buzomi, came over from Macao that any real impression was made. This was in 1615. His preaching presently drew attention, and several converts—one of them a rich female, whom they name Johanna—were the result. The king, the son of the first independent Choua, was favourable, and threw no obstacle in the way of the missionaries. But still the work was soon stopped by the jealousy and hostility of the pagan priests. They began to murmur against the new worship, and to cry out that the gods were angry; and they used the opportunity of a dearth to stir up a flame of indignation which the king could not withstand. The missionaries were ordered away, and would have gone had not contrary winds detained them. It was when he was in sickness and poverty that F. Buzomi drew towards himself the notice of a new friend, the great governor of Pulo-cambi, who having come up to the capital, and chanced to see the missionary, viewed him with an extreme interest and affection. He took him back with him to

Pulo-cambi, which is the country in the vicinity of Quin-hon, treating him with great honour, and delighting to pour out on him the proofs of his high admiration and love. He urged his subjects to listen to the preaching of the father, and made them sensible that nothing would please him more than that they should embrace the religion he taught. One of the governor's first works was to build them a church, and there is something so quaint in the account of the missionary respecting this proceeding, that we will give it in his own words. 'Turning to us,' says F. Borri, a companion of F. Buzomi, 'the governor again desired that we would determine a place for the church, that he might give orders for setting it up. We showed him a place that seemed convenient enough, and he, approving it, went away to his palace. Before three days were over news was brought us that the church was coming; we went out with great joy, and no less curiosity, to see how a church should come; for though we knew it was to be made of wood, as had been agreed, yet it could not be other than a great pile standing on ample pillars. On a sudden, in the field we saw above a thousand men, all loaded with materials for the fabric. Every pillar was carried by thirty lusty men; others carried the beams, others the planks, some the capitals, some the bases, one one thing, one another; and so all of them went in order to our house. . . . The architect came, and taking out a line, viewed the ground, marked out the distances, and calling those that carried the pillars, fixed them in their places. This done, he called for one part after another, that every man might render in what he brought, and go his way; and thus, all proceeding regularly, and every man labouring his best, all that great pile was set up in one day.'

This kind mandarin seemed never tired of the good offices he could do to the fathers, and whatever request they made to him he was forward to gratify. He came one day to their house, and, as a mark of honour, held a public audience in the court. Two criminals were sentenced to death. The fathers interceded for them, and he pardoned them. 'To these holy men,' said he, addressing the bystanders, 'I can refuse nothing. I am longing to get rid of the hindrances that prevent my being baptised, and receiving their holy faith. It is what you all ought to do, if you wish to please me.' And yet, notwithstanding these good dispositions, this mandarin died without baptism. He fell sick after a day's hunting, in which he got over-heated, and in three days he was dead. The fathers visited him, and proposed baptism; but he was not aware of his danger, and delayed it, and it was too late.

Soon after, when the fathers were suffering from the loss of this friend, help reached them from another quarter. One day there was seen at the door of their house a grand cavalcade—elephants, numerous attendants, with a female of high rank, the wife of the ambassador to the King of Camboia. She had come to ask the fathers to baptise her. She had heard some of the truths of the Christian religion, and they had moved her greatly, especially the ideas of heaven and hell, and she had a great fear that she might die and be lost. The fathers kept her under instruction, and quickly prepared her. And when she began to know 'Jesus Christ, true God made man, and humbled for the sake of man,' her heart was more moved than ever. Then she tried to imitate something of that humility which so touched her; so when she visited the fathers to hear their lessons she ceased to come in her first grand state, mounted on an elephant, but she walked with naked feet through dirt and over stones, obliging her attendants to do the same, though the distance was considerable.

Her husband, too, followed her example. He paused a moment when he heard that he must give up his many wives, but he made the sacrifice, and, as the missionary tells the story, the simple honesty and resolute will of the man are conspicuous.*

Another convert to be noticed is a pagan priest. What won over this man was the doctrine of our Lord's resurrection. His residence was near the missionaries', and he frequently conversed with them. What they told him made him more curious, and more eager for instruction. And when he heard of our Lord's resurrection, and that He rose that we might all rise with Him at the last day, he was exceedingly touched. He eagerly asked for baptism, and he and all his family were baptised. The man was full of devotion. He was on his knees all night,

* All this is taken from Father Borri, a missionary of the time.

First Missionary Work.

repeating over and over again the words, 'Tuii ciam biet,'—'I knew you not;' or, as the good father interprets it, 'Forgive me, my God, for till now I never knew You.' 'This man,' adds F. Borri, 'had but one wife, and had lived about thirty years, which was his age, so strictly up to the law of nature, that he had never, as he said, up to that time knowingly deviated in any matter of consequence from what was just and upright; and his adoring idols was because he thought it contrary to reason not to adore them. He is a proof of what divines say, that God never fails to have baptism administered, either by the hands of men or angels, to a heathen who lives a moral life, according to the dictates of reason and the law of nature.'

In 1639 F. Buzomi died, and his work was taken up by that great missionary of these parts, Alexander of Rhodes. Conversions proceeded rapidly; from twelve to fifteen hundred every year. By the middle of the century there were fifty thousand Christians, and before it had closed they had risen to eighty thousand. There were frequent persecutions, and several martyrs. The first martyr was the catechist Andrew, a young man only nineteen, but full of fervour and resolution. Alexander of Rhodes was by his side at his execution. He died 1644; and the next year two other catechists, Ignatius and Vincent. In 1661 there was a more serious persecution, and it continued some years. It was in the reign of Hien-Vuong. Peter Dang was one of the martyrs of this date. He was a soldier, and with three companions was led up before the king to receive sentence. The others were greatly terrified, but Peter had no fear at all. 'Prince,' said he to the king, 'I am, in the first place, the subject and servant of the King who is supreme Lord of heaven and earth, and, after that, I am your majesty's.' The king at first did not seem to notice what he said, and he repeated it; when the king, much enraged, exclaimed, 'I am supreme in my own kingdom, and govern it as I please; and I depend not on any Lord of heaven and earth.' And Peter was ordered out to execution.

In 1665 the king gave the order that all the Christians should be forced to trample on the cross, and that those who refused should lose their heads or be thrown to the elephants. There were in prison some Christians, who were now brought out to make their final choice, and when asked to trample on the cross, 'No!' they exclaimed; 'our resolution is unchanged; gladly do we offer our lives to God, and if we had a thousand we would do so.' Amongst these martyrs were two brothers, Raphael and Stephen, one sixteen, the other only twelve, and none were more forward in offering their lives. Raphael, speaking for himself and his little brother, said, 'We are orphans, and we beg of you to send us to heaven, where our Father is.' 'Who is your father?' asked one of the judges. 'God,' he replied, 'the Lord and Creator of heaven and earth.' Another of these martyrs was a young girl named Jane. She had come herself, full of enthusiasm, and acknowledged herself a Christian, and asked to die for her faith. Driven back, she returned, and, refusing to profane the sacred image, was added to the company. They were twelve in number, full of joy and courage. With equal fortitude they laid down their necks for the sword or faced the elephants. Jane, Raphael, and Stephen were chosen out for the latter fate. It was thought that they would never dare to stand up before the formidable beasts. But they did not shrink. While they stood waiting, a young girl named Lucy rushed in, and threw herself at the feet of Raphael to kiss them. The boy, thinking that she wished to turn him from his purpose, said, 'Grieve not, my sister; we are going to heaven;' and little Stephen, turning to those around, added, 'We are glad to suffer; it is for the faith we love. We wish to go to our Father in heaven.' The boys suffered last. They saw their companions despatched by the great beasts, but they were not frightened. They made the sign of the cross, and presently they too were trampled under the feet of the elephants.

Lucy was the daughter of Peter Ki, who had died for his religion shortly before. He was a mandarin of rank, but degraded to a common soldier on account of his being Christian, for which he in the end forfeited his life. Lucy was full of his spirit, and wished also to be a martyr. A little while after, she stood by when four more bold confessors were witnessing for their faith. The mandarin reproached them for leaving the religion of their country to embrace that of the Portuguese, and Thomas, one of the party, defended himself. 'It is not the religion of the Portuguese,' he said, 'nor of any one nation, but the law which the Lord of heaven and earth has given to the whole world. Just as the sun which shines on Cochin China is not the sun of this kingdom alone, but is equally the sun of other countries, so the religion of the Portuguese, being a religion coming from God, is not a religion for them only, but for the whole world also.' A proof of which was seen, he said, in the fact that it was not only the Portuguese who brought it to them, but Italians and French, and also Japanese. 'It has too,' he added, 'the stamp of truth and holiness; so that there are no people, however little reason they may have, that will not, when they consider it, find it easy to embrace, because it promises happiness here on earth from the regulation of our passions, and it leads to eternal happiness, which cannot otherwise be attained.' Thomas was a man of rank, and was dressed in a rich silk dress. The mandarin, angry at his bold profession of faith, ordered it to be stripped off. But Thomas was no way displeased; he thought himself more like his divine Master, who in the hour of His Passion had His garments torn off too. Lucy was standing by, and heard and saw all this, and, her heart moved with a holy zeal, she could no longer restrain herself; she went up to the seat of the judges, and said, 'I am the daughter of Peter Ki, whom the king put to death for being a Christian; I sigh for a like happiness; but because I was so young the mandarins refused to stain their swords with my blood. Now I am come with this other woman' (for

First Missionary Work.

she was not alone) 'to ask you to give us up to the elephants, that we may come the more quickly to the joys prepared for us in heaven.' The judges were surprised and angry at boldness like this. They ordered her to be led off with the rest to punishment, and before the elephants she was as fearless as she had been before the judges. Twice the elephant had to be driven towards her; first he maimed her with his tusk, then taking her in his trunk, he tossed her in the air, and the fall killed her.

But of all the early persecutions there was none that equalled the severity of that which arose at the end of this century, in the reign of Minh-Vuong. Before that, there had been an interval of rest, and this king's father had been particularly indulgent. Cochin China had also, during this season, been formed into a separate vicariate, and had its own bishop, and several French priests, in addition to the Jesuit missionaries. Minh-Vuong, from the beginning of his reign, had viewed the Christians and the missionaries with jealousy, and had come to the resolution of putting them down. He was restrained for a time by his high regard for F. Arnedo, who was a skilled mathematician, and was useful to him. But in 1698 he became an open enemy, and commenced a most vigorous persecution. All the missionaries that he could get into his hand were thrown into prison, and F. Arnedo amongst them. Five missionaries were in prison in the capital. The Christians were required to renounce their religion, and, in sign of it, to put their foot on the cross. Death was the alternative, and the mode of death that he selected was starvation. We have a minute and interesting account of some of the acts of the martyrs of the time drawn up by the missionaries, and some of the circumstances shall be here narrated. There was in prison with the missionaries a numerous body of captives, such as had stood firm under their first trial, and had refused to profane the honoured emblem of their salvation. These, with the missionaries, were one day led out before the king, sitting in state, to hear from his mouth their sentence. They came before him as culprits, with cangues on their necks and irons on their feet; by the side of each was a soldier with a drawn sword. It was taken for granted that the missionaries would not renounce their faith, and they were not asked, but the rest were told that if they would not do so they should die. There were thirty-seven in all, and half of them now failed. The others boldly insisted that they would rather die than abandon the religion of Jesus Christ. But the king would not then take their answer; he sent them all back to prison, to consider it more at leisure, and required that it should be given in writing. Four days later they were again summoned, but then there was a melancholy change. Seven out of all the number were now alone firm; the rest consented to submit themselves to the will of the king. But these seven were really full of an heroic spirit. Three of them were women, earnest as any, eager to make the sacrifice of their lives; but this was denied them: they were let off with a beating, and the mutilation of their fingers and ears; and one who through favour escaped this infliction thought herself unfortunate. But the four men died. They had to go through the painful horrors of starvation. Shut up in a small island, they lingered on for days. They could see water all around, and it was water they wanted, for they were tormented with thirst. Their guard asked them to drink, but they knew they could not do so unless they would first tread upon the cross. In their agony they threw themselves on the ground, digging into it with their hands in search of moisture. But they never faltered in their constancy. One after the other, as weakness overcame them, they yielded up their lives, the last surviving to the eighteenth day. The island was close to the capital, and the sufferers were the objects of great interest. Crowds went out to see them, pagans as well as Christians, wondering at, and instructed by their words and example.

It was a terrible ordeal, and all were not able to pass through it like these noble martyrs. There was one, a catechist, who showed himself very resolute for a long time, but who failed when he was put to this proof. For many days he submitted to the intolerable pains, but at length he could bear them no longer. When for eleven days he had been without meat or drink, his craving for water became irresistible; he was maddened by the heats of his body; and to obtain relief put his foot on the cross. He was a pitiful sight in the extremity of his distress. ' He was so pale that he looked like a corpse. His eyes were languid and sunken in his head; his skin was dried up as if it had been in a fire; and the inward heats by which he had been consumed had been so excessive, that blood was issuing from his mouth, his nostrils, and his ears. His whole frame was altered and weakened, and he had become deaf.' Such is the description that has been given of him. But to gain relief he inflicted on himself a prolonged misery; he would look back with shame and sorrow on the act by which he forfeited the martyr's crown.

The story of Paul Kien is pathetic. This man was a soldier, the colonel of a regiment. He had distinguished himself in his own province for the resolute manner in which he withstood all solicitations to abandon his faith, and the king had him brought up before him in the capital. There, as he stood before Minh-Vuong in chains, the king thus appealed to him. 'Colonel,' he said, 'I do not choose that any of my subjects should be Christians. I have forbidden it by an edict that has been published throughout my kingdom. Of this you are aware, and have disobeyed, and that notwithstanding the favours you have received from me. You deserve death. You must, then, abandon this strange religion, or die. Make your choice.' 'Sire,' replied the officer with a generous freedom, 'there is nothing in which I would not obey your majesty except in a matter that concerns my conscience. In respect to the Christian religion only, I must go against your order; for I cannot relinquish it without disobeying the sovereign Lord of heaven and earth, and without losing for ever both body and soul. By a singular grace of the Lord of heaven I have received this religion from my parents. I must prefer it to everything, even to life, that I may not deprive myself of the eternal happiness promised by God to such as are faithful.' This firm reply was, in the ears of the courtiers who heard it, the excess of disloyalty; they were full of indignation, and asked to be allowed to avenge the affront by cutting the offender to pieces. But the king forbore, contenting himself with sending back Paul to his province, with the order that he should be put to death. But on his return home a fresh trial met him. His wife and children and friends came round him, and entreated him to obey the king's command. The general of the troops added his persuasions. All the misery that would fall upon his wife and family was pressed on his attention, and it was represented to him that it was not the resignation of his faith that was required, but simply the satisfying the king by some slight mark of submission. It was not necessary, they said, even to touch the sacred image. If he would only put out his foot, and seem to do so, it would be enough. And these importunities prevailed. This brave man, after his long resistance and his display of courage, in the end gave way. He put his foot on his Saviour's image, and though while he did so he protested that he did not mean to abandon his faith, yet thus he lost the crown of martyrdom which God had offered him. But he did not preserve his life. The king, when he heard what had been done, was not appeased. He was rather angry that the colonel had done at all what he had refused to do on his own demand, and he reiterated his order that he should die. He died a penitent, if not a martyr, with his eyes opened to see the folly as well as the sin of his act, resigned and firm, and loudly insisting that he died a Christian.

After some years the persecution relaxed; the missionaries who were not dead were let out of prison, and were not molested; but the jealous feelings of the king remained, and if he had not died he would have recommenced it. The two next kings were favourable, and there was a long calm. A specimen of the favour the missionaries attained at court is furnished in a letter of M. Siebert, who at the particular request of Vu-Vuong came over from Macao to the Cochin-Chinese capital. M. Siebert tells us the manner of his reception. 'From Nuoc-Man we sent a message to Sinoa (Huè), the capital of Cochin China, to inform the king of our arrival. There was general joy at the court, and the queen-mother, in her delight, said to the king, "For seven years your father was earnestly requesting the presence of this wonderful man, and without success, and now at the very beginning of your reign he has come." Soon we left Nuoc-Man for Sinoa, with a mandarin whom the king had sent to accompany us, and with marks of distinction that reflected honour on our religion. On my arrival at court, F. Emmanuel de Brito presented me to the king, who accosted me with great kindness, and made me a present of a Cochin-Chinese dress and a doctor's cap.

'There was an old custom in Cochin China requiring all who held office or rank at court to go and take an oath of fidelity to the king, invoking at the time some pagan deity. For this I was called before the king. At once, I openly declared that I could not take such an oath, for my conscience would not allow it; that I would rather resign my dignity, and my life too, than do a thing so offensive to God.

'The king was not at all displeased at what I said, but, turning to the officers and mandarins around him, said, "The master does not permit the Christians to take such oaths, and of course he cannot take it. For the future, we will not ask Europeans to take these oaths. The father need not be at all uneasy about it." Then the king told us an anecdote. He had threatened F. de Brito, some time before, he said, to have him thrown into the sea if he would not worship the idols of the country. And the father had said that he would rather die than deny his God. He had, next, made a like threat to a bonze if he would not become a Christian, and the latter had made no objection. "See," added the king, "how different those masters of Europe are from our own; how faithful and firm they are, while ours are weak and inconstant."

'Afterwards, the king put the question to me why the priests forbade such oaths to the Christians. "It is not the priests," I said, "but God Himself that forbids them." And I took occasion to explain to his majesty the commands of the Decalogue. When I came to the fourth commandment, the king stopped me, and turning to those about him, exclaimed, "Why, then, do you charge the Christians with refusing to give honour to their parents? You see that they teach just the reverse." "It is true," said a learned mandarin who was present, "that they permit honour to them while alive, but when they are dead they refuse it."

'I then took upon myself to answer this objection, and explained the Catholic doctrine about prayer for the dead. "It is true," I said in conclusion, "that we do not place food on the tombs of our dead parents; for of what use could it be to their bodies when they have become food for worms? And which of you ever saw them taste of the delicate meats you offer them?" "That's not the thing," eagerly interposed one of the chief bonzes; "what they eat is the substance or essence; they leave the accidents." "Very substantial accidents," I said with a smile; "enough to intoxicate and fatten the bonzes who daily feed on them." And the whole court burst into laughter, to the discomfiture of the bonze. It seemed that these last words hit him hard, and that all were sensible that they did so. Then the king ended the discussion by saying, "Master, what you say is true."

'Afterwards the king inquired of me how our priests got the power of pardoning sins, which were offences against God. Then I explained to him the power of the keys in the Church, and my answer pleased him much. Then he wanted to know how many times a sinner could obtain pardon; and as I spoke of the boundless mercies of God, who is never tired of pardoning, the king appeared deeply moved, listening with attention and interest.'

'As to the number and condition of our Christians,' says this same missionary, 'many of them are nobles of rank. I could name two princes of the blood, brothers of the late king, who with all their families are converts; a councillor of state, who is also governor-general of the whole kingdom; the viceroy of Dinh-Cat; the general commanding the strong walls between Cochin China and Tonking; another general, two colonels, a dozen lieutenant-colonels, and a number of captains of repute, who are all personally known to me.'

M. Siebert was especially valued by the king on account of his mathematical knowledge and his medical skill. He was styled court mathematician and physician, and was made a mandarin of the first rank. But he died prematurely in 1745, only four years after his landing in Cochin China.

The religion was at that time advancing. There were five churches in Huè alone, and one of them in the inner city, where the king's palace was. We have a specimen of the virtues of the missionaries in F. John Grueber, whom M. Siebert speaks of in terms of high respect and praise. This father's great zeal was the cause of his early death. He was sick himself, but he undertook a long journey to visit a sick person who sent for him. He was in time to give him the last sacraments, but it cost him his own life. The fatigues of the journey were too much for him. His illness increased; he had an attack of dysentery, and fell under it. And his whole life had been in harmony with this last act. Once, when he was sick, he was being carried in a filet, the name given to a sort of hammock which they use in this country for a palanquin, to visit a dying person. One of the bearers became ill, and was unable to proceed; then the missionary got out, and made the man take his place, and assisted in carrying him to the place where he was going.

This father's manner was so agreeable that he was much loved. The Governor of Dong-Nay liked to converse with him, and often had him with him. At length, M. Grueber, seeing his visits resulted in no real good to the mandarin, spoke to him plainly and decisively,—telling him that, honoured as he felt himself by these visits, he dreaded their consequences, and that they would turn to his condemnation from the little fruits he drew from them. 'The conversations we have had together on religion,' he said, 'make you the more in fault, and you cannot now put down to ignorance your forgetfulness of your duties, or your delay in embracing Christianity.' And he told him he might justly fear some stroke of the divine justice. What followed gave meaning to his words. The mandarin was accused of some fault, and required to explain his conduct to the king. Troubled at the summons, he fell sick, and in his sickness sent for the missionary. M. Grueber went to him, and took with him some earth from the tomb of the B. John Nepomucene; and scarcely had the sick man touched the blessed earth, and made a vow to embrace the Christian religion, when he found himself recovered. He went to court, explained himself to the king, who was perfectly satisfied, and left him in his post.

Vu-Vuong was not always what he was when he so graciously received M. Siebert. The happy days of his early reign passed away, and he too became a persecutor. In the beginning of his reign Christianity had reached the climax of its successes. The number of bishops, and priests, and churches, quite surprises us when we contrast it with what we see in after years. There was a vicar-apostolic, and a coadjutor; there were twenty-seven European missionaries, and several native; there were three hundred churches, fifty of them spacious and handsome. The Christians had swelled into a large body, and, all of a sudden, down came a blow that blotted out the fair picture—destroyed the churches, drove away the missionaries, and deprived the Christians of their ministrations. Vu-Vuong had taken into favour a man who hated them, one Kai-An-Tin, and by him he was persuaded to adopt the old resolution of driving them out of his kingdom. He arrested all the missionaries, with one exception, F. Koffler, who was retained in his post of court physician. All the rest were banished—the two bishops, nine Jesuits, nine Franciscans, and nine other priests; they were put on board a vessel, and amidst the tears of the Christians, who flocked together in crowds to bid them their last farewell, were sent off to Macao. This was the worst stroke the Christians had received. They had rallied from the effects of previous persecutions; but from this one they did not rally. The Jesuit Order was broken up towards the close of the century. The stream of missionaries did not set in as it had done before. Vu-Vuong continued to shut out strangers resolutely, and it was only by stealth that they could find entrance. So it was that, after this, Christianity considerably declined. The number of Christians came down to scarcely more than forty thousand, with two little bands of labourers, one of them having their headquarters in Camboia, and the other in the neighbourhood of Huè. A Jesuit father or so lingered on for some years about Huè. F. Koffler did some missionary work, though quietly, and after him F. Loureiro. Then the care of the Christians here fell into the hands of the French missionaries. There were two that came out to Cochin China almost together, about the year 1776, M. Longer and M. La Bartette. Their names are names of note in these annals, for both of them for upwards of fifty years lived on in this country.

The vicars-apostolic of Cochin China, since the persecution of Vu-Vuong, had made Camboia their home. It was a safe harbour for them, for the ruler was still an independent monarch, and able to protect them. Thence, as they had opportunity, they issued out into Cochin China, passing on to the middle provinces, where the Christians were most numerous. One of these expeditions is referred to in a letter to Mgr. Piguel, the immediate predecessor of the Bishop of Adran; and the letter is valuable, as it not only supplies a testimony as to the sort of work then done, but it reveals to us the beauty of the character of one of those humble and ardent men who toiled on unknown in that distant country, with little record of their virtues or their deeds. 'Part of last year,' he says, 'I passed in Cochin China, and the Lord granted me abundant consolation. The crowds of Christians that kept flocking to me were so numerous, that when I had been two or three days at a village, which was all the stay I could make, there was not house-room for them. During this journey seven thousand persons were confirmed, and more than six hundred adults were admitted to baptism. As for confessions and communions, I could not count them. Pagans came asking for instruction and baptism. My health is now always bad, and not only casually as it used to be, and so I am unfit for much fatigue. A priest in my state in Europe would be dispensed from all heavy work. But, in whatever state I am, I must travel; sometimes I am in a boat, at others on horseback, most often I walk, and then I am at times deep in the water, or with naked feet struggling through the mud, and on occasions I must sleep in the open air; and all the while I am scarcely ever free from fever, or there is some other pain, as for instance asthma. I do not mention these things to complain; for, far from it, I esteem them precious graces of which I am not worthy, but I speak of them to make you understand how much need I have of help.' This letter of the Bishop is not the only insight we have into the graces of his character. There is another letter from a young French missionary, written just after he came into the country, who regarded him with hearty admiration. 'One who has never been out of Europe,' he says, 'would have difficulty in imagining the poverty and discomfort of this Bishop's dwelling. There is not a table or chair in the house. The Bishop, like every one else, sits on the ground. The covering of the house is of leaves, and these so scanty that they scarcely afford shade; and should it chance to rain when we are sitting at meals, we must move about to get a spot where the rain does not penetrate. His lordship had the condescension to go into his boat to rest, giving up his chamber to me. The walls were of leaves, as well as the roof, and they were so thinly spread, that with door and window closed light came in, and more wind too than one liked. The Bishop's wardrobe was no better than his dwelling. Counting over to him one day the things I thought I wanted for the college, I made a contrast between our scholars and those of Siam, who had plenty of everything, while ours had no more than three or four shirts and two or three handkerchiefs each. "What," said the Bishop, "two or three handkerchiefs! I have but one, this which you see here, and it is torn. Three or four shirts! I have only two, the one I have on, soiled with constant perspiration, and that other which is drying on the hedge. But think not," he went on, "that I am blaming this tenderness of yours towards these children. No. In this I am not behind you. They are no less dear to me than to you. It is my wish that, so far as our means allow, they should not be wanting in anything." And then he drew out a small purse, and put it in my hands, saying, "Here is all I have; had I more you should have it: what I retain is only what is sufficient for to-day's provisions." At such an instance of generosity I was greatly moved. I was most unwilling to take the money, and tried to return it. "You must not refuse," said the Bishop; "it is for your dear children, mine no less than yours. Do not fear that we shall want anything; have no concern; a poor missionary has always the never-failing treasury of Providence. It has never failed me."'

Mgr. Piguel had the title of Bishop of Canathe, and lived for ten years in Camboia. He commenced his episcopate about the time of the death of Vu-Vuong, when the severity towards the Christians relaxed. By the time he died the civil wars had commenced, the Taysons had become formidable, and, shortly after, they attained that supremacy which for so many years, to the exclusion of the family of Vu-Vuong, they were able to preserve.

CHAPTER III.

THE BISHOP OF ADRAN.

WE have some letters of M. Pigneux, which make us aware of the strong and ardent feelings with which he entered on his missionary life. The first is dated December 1765, and he excuses himself in it for having left his parents without informing them of his purpose. 'If,' says he, 'we are not now the slaves of the devil and in the darkness of idolatry, it is because apostolic men, moved by God's Holy Spirit, courageously left their country to bring us the light of the Gospel. They were not deterred by love or thought of parents, nor did their parents allow any natural feeling to frustrate the influences of grace. And now there are vast numbers of souls still in darkness, stretching out their hands, and crying to us to give them a share in the blessings we have. And we cannot as Christians, without being dead to every sentiment of faith, but feel an earnest longing to preach amongst them our holy religion. All should take part in this work; and if God has not chosen you as the instruments to succour these forlorn persons, you may at least rejoice in the knowledge that He has accepted the services of your son. For many years I have had a strong desire, urging me to go and labour for the salvation of those crowds of unhappy souls who are the victims of Satan and his delusions. I hope you will approve a design which agrees so well with what you feel yourselves, and that you will not refuse me your blessing. I did not wait to take leave of you, because I know my own weakness and the greatness of your love.'

He repeats these expressions in a second letter written a few days after. 'It cost me much,' he says, 'to go away without telling you of my purpose; but from the fear that you might oppose me, I thought myself bound to keep my plans secret, that I might not run the risk of the loss of my vocation. Now that I have started on my journey, I bless the Lord daily, and I ask you in your kindness to do the same. I know your sentiments too well to doubt your approval of the grand work on which I am entering, and am sure that you will readily pardon a failure of submission, when my only aim has been the glory of God and the salvation of souls.' And after he had completed his voyage he wrote again from Macao in the same strain. 'Have you pardoned me for leaving you in the way I did? I know you have. I cannot forget the religious lessons you gave me, and I am sure they have taught you to master the feelings of nature. We must not grudge suffering a little pain for God, who is so good in bearing long with us. And when He Himself provides us with the occasions we must not reject them, but with full resignation adore His holy will. We are reconciled, then, I will think, and you love me as tenderly as ever, and, for God at least, you would rather I should be out here labouring for the salvation of souls than anywhere else. And, perhaps, if you knew the extreme want of these poor people, how many there are, and what darkness they are in for want of missionaries, you might even wish that one of my brothers should have a call like mine.'

For some years M. Pigneux lived in Camboia. He was not engaged in active missionary work, but was employed in the quiet duties of college. There, with a little band of young scholars, drawn together from Cochin China, Siam, and Tonking, he gave himself up to tuition, preparing them for the priesthood. Another letter of his refers to this time of his life: 'If it was not for the work of the college, I might live here as unknown and as quiet as the Fathers of the desert. The house in which we live was built by the scholars, and it just serves to shelter us from the weather... We have almost nothing; but we are free from care, for the supplies of divine Providence are riches enough. Admire, then, God's goodness, and cease not to thank Him for the care with which He watches over your son. If I had remained in France, I might have become attached to the poor goods of the world; while, by coming to this country, I have learnt the happiness of being obliged to depend on God alone. O my God, what return shall I make You for so great favours? How dear to me is the solitude in which I live! Everything reminds me of the greatness of the Creator—nature, the trees, the birds, the very silence which reigns here.'

The docility and fervour of the scholars under M. Pigneux's direction are spoken of by a priest who visited the college in 1769, and was very much impressed by what he saw. 'At Hondah,' he says, 'where our college is, MM. Pigneux and Morvan came out to meet me at the head of their dear scholars. What consolation for them to have under them so precious a charge! They are, in truth, the hope of our missions, of Cochin China especially. If I had only heard it, I declare that I could not have believed what I have seen to-day. The fervour of these youths is so great, that I was never more edified in any seminary in France. Ever exact to their rules, these poor children preserve quite an angelic composure at their prayers, and at their studies there is more often need to check than to stimulate them. At recreation their gaiety is moderated, and free from all impropriety, and they avoid particular friendships. But nothing struck me more than the instant silence that prevailed on the sounding of the hour for finishing recreation, and also a way they had, and that without any prompting, of at once raising their hearts to God on the stroke of each hour.'

We get some insight into M. Pigneux's character from his preceding letters, and during his college life his character still further unfolds itself. It was the period of the civil wars, and the Cochin-Chinese soldiers penetrated into Camboia, and disturbed the tranquillity of his repose. In one of these inroads he fell into their hands, and for some months remained a prisoner. A letter of his, dated 1768, refers to this imprisonment. 'I have had the happiness,' he says, 'of passing the Lent of this year in prison, with a cangue of six feet on my neck. The Christians who came to see me shed many tears, nor could I console them, though they might easily perceive that my own heart was full of joy. For four months I was laid up with fever, but I am now quite well. Again and again you should bless God for the honour conferred on your family. Thank Him for yourselves, thank Him for me. Beg of Him that I may go back to prison, there to die for His holy name.'

In another irruption of these Cochin-Chinese M. Pigneux's life was in danger. He was indignant at witnessing their brutal conduct towards such of their countrymen as they discovered in Camboia, and he remonstrated with them; but they only threatened him in return, and told him that if he did not give up every Cochin-Chinese in the college, they would take his life. 'Kill me,' said he, 'if you please, but I will not betray one of them.' What might have been the consequences, we do not know; but he managed to escape in the night, and to carry off with him the whole body of his scholars.

It was in their flight that he was exposed to another peril, which one of his brother missionaries has mentioned, who speaks also of the singular calmness and intrepidity that he manifested in the emergency. They had to pass a stream, and, in crossing, the raft, on which M. Pigneux was, came to pieces, and he was immersed in the water. Twice he sank, and twice he recovered himself. His companions gave him up for lost. But he came safe to land, and, taking no notice of what had happened, proceeded unconcernedly on his path. This composedness in danger, which was usual with him, and his unfailing resolution, contributed to inspire that extraordinary confidence which he soon after gained, and which was felt universally amongst the adherents of the king.

On the death of Mgr. Piguel, M. Pigneux was named Bishop of Adran. His influence shortly became very sensible. There were two small potentates in that part of the country, who were rivals for his good will. Both alike wished to induce him to fix his residence in their territories. One of them was the King of Camboia, the other was the Governor of Cancao, a somewhat important person in those days, though only a vassal of Cochin China. The Bishop's position was gradually improving, and soon became very different from that of his predecessor. The Christians were a favoured body. The Bishop lived in a degree of state. He had ample means; he was surrounded by numerous dependents. His wishes were respected by the two neighbouring rulers. And so it was that, when the young Cochin-Chinese prince fled before his enemies, and sought a refuge, the friendship of the Bishop of Adran was really valuable to him. But it had a further and a greater value from the influence it had on the prince's character. He then learnt to defer to the Bishop's counsels, and to respect his wishes; and the Bishop taught him to curb his impetuosity, to exercise greater prudence, to deal more courteously with the mandarins whose support he required, and to get the better of many faults that were injurious to his fortunes. He also animated his courage, and supplied him with lessons of policy that went a good way to establish his cause.

The first successes of the young prince took place when the Taysons were engaged in the conquest of Tonking. But that conquest was short work, and they were soon free again. Then they came down upon him in full force, and he was powerless against their overwhelming numbers. He was obliged to fly, and the Bishop too; and both of them for more than a year were wanderers on the waters of the great Gulf of Siam, or in some temporary resting place in one of the numerous isles with which that gulf is strewed. Those were the days of this prince's greatest distress. His enemies followed him out on the seas, and entirely crippled him, destroying almost the whole of the vessels with which he had first fled. Then, in the most wretched plight, he roamed here and there, with a single vessel of any size, and a few smaller ones, and with no more than six or seven hundred followers, and these reduced at times almost to starvation. The Bishop was much better off. His wise forethought had made provision. He got away with his scholars, lodged a portion of them in Siam, and with the rest made for a distant island some two hundred miles from land, and there, for nine months of the year, he lived with them in secure solitude. A letter we have of Mgr. Pigneux speaks of those days; and a part of it may be here given. 'It was the Feast of St. Joseph, the patron of the mission, and we had celebrated High Mass, and confirmed four hundred persons. Just then, tidings reached us that the rebels were at hand. This I had been expecting, and I had made my preparations. Next day, when I offered Mass, I commended our flight to God, and in concluding my instructions to the Christians present, I advised them to go back to their homes, but I did not say a word about my purpose of leaving them. The port of Brissac was the point I then sought, and I reached it in two days. There were four hundred Cochin-Chinese Christians there, and for seven years they had had no ministrations. I stayed with them a week, fully engaged in trying to revive their religious fervour, but the coming of the king with fifty vessels obliged me to go and seek a more retired spot. Easter we kept in a large island in the Gulf of Siam. Since I came to the Indies I have not enjoyed such peace as I did in that isle. We were there from the Wednesday in Holy Week to Easter Tuesday, and throughout that time I had but one thought, my own salvation and that of the people with me; and they, too, quite resigned themselves to the trials which the providence of God seemed to have designed for us; and soon we felt them in a manner that keenly touched us. We had landed in a spot suited for the laying-up of our boats, when every one of our party, sixty-nine in number, with only one exception, was seized with dangerous sickness; two of our attendants we lost, and a scholar in whom we placed great hope, who had just completed his studies. This young man was twenty-seven years of age, and he died in the same good dispositions in which he had lived. Seeing me sad and discouraged, two days before his death he addressed to me words which I shall never forget. "Why is it, my father, you seem to have lost all your usual constancy? Have you forgotten the mercies of the good God? To-morrow or next day I shall die, and go before the judgment-seat of God. But a chief confidence I have is that you are suffering here for me, and that the state in which you are is so pleasing to God that He will not refuse you the salvation of my poor soul. Be not out of heart; these pains will soon pass away, and the merciful God will in the end crown your labours." At this discourse, one that I little thought of hearing from him, I was greatly moved; I was so confused that I went away and hid myself in the woods, and there I passed the rest of the day lamenting my own weakness.'

In this same letter the Bishop recounts an incident which makes us see the excess of distress in which the prince was at that time, and also the reason of the deep gratitude which he ever seemed to feel towards the Bishop of Adran. They met on the waters. The Bishop had still supplies, and he could spare something from them. The king and his followers were quite destitute. They were trying to satisfy their hunger with the roots they could dig up in the desert islands. 'I was obliged,' says the

Bishop, ' to offer him a part of my stock, and the few gifts I could bestow were received with a thankfulness and a depth of feeling that I could hardly have imagined. So greatly was the king affected, that when I went to him the next day, he would not let me go away, but kept me with him for a fortnight.'

It was in those days that the ties between the Bishop and the king were riveted so closely; it was then that the prince was led to that extreme degree of confidence, the giving into the hands of the Bishop his son, a boy of six years old, for his education and protection. The child was taken away by the Bishop to France, and presented to Louis XVI.; and when Mgr. Pigneux returned, he came with new proofs of friendship, ships and men and supplies of war, that went very far to secure the triumph that was in the end attained.

But before the return of Mgr. Pigneux the cause of Gia-laong—for we may call him by the name he afterwards assumed—had mended. In the interval he had not been idle. He had first gone to the court of Siam, but seeing his hopes of assistance in that quarter vain, unwilling to waste his time, with a few followers he threw himself upon the affections of his subjects. The moment was favourable. The Taysons were then quarrelling amongst themselves, and they had not leisure to notice him. The two younger brothers were discontented with the elder Nhac, who kept the spoils to himself; and the third and youngest, who was also the most skilful and bravest, and the real conqueror of Tonking, determined that he would not give up the kingdom he had won. These dissensions ruined them. For Gia-laong quietly made his way further and further; he regained, one after another, the provinces ruled over by his ancestors; and at length, soon after the return of the Bishop, headed by a French vessel, suddenly his fleet sailed into the port of Quin-hon, and surprised, captured, and destroyed the whole fleet of the Taysons.

But the war was not ended. For ten years it lingered on; Gia-laong sometimes making further advances, but again driven back, for the united forces of the Taysons were much more numerous than his; but at length, after Nhac and his brothers were dead, and Bahalong, one of his nephews, was at the head of the usurpers, the onward move of Gia-laong became steady and consistent. The battle-field was exchanged from Quin-hon to Touron. Touron and Hue were taken, Upper Cochin China was overrun, Tonking was entered, and, almost as soon as it was entered, the cause of the Taysons was lost, and Gia-laong had not only recovered the throne of his ancestors, but had become the sole ruler of the whole dominion of the Vouas.

The Bishop of Adran returned from France in 1789. 'Our arrival,' says one of his companions, 'was a sort of triumph. But as we brought back the king's son, and raised the hopes of the people of the country at a critical moment, it was not surprising that we should be so received.' But when the enthusiasm of the welcome was over, still the missionaries felt the consequences of the high regard in which the Bishop was held. They found themselves the objects of honour and esteem. They were reputed men of probity, whose words might always be believed. Persons of the highest rank treated them with politeness, governors of provinces deferred to their wishes, mandarins came to visit them, and considered it an honour to receive visits from them. 'The king,' says one of the missionaries, ' goes beyond all others in his attentions. I never meet him but he bends his head with a gracious smile, and whenever I go to the palace he bids me be seated, and offers me tea and refreshment.' His regard for the Bishop was unbounded, and his desire to oblige him proved by his immediate attention to every request. 'Scarcely a day passes,' says M. Lelabousse, a missionary whom the Bishop had lately brought with him from France, 'that the king does not give him some proof of his affection. There was lately a revolt in a recently-conquered province of Camboia, and the king gave orders that there should be a general massacre. A considerable body of troops set off to execute the commission. The Bishop heard of it, and went to the king, and asked a general pardon. Angry as the king was, he immediately revoked his orders, and numerous lives were spared.'

The young prince whom he had taken to France remained at first under the Bishop's care. The boy had a strong affection towards him, and reposed in him full confidence, going to him frequently, and telling him all his little troubles, especially how sorry he was to be living amongst pagans, and to witness their superstitions; and he would say that he would like to be back again in France, if it were not for the hope he had that he might one day make his people Christians. He wished to be a Christian himself; he said Christian prayers; his page was a Christian, and every evening they said their prayers together. The Bishop one day pointed out to him a young man of his household who had that day been baptised. 'How happy he is!' exclaimed the boy. 'I wish I was in his place.' He was apt and intelligent, as his remarks sometimes showed. His mother one day asked him who made the elephants, and he told her God. But she said it was not God, but the king. Then the boy, turning to the king, said, 'Well, papa, you need have no fear of the rebels; elephants are their chief strength. They have three hundred; make two thousand, and you may be at ease.' On which the king laughed, and said, 'You say well, my son; it is God who made them.'

After a time the mandarins became jealous of the Bishop's influence, and were afraid the prince would become a Christian. The fear was particularly excited by the conversion of one of the principal mandarins. We have the story at length from M. Liot, one of the older missionaries, and we may give it in his words. 'The king last year' (1794), says M. Liot, 'wanting to send his son on some business, requested the Bishop to go with him as his guardian. And, as the provinces where he was to go had not for a long time had any ministrations, the Bishop willingly consented. The chief judge, named Ong-giam, who was highly esteemed by the king, and in great repute for his superior learning, was of the party. Up to that time Ong-giam, though he had a regard for the Bishop, and did sometimes visit him, had a particular antipathy to the Christian religion. On this occasion, however, being brought into closer contact with the Bishop, he not only learnt to esteem him more highly, but he entirely changed his sentiments about his religion. After they had talked over the subject of the worship of ancestors and the doctrine of Confucius, Ong-giam went to the king, and said, "The master reasons very well about religion; his ideas are more elevated than our own." Then, after recounting what the Bishop had said, he acknowledged his belief in its truth, and declared that it was in every respect agreeable to reason. Two days after, the king repeated this to the Bishop, and the Bishop again went over the same arguments, which were not new indeed to the king; but, whether from human respect or any other motive, however he might feel their justice, he made no expression of his sentiments. On his return to Saigon, before the whole court the king said, "See what the eloquence of the master has done. It has persuaded Ong-giam. What may it not do with us?" And this reflection increased the fear of several of the mandarins that the Bishop would make a Christian of the prince. Three of them then wrote out a paper, which they got a dozen more to sign, and presented it to the king. In it they besought his majesty not to intrust the education of the prince to the Bishop, nor to allow him to visit the Bishop more than twice in a month, nor the Bishop to visit him, except occasionally. The king was very much displeased, and in fear that the Bishop should hear of what had taken place, and be induced to leave the country, or at least discontinue the care of his son. But, though the king tried to prevent it, the Bishop got intelligence of it, and, as was foreseen, requested permission to quit the kingdom, and, dropping his visits to the prince, would hardly receive him when he came to visit him. The king, very much irritated with the authors of the writing, obliged the foremost of them to go to the Bishop and apologise; and he sent several others, and among them the queen and the queen-mother, to petition him not to alter his way of treating the prince. But their intercessions were to no purpose. The Bishop was inflexible. At last the king went himself, and so moved was he that scarcely had he seated himself when he rose again, and, with tears, earnestly asked the Bishop to pay no attention to the writing of a few weak wretches. "Although all the court go wrong in this matter," said he, "what is it to you? Let the master be content that I am his friend." So strong an appeal the Bishop was not able to resist, and he agreed to stay. The next day the king went away to the war, and the Bishop going with him to the gate, he then said, "I would wish you to be perfectly at ease, and tell you the plain truth. I honour you above every person in the kingdom. Of this the mandarins are not jealous, for they know how different their case is from yours, and what important services you have rendered to me and my son and the state, and that your understanding and prudence are a thousand times greater than theirs. It is only about religion they cannot agree. Laugh at them then. I know what to do about religion, and I have perfect reliance on your prudence.'"

The Bishop also has given us his account of these transactions, and has added some particulars which M. Liot has not mentioned. 'This year,' says the Bishop, 'I have had to manage an affair of much delicacy. About nineteen of the principal mandarins, amongst them the king's uncle and another near relative, in their zeal for the religion of the country, combined to represent to the king that he could not any longer with prudence allow me to retain the charge of his son ; that as I was a stranger, and of another religion, I could only rear him up in my own principles; and that therefore they entreated his majesty to break the connection existing between us, and to place the prince under literate mandarins, who would bring him up like his ancestors. A month had not passed before two of the officers who were of the party were condemned to lose their heads. The sentence had been already passed, and confirmed by the king. It was the persuasion of the whole court that no one but myself could get them off; but that, as they had joined in signing the writing, it was vain to hope for my intercession. But I proved to them it was otherwise ; for, as their fault was simply a matter of discipline, and might be overlooked, I exerted myself for them, and obtained for them not only life, but the restoration to their former posts.'

Then the Bishop speaks of the conversion of Onggiam. 'The alarm at court was in consequence of the conversion of the principal of the learned mandarins, who had been previously much opposed to our religion. So wedded was he to the doctrine of Confucius and pagan worship, that he was impatient of all sentiments different from his own. But from frequent conversations we had during eight or nine months which we spent together, he found that instead of converting me, as he had proposed, his own ideas became quite changed, and so far, that he even suggested to the king the dropping of some of the superstitious customs of the court. I had hope that this conversion would have turned out happily for religion; but God, whose designs we cannot penetrate, ordered it otherwise. This mandarin was with the prince in a town where we were besieged by 30,000 of the enemy. When the siege was raised he was very sick, and could not go back with us to the royal city. Throughout his sickness, which lasted a month, he was continually asking for me, saying that could he but see me once more he should die content. In consequence of his repeated desires, notwithstanding his extreme sickness, they did their best to satisfy him. But it was a journey of fifteen days, toilsome even to one in health, and the fatigues were too great; so that before he got more than a third of the way he expired in his palanquin. Although he had not been baptised, I have the hope that his desire will supply the want. Perhaps already he has received the reward of all he has said and done for religion since his conversion. He was sixty years of age, grave, thoughtful, laborious, and noble as well as simple in character. He died poor, though through life he had held high offices, and his reputation for integrity was untainted. He was the first of the literates in learning as well as rank. The king had full confidence in him, and constantly consulted him. All this made his conversion the more startling. There was a general murmur: "If a man like this could not resist the arguments of the European Bishop, what will become of the prince and the king?"'

M. Liot has told us one or two more stories, which we will repeat. They refer to a period a little later, and they show us that the king's mind gradually turned more and more away from the Christians. He protected them only out of his respect to the Bishop of Adran, and from his strong wish not to disoblige him; but he had no relish for the religion itself, and this became more and more apparent. 'It is a custom,' says M. Liot, 'on the first day of the year, in each township, to raise general contributions for sacrifices made in the temples for the welfare of the kingdom. It is generally very difficult for the Christians to get freed from this payment, and, when unable to make terms with the village chiefs, they are subject to much ill-treatment, and cannot obtain redress, for the usage is regarded as a fundamental law, from which even the king cannot exempt you. We hit on an expedient three years ago for relieving the Christians from this embarrassment. On the preceding eve the missionaries requested a visit from the village chiefs, met them affably, and asked them to be present on the following day at the prayers the Christians would offer for the prosperity of the kingdom. Then Mass was celebrated with as much pomp as possible, and afterwards a hymn was sung by the children, asking every blessing of God for the king and royal family, the mandarins, and the whole kingdom. The ceremony over, an entertainment was given to the visitors, and after a discourse on religion, a request was made that the Christians should be exempt from the contributions. The plan succeeded. But the next year, in a village where there was no missionary, the Christians had a dispute with the pagans on the subject of this contribution, and as they could not agree, the matter came before the governor of the province, who gave the pagans a document authorising them to compel the Christians to pay. Aware that an order like this would be mischievous to the other Christians, the Bishop sent me to the governor, with whom I had some acquaintance; and without difficulty the order was revoked, and the proceedings against the Christians were stopped. Months after this, in another village of the same province, the village chiefs wanted to oblige a catechist to pay towards some superstition, and the catechist imprudently went to the governor about it. The governor was no friend to the Christians, and was not pleased with what he had already done; and, glad of this new opportunity, ordered the contribution to be paid, and brought the subject before the king.

'The Bishop of Adran had always resisted the importunities of the missionaries that he would ask the king for legal exemption from these contributions; for he considered the request imprudent, and very doubtful in its results. But in the present instance he gave way, and directed me to take with me F. Paul, a Cochin-Chinese priest, and to go to the king and learn what the governor had said, and at the same time to make this petition. We went to the king, and addressing him in a low voice, asked the indulgence. He did not at once reply, for he was evidently embarrassed; he did not wish to displease the Bishop by a refusal, nor the mandarins by granting the demand. So he repeated aloud what we had said, and interrogated the mandarins whether a law of this kind could be passed. They all declared that it could not. And nothing I could say was of any use. All I could obtain from the king was "that the contributions might be dispensed with if the towns pleased, but if they chose to enforce them they had the right; it was an immemorial usage." A reply like this embarrassed us, for we feared the people of the towns might take advantage of it, and that the difficulty of coming to terms with them would be increased.'

Another incident M. Liot has reported is as follows: 'At the request of some of the mandarins, the king rebuilt a temple of Confucius with considerable splendour. He issued an express order that every literate mandarin should contribute towards the expenses. This perplexed us exceedingly, and it puzzled us much to decide how to act. In the end F. Paul and myself went to the queen-mother, and requested her to put into the hands of the king a petition that he would exempt the Christians from this contribution, and instead accept from them a sum of money for state purposes. She as well as the queen acceded to our wishes. The king was altogether disinclined. "Every person," he said, "who had learnt letters must aid in building a temple of Confucius, the patron of letters. It was for the public interest." Two days afterwards the king inquired of a Christian mandarin if he had paid his contribution. "No, sire," he replied; "I cannot do it; but I have here a sum of money which I request your majesty to accept for purposes of state." "Give it me," said the king; but two or three of the mandarins objected, saying the levy was not for state purposes, but for the temple of Confucius. And the king insisted it should be so. The Christian, however, stood out, and did not pay the contribution; and the matter ended without the trouble that had been anticipated. The missionaries were for a time very uneasy, and the Christians had to battle about these payments for which they were importuned; but the king evidently wished no more than not to offend the mandarins and shock one of their strong prejudices.'

The king was not always so lukewarm in favour

of the Christians as he was at the time of these events, *i.e.* about the year 1797. Once he was much more active in their behalf. The Christians were said to deal in charms, and it was a current report that they killed children, to take out their eyes and make charms. A rogue of a fellow went to the king, and accused the Christians of causing the loss of his speech by their charms. The king made as if he believed him, but told him he knew of a cure. Then he mixed a little dust with water, and gave it to the cheat to drink. After a few gesticulations, the fellow pretended to have recovered his voice, and the king, saying he had another medicine for him, ordered him a sound beating.

But the missionaries had no longer any such tales to tell. The language of M. Lelabousse seems to represent that the condition of the Christians was really painful—that their enemies were allowed to exercise their spleen unopposed, and that the king had ceased to be their friend. 'Persons suppose,' says this missionary, 'that we can do just as we please, and that we are in such favour that we can practise our religion openly and without restraint. It is true that we are not in prison, nor do we wear the cangue, but we are persecuted in no slight degree; for there are mandarins who are never tired of annoying us, and delight in paying off on the Christians the insults that they say are offered to the idols by our refusing to bow before them, and there are, besides, the devotees of Phat, women with tongues of venom, doing us all the harm they can.'

Again, speaking of the king, he says: 'He has forgotten the attachment which the Christians have always shown him, and the important services they have rendered at the most critical seasons, and he views them only with hatred and contempt. It must be granted that he is being ever urged on against them. Crowds of bonzes swarm in the country, and are constantly seeking to raise up a persecution, multiplying their efforts to gain their ends, and influencing the females of the court, who, being earnest followers of Phat, are ready enough to be led, and go on incessantly murmuring that a handful of Christians ought never to be allowed to contemn the idols, and ought to be exterminated.'

The Bishop himself was sensible of a change in the king's behaviour, but he put it down to a refinement of policy, with a view of inducing the Bishop to resume the superintendence of his son.

The few years that had passed since he had been removed from the Bishop's care had been most unfavourable to the young man. He had grown almost into manhood under the contaminating influences of a corrupt court. All the simple modesty of his character was gone. 'He is entirely altered,' says M. Lelabousse. 'He has not now the quick lively understanding he once had, nor the soft affectionate heart; the poisonous air of the court has blasted them; they have disappeared under the influence of female seductions.' He had not, however, lost his love and respect for the Bishop, and the king desired again to use this influence for his advantage. A letter of the Bishop gives us his view of the king's conduct, and supplies us with some interesting information. 'When I made my visit to the king, on the first day of the year, to offer him my congratulations, he took occasion to speak to me on public affairs. In this conversation he spoke of a military expedition he had in view, and he tried to fathom whether I would be willing to go with his son, whom he proposed to employ in the business. I had not forgotten the old jealousy of the mandarins, and evaded the subject, and so displeased him. But he commanded his feelings. Some three weeks afterwards he asked me to ride out with him, and then expressed himself more plainly; and so I found it necessary to speak. Still I excused myself, and asked him not to employ me in this way. The king said nothing, but it was evident that he was bent on forcing me to comply with his desires. When we returned to the palace, he began speaking in a disparaging manner of our holy religion, and said, that out of regard for me, and in the view of my services, he had forborne to persecute it, and had granted it toleration. But, as if with the purpose of shaking my resolution, he added that he was thinking seriously of changing his conduct.

'A few days after, he used some force with a Christian officer, who for more than twenty years had practised his religion unmolested, to induce him to offer worship to the king's ancestors in a temple just consecrated. He employed two old mandarins, who he knew would do the work with a relish. The feast was prolonged for three days, on which religious honours were offered. The first two days the mandarin did not obey the orders he had received to take part in this worship. The third day was the prince's birthday, and the Christian mandarin could not avoid coming with the other mandarins in his robes of state to the civil ceremony. When he had saluted the prince, and was about to retire, the two mandarins would not let him go, but forced him onward to the temple of the king's ancestors. Then they said to him, "Salute the ancient kings, my brother; salute the ancestors of our sovereign. What harm is it? The king does not oblige you to salute the idols, nor the genii, nor the demons." "I see no ancient kings," said the mandarin, "nor do I believe there are any here. How can I salute them?" "Do not persist in refusing," they replied, "or the king will be angry." "You know," said the Christian, "that I have never been present at these ceremonies; why, then, do you use force?" "It is the king's order," they insisted. And then, using force, one holding his arms, the other bowing down his head, they led him back to the king, and reported that they had induced him to make his salute, but that while he did so he had prayed to his own God. To which the king replied, "What matters it, provided he has saluted?" Then, turning to the Christian, he addressed himself to him with a mild reproach: "Why is it, when I have so long provided for you, and bestowed on you many honours, you refuse to salute my ancestors? I have not forced you to abandon your religion, nor ordered you to worship idols or spirits; all I have asked is that you should join in paying public honour to my ancestors." "I acknowledge your majesty for my king," said the mandarin, "and hold you in the most profound respect; and how could I dare to show any disrespect to the ancestors of my king? But they have been long dead, and I do not believe that they can return; and my religion forbids me to salute them in a place where I do not believe they are." "Do you not salute the saints?" asked the king. "How do they differ from my ancestors? They are dead also, they cannot come back; how can you salute them, and refuse the same honours to my ancestors? I do not believe that my ancestors are present here, or that they eat the meat I offer them; but I salute them only by way of public recognition."'

The Bishop of Adran did in the end consent to the king's wishes, and went with the prince, and the result was that the king's coolness towards the Christians vanished. The presence of the Bishop was valuable even with respect to the conduct of the war, and this had been often proved. In the earlier contests the Tayson forces were much more numerous than their adversaries, and they often tried to intimidate by their threats and vaunts, swarming up to the lines by which the king protected himself, and uttering their proud insults; and then the Bishop's quiet composed manner was a stay to the fainting hearts of the king's followers, and at the same time his ingenuity and presence of mind extricated them from dilemmas. Once a spy made his way into a fortress in which the king with a party of his troops was beleaguered by very superior numbers, and if it had not been for the Bishop the man would have gone back and reported the feeble state in which they were; but the Bishop showed a bold front, and sent the fellow off with quite a different idea from the truth; and the ruse succeeded. But the young prince especially wanted a stay, and would have been quite unfit for the charge which the king now intrusted to him, which was in an advanced and important position, if he had not had the Bishop by his side to counsel and support him. But these duties were the last in which the Bishop was engaged. In this expedition he fell ill of dysentery. The disorder proved dangerous, and he could not throw it off; and at last it became very evident that this good and great Bishop's death was at hand. The king sent his physician to him, but it was in vain. No human skill was of any use. We have an account of his last days, from the pen of M. Lelabousse, so interesting and instructive, that it must be here introduced.

'The Bishop of Adran,' says M. Lelabousse, 'calmly contemplated the approach of his last hour. "This," said he, "is the end of that course of busy labour which, in spite of my repugnance, I have been so long leading. So at last are my pains terminated, and my happiness is commencing. Willingly do I leave the world, where I have been considered fortunate. I have been admired by the people, respected by the great, esteemed by the king; but I have no regret for these honours; they are only vanity and affliction. Death brings me repose and peace, the sole objects of my desire. I await it with impatience. If I am of use here on earth, I refuse not the trouble. I am willing to bear all the crosses I have found in the midst of my dignities; but if God pleases to call me to Himself, I shall have my chief wish. Although I dread the terrors of His judgments, I have a greater trust in His mercies." '

The king had sent his physician to him, who used every means he could think of to preserve a life so valuable to his master. The king also came himself, with his son, to visit him, and shed tears on perceiving the fruitlessness of all skill. When the physician saw there was no more to be done, and was about to take leave of the Bishop, the latter said to him, 'Be not sad because you are not able to cure me; you have done what you could, and I thank you. Go to the king, and tell his majesty what you have seen; tell him that I have no uneasiness, no fear; that he may know that a European knows how to live and die.'

There was much talk about these words at court. 'The master,' said the king one day, 'had but one fear during his illness that he should become delirious, and so fall into some act unfit for one whose conduct has been always worthy of praise.' 'But it was not so,' says M. Lelabousse. 'The Bishop of Adran always scrupulously observed the most exact modesty, and he was afraid that, should he be delirious, he might some way outstep the bounds of a virtue he loved so much. Although the nature of the climate and the state in which he was might have excused some deviation from his strict rule, he would not for the sake of ease in the least relax it. He was so careful to keep himself always decently covered, that even when he had lost the use of reason he still clung to his old habit. His fervour was not less than his modesty. I do not believe that during the three months of his illness a single hour passed without his thoughts being turned to God and the happiness of heaven. As he seldom slept, and if he did, only for short intervals, he was meditating day and night. The chapter, "Vidi civitatem sanctam Jerusalem," and the hymn of the Dedication, "Cœlestis Urbs," were frequently the matter of his contemplation and the subject of his discourse. He was so full of the idea of this heavenly Jerusalem, his imagination represented it in colours so glowing and moving, that you would have believed him there already, while he was speaking of it. One day especially his discourse was so sublime, I had never heard anything like it; never had he preached so well. I could have thought it was St. Augustin or St. Ambrose that was by me. The deep love that lighted up these thoughts gave him an unfailing patience amidst the violence of the most wearying pains. God, to prove his constancy and to purify his virtue, permitted that he should be harassed with unmitigated colic, accompanied with fearful convulsions; but his great soul supported all with a courage such as I had never before seen. There was not a groan, not a sigh, however acute the pain; not a single word that could sadden any of those who came near him. I never heard him complain, except of the trouble he was causing us; we, however, felt none, except at seeing him suffer.

'The Bishop, towards the end, could not make use of the lightest nourishment; for about a month he drew in a little very mild rice-water through linen at the end of a reed, and that was at length changed for warm water. This linen represented to him the sponge offered to his divine Master when dying.

'Of his robust and vigorous frame there was now left only skin and bone; all the strength was gone. Yet though the outward form was so reduced, in spite of the sharp pains that were wearing him away, still his understanding was sound and vigorous as ever. He thought of everything; he arranged everything with perfect presence of mind. This was so till the last four or five days of his life.

'After receiving the last rites of the Church with much devotion, a little before his death he asked me to bring him a crucifix. When I had given it to him, he took it in his hands, and with the lively faith that has been the principle of his life he addressed it in these touching words: " Precious cross, that hast been my portion through my whole life, and that art now my consolation and my hope, permit me to embrace thee for the last time. Thou hast been outraged in Europe; the French have overthrown thee, and cast thee out of their churches, no longer holding thee in respect. Come, then, to

Cochin China. I would desire to make thee known to this people, who are rather ignorant than wicked; and to plant thee in this kingdom, even on the throne of the king. But my sins have not allowed that I should be the instrument of this great work. Plant it, then, Thyself, my Saviour, and raise Thy temples on the ruins of those of the devil, and reign over the Cochin Chinese. Thou hast appointed me to preach to them the Gospel; now that I leave them to come to Thee I give them back into Thy hands. I ask of Thee pardon for all the faults I have committed during the thirty-three years I have had the care of them, and also the grace of dying in Thy love."

'After this short prayer he bowed his head to the crucifix, watering it with his tears. As I knelt at his feet, my tears streaming over his hands, those paternal hands so often raised to bless me, I cried, as far as my sobs would permit, "My father, my father, the chariot of Israel, and the driver thereof."

'He replied to me with dying voice, "I have no mantle to leave you; I will give you the best I have —my blessing; and I pray God to fill you with His Spirit, to direct and sustain you in the painful course which is before you. You lose in me a friend who loves you tenderly. In your pains I could console you. I know your heart, and you know mine. Henceforth you have no one; ... but take courage; soon we shall meet in heaven."

'This was the last time the Bishop of Adran spoke to me with full consciousness. After this he became delirious, and in a few days more was in his agony, which lasted nearly forty hours. At length, on the 9th of October, on the Feast of St. Denis, having edified us by his patience and fervour and steady contemplation of death, he expired in my arms, about half-past ten in the morning, at the age of fifty-seven years and ten months.

'As soon as he was dead, we bore the sad news to the king, who on hearing it sent a splendid bier, with pieces of damask and silk for the burial. On the 10th of October the coffin was carried, with lighted torches and much ceremony, to the house of the Bishop. It was placed in the great hall, and there exposed to satisfy the wishes of the faithful. Every day Mass was celebrated there for the Bishop, and other Masses were said in the church close at hand.

'The king's son caused a great building to be erected in the court, to receive the mandarins and all those who wished to pay funeral honours to the illustrious master. The Christians from all parts of the province came in crowds to shed tears of love and gratitude over the mourned remains of their good pastor. The prince had placed a guard there, to prevent the Christians receiving any molestation.

'The king gave orders that everything should be done for the Bishop which religion directed, and that nothing should be spared to give splendour and magnificence to the ceremonies. Whatever was wanted was to be given us. He wished solemn Masses to be sung, and they were accordingly. On the eve the missionaries in cope and the scholars of the seminary in surplices proceeded to the church, where a vast crowd of Christians were assembled. The French officers and Christian mandarins were present in official dress. Matins and Lauds were sung. Then with strains of solemn music we went in procession to the hall where the coffin was, there sang the "Libera," and then returned to the church. The darkness, the silence of night, the lighted torches, added to the effect of the ceremonies, and the pagans, who in religion are much affected by outward things, were immensely struck with all they saw. The next morning there was again the same order, and Mass being over, there was anew a procession to the Bishop's house, where as before the "Libera" was sung after the recitation of some other prayers. When the ceremonies were concluded, the prince invited the mandarins to a grand repast, as is the custom of the country when at the king's orders they attend on such occasions.

'The funeral was on the 16th of December. The State combined with the Church to bestow on the Bishop the honours due to the rank he held in each. The king gave orders to his son to superintend the funeral. We began to move at two in the morning. The coffin, covered with superb damask, and placed on a handsome rest twenty feet long, with double rows of lighted candles on each side, was borne by eighty chosen men. Over it was an embroidered canopy. A large cross, formed of branches artistically arranged, headed the procession. There followed six niches elaborately sculptured, each carried by four men. In the first were written four letters of gold, signifying "To the Sovereign Lord of Heaven." The second contained the image of St. Paul, the third of St. Peter, the fourth of the angel guardian, the fifth of the Blessed Virgin, and last came a standard of damask, about fifteen feet long, on which were embroidered in golden letters the titles which had been conferred on the Bishop of Adran by the Kings of France and Cochin China, with his rank in the Church. His cross and mitre were in the sixth niche, which was borne immediately in front of the coffin. By the side of these niches walked a large number of Christian youths, accompanied by the principal catechist of each church. The whole of the king's guards, numbering twelve thousand, were under arms, and ranged in two lines, with cannon in front. One hundred and twenty elephants, with their attendants and standards, marched on the two sides. Then there were all kinds of military music, firing of muskets, and fireworks, while lanterns, torches, and candles lighted up the procession. At least forty thousand persons, Christians and pagans, were following. The king was present with the whole body of mandarins, and, what was more unusual, his mother, his sister, the queen, his concubines, his children,—the whole court believed that for a man so above the common they must go out of the common way—all came, and went on even to the tomb.

'This magnificent funeral, such as had never been seen in Cochin China, brought together so large a crowd of spectators, that it is impossible to tell the number.

'The Bishop had chosen for the place of his burial

a garden about a mile from the town. This he had cultivated and beautified with his own hands. In this retired spot, suited for quiet reflection, he had thrown off all care; here at times he brought his royal pupil for recreation; here with his missionaries sometimes he would take repose. When the procession arrived at the garden, they rested the coffin beside the tomb. The king made the people retire while the last prayers were said. On M. Liot approaching to cast a little earth in the grave, as a signal for filling it, the king also approached, and threw some earth into it. The Christians coming forward with loud laments, the mandarins would have obliged them to be silent and to go back, but the king said "Leave them alone; do not hinder them." At last the king advanced with a grave and solemn step, grief plainly marked in his countenance, to pay his final address to the prelate; tears flowed down his cheeks, and a grand mandarin, up to that unmoved, said aloud, "If we do not weep for the bishop, we must weep for the king."

'When all was concluded, a sumptuous repast, at the king's expense, was served in tents prepared for the purpose, to the mandarin and troops and all who had been present at the funeral. The king himself stayed within his own chamber, giving vent to his grief.

'Afterwards he caused a magnificent mausoleum to be raised in the garden at a great expense, and, as a further testimony of his love and admiration of his lost friend, he caused a patent of distinction to be written out, declaring the high honours conferred on this Christian Bishop.

'It runs thus: "I had with me a wise man, the sharer of all my secrets, who from a distance of thousands of miles came to this country, and never left it, even when fortune was most adverse to me. Why is it that now, when I prosper all at once, he has been taken from me by a premature death? I speak of Peter Pigneux, honoured with the rank of Bishop and with the glorious title of Plenipotentiary of the King of France. In the remembrance of his former virtue, I wish to give a new testimony to him. I owe it to his rare merits. If in Europe he passed for no common man, here, in the court of Cochin China, he was regarded as the most illustrious stranger we had ever seen. In my early youth I had the good fortune to meet this valued friend, whose character was so well suited to my own. When I made my first effort to mount the throne of my ancestors, I had him by my side. He was to me a mine of wealth, whence I could draw counsel to direct me in every need. But suddenly came down on me a thousand ills, and my feet tottered as those of Thieu-khang of the dynasty of He. Then he had to take a course that separated him from me as the heaven from the sea. I gave into his hands the prince my heir, and truly he was worthy of the dear pledge I confided to him, that he might interest in my favour the great king who ruled in his own country. He succeeded in obtaining help for me; already had he got back half-way, when his plans were thwarted, and he was not able to fulfil his wishes. But looking on my enemies as his own, in his attachment to my person, he came and joined me, that we might devise the means of combating them.

"The year in which I returned to my kingdom, I looked out impatiently for the rumours of his return. The next year he arrived, as he had promised. By the engaging and gentle way in which he had trained the prince my son, whom he brought back, it was easy to see what wonderful talent he had in bringing up the young. Day by day my affection and esteem for him increased. In times of difficulty he found out means which no other but himself could discover. The wisdom of his counsels and his virtues, which shone even in the pleasures of conversation, endeared him to me more and more. We were so united in friendship, that whenever business required me to go abroad, we rode together in front of the rest. We had but one heart. From the day when by the most happy fortune we met nothing has ever cooled our friendship, nor has been a cause of a momentary displeasure. I thought from his vigorous health that I should long enjoy the fruits of this close union; but now the earth covers this precious tree. How much to my regret!

"To make known to all the world the great merits of this illustrious stranger, and to spread abroad the good odour of his virtues, which he has ever concealed, I give him this patent of *Director of the hereditary Prince*, with the first rank after the royal family, and the surname of *Incomparable*. Alas, when the body is in the tomb and the soul has flown to heaven, what have I remaining with me of him! I have finished my eulogium; the regrets of my heart will never cease. O beauteous soul, O Master, accept this favour."'

The Bishop's burial-place was about four miles from Saigon. A guard of honour of two hundred soldiers was stationed to watch the tomb and monuments, and as long as Gia-laong lived they were not withdrawn.*

* Crawfurd's *Embassy to Cochin China*. Mr. Crawfurd visited Cochin China more than twenty years afterwards, on the accession of Minh-Menh.

CHAPTER IV.

MISSIONARY WORK.

THE missionary work done at this period in Cochin China was not much. The circumstances of the time were not favourable, and the missionaries were too few. There were three separate clusters of Christian population. One only was within the jurisdiction of Gia-laong. The second was amidst the battle-field, where for years the success was constantly varying, alternating this way and that, but gradually coming more and more within the sphere of the missionaries of the Bishop of Adran. The third, and the largest body of Christians, was wholly out of his reach.

In the southern provinces M. Liot, an old missionary, was stationed, with the care of the students of the college; and of course he could not do much missionary work.

The active missionary of the season was M. Lelabousse. He was one of seven fresh priests whom the Bishop of Adran brought back with him from France in 1789. But three of them died very shortly, and not one of them, except M. Lelabousse, was alive at the time of the Bishop of Adran's death. M. Lelabousse was occupied in the provinces that had felt the desolating effects of the war, where he saw much to fill him with sorrow. The numbers of the

Christians had been sadly reduced; some had been pressed as soldiers, some had gone into exile, some had abandoned their religion.

We have several letters of his, which show what might have been done if only there had been more labourers, and the war had not offered such impediments. There was a great disposition among the pagans to receive the Gospel; the Christians were themselves fervent; and, notwithstanding all obstacles, there was a steady flow of conversions, and wherever he went he found more ready to listen to him and submit to the faith than he was able to assist.

The first of his letters gives his early impressions. 'In these unhappy times it is difficult for the Gospel to make much progress; there are pagans, however, who are willing to submit themselves to the yoke of Jesus Christ. I have been but a year and a half in the province, and have had the consolation of admitting a hundred to baptism. The Cochin-Chinese listen willingly to religious teaching, and show a good deal of curiosity on the subject. As soon as a missionary appears in a place the pagans flock around him, multiplying their questions, but not rudely, for they are very respectful and deferential. They are by no means a barbarous people, as some might think, but are very studious of etiquette according to their own habits. There are persons, of course, here as everywhere, who are wanting in honesty and decency, but for the most part they are courteous and well behaved.

We might preach here with fruit had we only peace. The public works into which the people are forced, the constant state of alarm, and more than all the too great proportion of Christians for the small number of missionaries, preclude the idea of doing anything for the pagans. There are eight thousand Christians in the province in which I am, scattered and far asunder.'

Again he writes: 'Amidst the general convulsions we must lament not simply the ravages of the war, but the loss of souls. But still, for His own glory and for our own consolation, the Lord has kept a great number faithful, notwithstanding the torrent of evil. There are indeed Christians that do honour to their religion. I wonder, and I praise and thank God, when I see so many pious fervent souls in a place where sin and the devil reign, and where temptations are continually rising, as I may say, under the feet, and that too when there have been no missionaries. For upwards of ten years these poor Christians have had no Masses, no instruction; have not made a confession; and now, when we are here, we are not enough to hear them all even once in a year.'

In 1795 M. Lelabousse puts down the number of Christians at sixteen thousand, and says that in the last two years his adult baptisms had been so many as nine hundred. Since the last report, Gia-laong had been advancing onward, which accounts for the increase.

In 1796 he writes: 'During the last seven years,

i.e. since the return of the Bishop, our Christians have increased at least a third. Our chief care is with the catechists and the young. We give them both little retreats, which produce a good deal of fruit. From these retreats the catechists go forth full of zeal, doing their utmost to recover souls for God. The Cochin-Chinese children are very susceptible, and when they are instructed give ample proof of virtue. I have known many whose lives are blameless, that might rival the most fervent in Europe. After a first communion, one of the party, a young girl about twenty, passed three whole days and nights without food. I asked her what she had been doing all that time, and if she had not felt hungry; she said she had spent it in meditation and prayer, and that she had been so happy that she had not thought at all of eating.'

Another missionary cites an instance of the ardent feelings of these Christians, in the case of a young woman who had given scandal by her bad conduct. She came to him full of shame and sorrow, asking him to impose heavy penances on her, prayers, fasts, and to require her to cut off her hair and make a public reparation. But the priest, satisfied with her good dispositions, did not choose to deal so rigorously with her as she wished. But next morning the woman appeared in church, and before the Mass began she knelt down, and with much show of sorrow asked pardon of the Christians for the faults which she had committed.

In 1797 M. Lelabousse says: 'In the country

now occupied by the legitimate king we have six missionaries from the seminary of Paris, without including the Bishop and six native priests. The Spanish Franciscans have one religious. In the country about Huè there are six religious houses; in the province of Phuen, near where I am, there is one. There I found twenty-five religious, living by the work of their hands, and unknown to the pagans. They live in a poor little house. It is not possible to visit all the Christians once in two years. Many have not seen a priest for four years. There are provinces that have been without a missionary for fifteen years. One of these I visited. I could stay only a few days, from the spreading of the war into it. Long after I left these people they would kiss the very traces of my feet. As we have not time for the care of the Christians, we are obliged to give up the pagans. Yet what numbers might we gain to God could we only go amongst them! We can form an idea of what might be done from the number who of their own accord come to submit themselves to the faith. There is not a Christian village where there are not catechumens to baptise every time we pass them. There are several where I have had the consolation of giving this grace to twenty-five or thirty adults. At this moment, while I am writing, there is a request to go to a little Christian village, where five or six persons are anxiously desiring to embrace our holy religion, who have already been instructed. Many others, amongst whom are the chiefs of the village, are looking out with impatience for my arrival, that they may put their questions to me and satisfy their desires for the knowledge of the truth. I know a village where there are two thousand pagans, who have long wished to be instructed in our holy religion. Thirty of them, tired of waiting to no purpose, came in the beginning of the year to find a place to live where they could be made Christians. Every year, in my own neighbourhood, I have baptised nearly two hundred, sometimes more.'

M. Lelabousse became the successor of the Bishop of Adran, but he did not survive him long. There was, indeed, a great mortality amongst the friends of the Christians, who might have had influence with Gia-laong in subsequent years. Of this number was Father Paul, a Cochin-Chinese, much valued and trusted by the Bishop of Adran, and who had been known to Gia-laong in the days of his adversity. And besides, just in the moment of victory, died the young prince whom the Bishop of Adran had brought up. It is said that he died a Christian, and that before his death a native Christian gave him baptism; but we have no reliable information on the subject. So when Gia-laong triumphed, and the whole country fell under his power, the Christians had lost many of the supports which would have been valuable to them.

CHAPTER V.

FIRST MISSIONARY WORK IN TONKING.

Tonking received the Christian faith very much about the same time as Cochin China. It spread instantly and rapidly. The first missionary of note was just the man to make an impression, one whose faith and zeal and enterprise were unbounded—Alexander of Rhodes, whose name was famous in these countries. His success began immediately. He had hardly landed before he had made two converts, and at the end of the first year he had baptised above twelve hundred. His labour was untiring. He preached four times every day, and often six. Whole nights he spent hearing confessions. This went on for four years, from 1627 to 1630. During these years there was no opposition. The king was favourable to the missionaries, and openly espoused their cause. The king's sister and several of the royal family became Christians. The number of Christians went on increasing; and then came a sudden change. The king became suspicious, and ordered the missionaries at once to leave the country, and they were forced to obey. All went away, and were absent for ten months; but they left behind them a body of zealous Christians, and amongst them were some who could sufficiently fill the missionaries' place, and maintain the work they had been doing. There were preëminently three, Francis, Ignatius, and Andrew, catechists; and Francis was set at their head. This man was a pagan priest when the missionaries first arrived, but they had not been long in the country before he understood his errors, and renounced them. He was present one day when Alexander of Rhodes was preaching, and heard him denounce the false gods of the country, and the words took effect on his heart. He at once seemed to recognise the impotence of his deities, and went to the fathers to seek instruction. He was an apt scholar, and so profited by the lessons he received, that when the fathers left, there was no one found more fit to set over the mission. Through the active zeal of Francis and the other catechists conversions multiplied during the missionaries' absence; and on their return they found that no less than three thousand four hundred had been baptised; and the fervour of these new Christians was surprising. A Portuguese who had an opportunity of seeing them was much struck, and said they were more like religious than simple Christians, and that there was nothing like them in Europe. Another Francis may serve as a specimen. He was in the employ of a brother of the king. From the time of his baptism he gave himself up heartily to works of charity, and one of his especial delights was to bury the dead. This work of his was displeasing to his master, who disliked the Christians; and he ordered him to desist from it, and to give up a religion that taught him such practices. But Francis would not comply. So first he was driven out from the prince's service, then he was severely beaten, and as he was not to be moved, his infuriated master ordered his head to be cut off. And so Francis was the first martyr of Tonking.

Amongst the converts were some who might have seemed most unlikely. One of them was a sorcerer, a man of some repute, who had often expressed his contempt of the Christian faith. But he was struck by what he heard of the great things done at times by the sign of the cross, or by holy water, or that followed from Christian prayers. It made him think, and then he studied the catechism, and became convinced, and embraced the Christian religion.

From 1630 to 1640 the converts kept rapidly increasing. The fathers were suffered to remain in the country, though not without occasional signs of displeasure. During these years the average number of baptisms was about ten thousand each year; in 1639 there were over twelve thousand, and the total number of Christians was then computed at one hundred thousand.

After that it went on multiplying at the same rate for many years; so that in 1658 they were said to have advanced to as many as three hundred thousand. Then a fresh reign had commenced, and the new monarch very soon formed the resolution that he would allow the missionaries to remain in the country no longer. They had at that time their fixed stations in different provinces; they had built a hundred churches. Some villages were entirely Christian; some not wholly Christian had two thousand Christian inhabitants. In Kecho there were nine thousand, and the religion had spread into the palace; some of the wives of the late king, the niece of the queen-mother, the wife of the governor of the city, were all Christian; several mandarins, learned men, captains, soldiers. The king let the missionaries know that they must go; but he permitted two, F. Borgès and F. Tissanier, to remain, on the condition that they should not leave the capital, nor engage in missionary work.

At this period the missionary work depended again on the catechists. The fathers could not go out of the city, nor give the sacraments to any that did not come to them.

F. Tissanier lived at Kecho for three years, and has written an account of the mission in his time, and it is from him we draw this part of our history. Amongst other things he tells us of a visit that he and F. Borgès made to the court on the first day of the year. 'The principal festival observed by the Chinese and Tonkinese,' says he, 'is that which celebrates the first three days of their new year; and as this is decided by the moon, they make it commence from the new moon nearest to the 5th of February. They are most particular on these occasions to put on their most handsome dress, and they will spare no pains, even though poor, to procure fine apparel. The last day of the year the king, attended by his guards, leaves his palace, and goes down to the river to bathe, and the next day it is the custom for him to receive his subjects in the palace who come to pay their respects.'

It was thought desirable for the fathers to go. 'So,' says F. Tissanier, 'I put on a violet robe and a great six-cornered cap, which is the prescribed dress for a visit to the palace. As this first day of the year is with them superstitiously regarded as a day of good fortune, the Voua is on this day carried with great pomp through the principal streets of the city, so that I saw together the two kings of Tonking with as glittering a show as is perhaps ever to be beheld in this part of the world, and certainly in Tonking. On the eve the whole court is engaged in preparations for the grand feast; soldiers, by the king's order, are stationed in all the streets through which the Voua is to pass, three thousand being so employed. Through the night there is the constant gleam of fireworks. At midnight the sound of a cannon announces that the new year has begun, and is a notice that the next three days are to be days of rest and pleasure. At break of day the troops begin their march, that they may escort the Voua from the palace to the temple, where solemn worship is to be offered, and there is a propriety in the ceremonies which even a European can admire.

'There were forty thousand soldiers, with arms perfectly clean and bright; their dress was of linen of various colours, though that of each company was alike. Behind each company was an elephant with a mandarin or prince of the blood on its back, his seat a gilded chair, which was fastened on the elephant by iron chains, many of them silvered.

'Following each regiment came a number of horses, richly caparisoned, led by the bridle. With this grand display the king was borne along on a gilded seat that was covered; around him the pick of his whole army, forming the Choua's body-guard; they were mounted on choice horses, and were accompanied by a hundred elephants, and these were managed with all the ease of the most quiet horse in France.

'Last came the palanquin of the Voua, surrounded by his guards, who was going to offer sacrifice in the temple. The king and principal mandarins were present at the ceremony. When the Voua had completed the sacrifice, three discharges of a cannon were the signal to the soldiers that the Voua was about to move back to his palace. Then they began to defile, soldiers first, then horses and elephants, and after them the Voua, mounted on a splendid throne, numerous yellow flags fluttering around. This monarch seemed rapt at the sight of the vast multitude and grand scene as he paraded through streets in which on this day only in the year he was permitted to appear. The Choua, as he was carried in his chair, sat silent, with a dignity that was not observed in the Voua. On this occasion there were more than three thousand horses, and full three hundred elephants, and some of them of prodigious size. But as we looked on, what gave us most sorrow was the thought that out of that great multitude of soldiers, captains, mandarins, and princes, there were few who were not idolaters.

'Several went on with the Voua to his palace, but the king returned to his house, that he might receive the salutations of the princes, mandarins, and the whole army. The crowd at the palace gate was so great that we had small hope of being able to enter; but we made our way into a court where the king was receiving the homage of his people. There were four thousand persons present, and before them we made our four low bows, cap on head; for in Tonking and China no one except a malefactor stands uncovered before the king.'

On the third day of the feast the missionaries repeated their visit to the Choua, and then the king noticed them and honoured them with a word, and that satisfied them that he was not displeased, and that he tolerated their presence in the kingdom.

The Voua, who was allowed to take the first place in these ceremonies, was the descendant of the old reigning dynasty of Ly, who, as is seen, had lost all authority, which was centred in the Choua. Their condition had become perfectly insignificant. The Choua was the real ruler, and it is of him the missionaries speak under the name of king. When Alexander of Rhodes came to Tonking, Trinh-Taong was the third Choua. His father, the first of the line of Trinh, was son-in-law of Nguen-Do, the originator of this double rule. Nguen-Do had been successful in putting down a usurpation that had deposed the family of Ly; but though he restored the house of

Ly, and allowed them the old title of Voua, or king, he kept the whole authority in his own hands. He was succeeded not by his son, who was young at the time of his death, but by his son-in-law. The son, however, named Nguen-Hoang, became governor of Cochin China, and there, imitating the action of his father in Tonking, he set up for himself and assumed independence, and was the founder of the royal dynasty.

F. Tissanier has singled out for mention a catechist who died during the time of his residence at Kecho. His name was Benedict, and he lived at Kien-Lao, a town of some size, about a hundred and twenty miles from the capital. The people of this district were a fine hardy race, and some of the best soldiers in the king's army were drawn from it. The Christians there were numerous; there were two thousand in the town, and in the neighbourhood as many as fifteen thousand. And this Benedict was conspicuous amongst them. He was thirty-three years of age when he embraced Christianity, and such was his first ardour that it was his wish to leave his family and go and live with the missionaries. But the fathers would not allow it, and they thought zeal like his would be useful in his own home. But Benedict had all the spirit, as if he had been living under the rules of religion. He entered fully into the promise of his baptism, and gave up the world and its pleasures, taking the cross of the Son of God as the principle of his life. The pagans laughed at his folly, but to him his austerities and prayers were his chief delight. He let the pagans deprive him of his property, and cared not for it; for their affronts and wrongs were acceptable to him, as he could so glorify God in following in the way of his crucified Saviour. The mandarin who was governor of this town was a pagan, and very much averse to the Christian religion. He came one day into the room where the Christians were assembled, for at that time they had not a church, and pleased himself by striking with a stick whoever came in his way. The Christians fled from him to avoid his blows, but Benedict knelt still in his place. His composure irritated the mandarin, who beat him well, but without disturbing Benedict, who told him that he was ready to suffer anything for the love of God. Benedict was afterwards chosen chief catechist for this town and district, and great results followed from his earnest zeal. The number he baptised was astonishing, sometimes four hundred in a day. He built a church, and then, as the number of Christians increased, he added three more, large, and decorated as far as could be. He urged on the Christians to all sorts of good works; he persuaded them to give up their enmities; he taught them to practise acts of charity, one of which was every Sunday to bring to the church a measure of rice for the relief of the poor and sick. The rice was poured out at the church door, and mounted up to a great pile. In his charity he would go out to seek the robbers that infested the rivers, and entreat them to give up their lawless ways, offering willingly to give them what they sought to gain by force. The power of his words and example was widely felt. Pagans as well as Christians would listen to him. This good catechist came up to Kecho to die. His illness was brought about by his great fatigues in visiting the sick. He knew that he should die, and he wanted to see the missionaries, and to receive the sacraments. They asked him afterwards whether he would go back to Kien-Lao, to die at home, but he said, 'My home is where I can be most near the fathers, and the greatest honour you can do me is to bury me in the church.' The last five or six days of his life he had a crucifix constantly before his eyes, and he died in F. Borgès' arms.

In Tonking there was never such persecution as we have seen in Cochin China; but the missionaries were not suffered to remain long without molestation. F. Borgès soon after was expelled, and for several years there were no Jesuit missionaries in the country. During this interval a new set of missionaries was introduced, the French missionaries, who after a time took the whole work into their hands. The first of the line was also the first vicar-apostolic, Monsignor Deydier, who, in the disguise of a sailor, secretly made his way into the country in the year 1666.

After this the condition of the Christians was very varied. Sometimes there was a number of missionaries busy and undisturbed; sometimes they were suddenly stopped by some strong edict, and not one was allowed to remain in the country. In 1695 a French priest, named Royer, came to Tonking, and was able to continue his work for twenty years or more. We have a scheme of some of the work he did. He baptised yearly about three hundred adults; some years from four to five hundred. His infant baptisms were something less. He heard seven or eight thousand confessions, and gave six or seven thousand communions. His work was done mostly in the night. It was then he heard confessions, and held what intercourse he could with his Christians. He was a man with the true missionary spirit, as is evident from a letter of his that has been preserved. 'I was never so happy in France,' he says, 'as I am in Tonking. Truly we have here nothing but God, nor must we look for anything else; but what happiness it is to say with all fulness of heart, with no other attachment to deceive, "Deus meus et omnia!" ("My God and my all!"), and to hear also within our own soul the response of God to this entire surrender of ourselves to Him! We are ever discerning the marks of His special protection and the plain proofs of His presence. God gives Himself to us, I may say, as we wish to give ourselves to Him, wholly, and the hundredfold which we receive in this present life surpasses every sacrifice we make out of love for Him.'

A letter of another missionary in 1715, M. Messari, a Jesuit, shows us what sort of labours these missionaries would endure in order to find a way into the country. 'Towards the end of April I left Macao for Tonking, where I am to have twelve thousand

Christians under my care. I have made this journey on foot; I have had much to suffer in my long tramp: my feet were inflamed, and the skin much bruised. This has caused me much pain, but has not delayed my journey. I have made the distance from Macao to Lien-Tcheou in twenty-six days. This town, which is in China, is only six days' walk from Tonking. I am waiting for the Tonkinese couriers, who are to guide me into their country.' This missionary died for the faith in 1723. He was not actually a martyr, for he died of an illness caused by the fatigues of an imprisonment. He was arrested with F. Buccharelli, and both of them were taken to Kecho. F. Buccharelli was a martyr, having his head cut off a few months after the death of F. Messari. Nine native Christians suffered with him; one alone of these had shown any fear, Francis Ram. In his first alarm he consented to put his foot on the cross, but quickly repented, and gave himself up to his judges, and suffered in the end courageously. Luke Thu had quite a thirst for martyrdom. He had from youth been eminent for his virtue. His reputation for piety and learning had made him dear to a young Christian female who was rich, but he was loth to change his own poor and humble state for one of wealth, and shrank from the alliance. But her virtues made her worthy of him, and they were after a time married. Afterwards, having no children, they agreed to divide their goods amongst the poor, and to keep only for themselves a small pittance, enough to enable them to live by a church, where they might enjoy the blessings of the Mass and the sacraments. When persecution revived, a great desire seized Luke Thu to shed his blood for Jesus Christ. So he presented himself before the judges, and declared himself a Christian, and when ordered to put his foot on the cross, he only replied: 'This crucifix is the image of the Son of God, who deigned to be made man, and to die for the salvation of the world. Never for anything would I consent to put my foot on this sacred image.' And so saying, he took the crucifix, and raised it to his lips with love and reverence in the sight of the astonished pagans. When he was told that such disobedience of the laws of the king would be at the risk of his life, 'I fail not in respect to the laws of my country,' he said; 'but my first honour is due to the King who is in heaven. By following His laws I hope to be with Him in heaven through all eternity. You have power to take my life, but tell me for what it is you condemn me. What crime have I committed? What law have I violated? Is it for embracing Christianity, and practising its rules, that you punish me? Then know that no human law can touch things of this sort. Laws which forbid them are an affront to the divine Majesty, and deserve to be condemned.'

Boldness like this brought down upon him the vengeance of his judges. He was beaten all over with heavy hammers. But he was firm and serene, and the severity of his sufferings only made more plain his patience and heroic spirit. He suffered a long imprisonment, but his cheerfulness never flagged.

His chief joy was when he was told that the sentence of death had been passed. Then he sent to his wife telling her not to grieve, but to rejoice for him, and to wear no mourning, for the hour was come which he had so long desired, and the great wish of his heart was granted.

Some years later, as another letter shows, the mission was in peace and prospering. F. Philip Sahiri, who visited Tonking in 1736, writes thus: 'The present king is more indulgent to the Christians than his father was, and has given liberty to some who were in prison. Our fathers have two hundred churches and chapels, which are under the care of zealous well-trained catechists. The Christians are full of fervour, well instructed, and firm in the faith, and in their holiness of life, their pure morals, and generous charity represent to us the early days of Christianity.'

But it was only the next year that there was fresh persecution, and four Jesuit fathers shed their blood for religion. They were four fathers only recently arrived from Macao. They fell in with a troop of bandits on landing, who, after pillaging them, gave them into the hands of the governor. This man, in spite of orders, out of motives of avarice, sent them to Kecho. Once there the hope of deliverance was passed. January 9, 1737, they were executed, and two Tonkinese Christians with them.

On the appointment of Vicars-Apostolic, Tonking was divided into two Vicariates, Eastern and Western. Eastern Tonking was afterwards given up to the Spanish Dominicans, Western Tonking remaining under the rule of the French bishops. The fifth of these bishops was Mgr. Reydellet, who, coming to Tonking as a missionary in 1749, in 1766 became vicar-apostolic. One change had then taken place which very much improved the condition of the Tonkinese Christians, the substitution of native priests for catechists, who in the earlier days of this mission were employed in the principal missionary labours. Mgr. Reydellet also became the founder of the college of Ke-vinh, which for a series of years was the principal episcopal residence, and the chief school for preparing catechists and priests for their work. Ke-vinh was then a small village, with three hundred inhabitants, all Christians. It was the centre of a considerable Christian population, for in the surrounding villages were numerous converts, and their numbers were constantly increasing. The young catechists of the college had their first practice in missionary work in these villages; for on Sunday after Mass a troop of young catechists would go out and exercise themselves in the business of instruction, remaining absent till the Saturday following; and with such zeal and spirit did they labour, that seldom a day passed that they did not bring back a stray Christian or baptise a convert. The college was a large establishment. It was a seminary as well as a college, the home of sick and aged priests, and the episcopal palace. Here at times the Bishop would attempt a grand ceremony. He instances Easter 1767, and treats it as an event to be com-

memorated. There were present two European and
two native priests. The Christians flocked in from
all sides to this Pontifical Mass, and the mandarins
took no notice. At that time, as the Bishop tells us,
they were enjoying quiet. 'The missionaries are
let alone. The old edicts against us are in force
indeed, for they have not been revoked. But the
governors in some provinces are friendly, and do not
notice us. Some chief mandarins at court are favourable to us, but are in too great fear of their colleagues to openly show their sentiments.' Conversions then averaged between five and six hundred,
mostly the fruit of the work of the native priests and
catechists. There were twenty-nine native priests;
the European were very few, but their number was
increasing. In 1779 Mgr. Reydellet died, after a
thirty years' residence in the country. A severe
persecution had disturbed the Christians during his
last years, and had caused much desolation. College
and churches had been broken up and destroyed.
Two Spanish Dominicans, one a priest, had been put
to death. But in 1782 the storm had passed, and a
letter of M. Blandin, a missionary of the period,
shows us that active work was resumed. 'We begin to breathe,' he says, 'and God has taken signal
vengeance on the enemies of our religion. All our
persecutors have come to a miserable end. The man
who wrote the edict lost his hand. He died in great
suffering, and his body has been cast into the river;
a terrible ignominy out here, where the dead are
worshipped. Another who was foremost in de-

spoiling our churches and doing us mischief has been degraded, and lies ignominiously in a dungeon loaded with irons. We have been busy, now peace is restored, in repairing the damages of the persecution. So we have proclaimed the jubilee, which on account of the persecution we were obliged to defer, and I cannot tell you what fruits have resulted. The Lord has shed down on the mission very great blessings, and many persons, even whole villages, who in the persecution had given up the faith, have come back to God. Every one has been eager to gain the jubilee, crowding to the exercises, pouring in from the neighbouring villages as soon as the missionary arrives.'

The next vicar-apostolic after Mgr. Reydellet was Mgr. Davoust. He was an old man, who had before been a missionary in Tonking, but at the time of his appointment was in France. It was 1784 when he reached Tonking, and his landing was a narrow escape. A vessel with a mandarin on board was on the look-out, and he was only saved from capture by the fortunate grounding of his own vessel, in consequence of the fall of the tide, which would not allow the other to approach, and before the tide was again risen some friendly Christian fishermen had taken him on shore in their boat. Soon after he was at Ke-vinh.

With Mgr. Davoust there came to Tonking a missionary named La Mothe. He was soon at his post, and has described for us his position. 'There is a great deal of work in the place where I am,' he says. 'It comprises two districts, in which are two Tonkinese priests, 16,000 Christians, forty churches, four houses of God, five houses of religious females, not to mention the 100,000, or perhaps 200,000, pagans who form the population of the country placed under my care. This is a great deal for a labourer like myself. It is a heavier weight than I had when I was a vicar in France. But the more work I have the greater is my consolation. I am filled with admiration at the works of grace I see. I see women who never leave the path of virtue, with daughters who outshine them, privileged souls about whose predestination there can be no mistake. I see sinners of long standing—ten, twenty, or thirty years—converted, and coming back by dozens. One whole village renounced its superstitions, and came to me for instructions and confession.'

In 1790 the rule of the Chouas came to an end. The Taysons overthrew it, and with ease; although the Chinese interfered, it was ineffectually, and the Chinese troops were beaten as easily as the Tonkinese. The change was advantageous to the Christians. For the Taysons, in the earlier days of their power, allowed the Christians a good deal of liberty, and, during the few following years, there being a considerable accession of ministers, the missionary work was particularly active and successful. Mgr. Davoust was dead, and had been succeeded by Mgr. Longer, up to this a missionary in Cochin China, but selected by the Holy See for this vicariate.

CHAPTER VI.

M. LA PAVEC.

M. LA PAVEC was one of five missionaries that came out to Tonking in 1790. His busy active work has been described by himself in a series of letters, which give us a good deal of insight into missionary life in Tonking, and we will draw from them freely. The first letter, dated 1791, tells us of his landing. 'In the October of last year we left Macao, five French and four Spanish misionaries, to go to Tonking. After a ten days' sail we anchored nine miles off land, near a place where there were Christians. As our ship was European every one was afraid to come near us, dreading that we were pirates. Signals were in vain. After waiting two days we let down a boat, that we might put the Tonkinese couriers ashore. But the sea was heavy, and they were frightened, and came back again. The next day we noticed a number of fishing-boats; so one of the Spanish fathers and myself, with the two Tonkinese, got down into our boat, to make out, if we could, whether there were any Christians amongst them. There were full fifty boats, with not less than ten men aboard, and great was our surprise to see them all take to flight. We went on to put our couriers ashore. As soon as they had landed, and the news

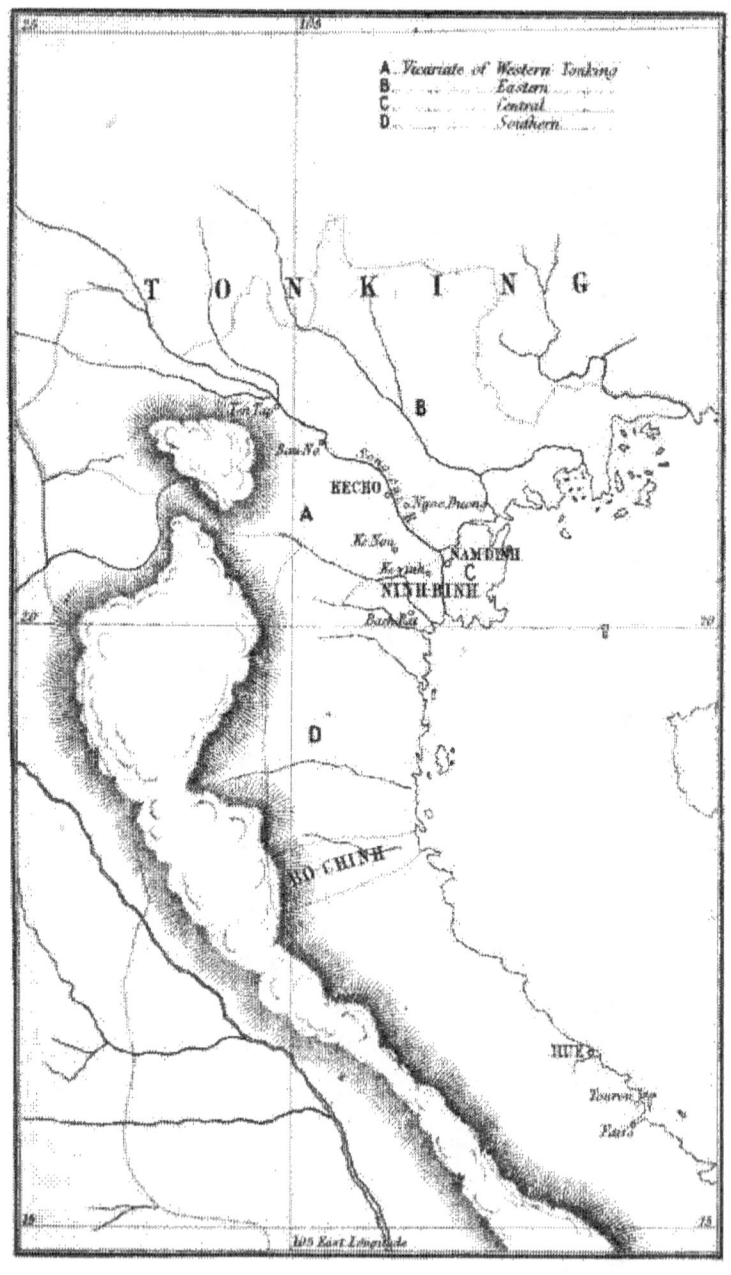

transpired that we were the missionaries, everywhere the cry burst forth, "Here are the fathers! There is no fear!" We were pleased and surprised to see the change in these men, just now so timid; they dashed into the sea to bring us to land; they shoved off their boats to hurry to the ship, and take provisions to the captain; they sent messengers to give notice of our arrival to the Tonkinese fathers. Every one was busy about something. Rough seas or rising winds were not now feared. They took us to the house of the Tonkinese fathers, which was close by, and, after dinner, to that of the Dominicans. The next day we had the pleasure of seeing our companions, who came with our effects. After celebrating the Feast of All Saints, we left for our own college of Ke-vinh, and there M. le Roy was awaiting us. A few days later came M. Sérard, the pro-vicar-general.'

In a little while M. la Pavec had his station assigned to him. It was a large extent of country—three whole provinces, the three northern—reaching up to the borders of China, having Eastern Tonking on one side, and Laos on the other. It would take him fifteen days to travel from one end to the other; it was intersected by rivers, while lofty mountains and trackless forests would add to the difficulties of passage. Numerous villages were scattered about, some of considerable size. The Christian population was about nine thousand, but from the absence of missionaries many were very ignorant, and many had left the faith. Three native priests were all the help they had, and two of them were disabled, one being sick and the other blind. The sight of a European priest was joy indeed to these people. 'It is sixty years,' they said to M. la Pavec, 'since we have seen a European missionary, and now in His mercy the Lord has sent us one. God be for ever blessed!' As he journeyed along, the Christians from the various villages flocked out to meet him, and many would not leave him, but went with him on his way. The pagans too were curious, and wanted to know what had brought him there; and when he told them that he had come in search of souls, they were full of wonder. It was a difficult thing to get away when he once reached a Christian village; they did not like to part with him; and once, when he was staying in a place where there was a small cluster of Christian villages, a deputation came to him, and seriously proposed that he should cease journeying, and stay where he was. The heat and fatigue, they said, would kill him; the Tonkinese priests, who were accustomed to the climate, might go out to visit the sick and give the sacraments, but he must stay at home and receive the visits of those who wanted him. But this would not suit M. la Pavec.

In a letter to his parents, written 1792, M. la Pavec has given a sketch of his daily life: 'About six in the evening I enter the confessional, and I do not leave it till dawn. Then, after making my preparation, and giving an instruction to the Christians, I celebrate Mass. After my thanksgiving I breakfast, and then hold interviews, first with the chiefs of the village on such business as may be necessary, then with any one who may have any private business to discuss with me. This done, I have my own duties. I read some theology, or portions of the Old or New Testament, or some spiritual book. Then comes dinner, palatable or not in proportion to the means of the Christian whose turn it may be to furnish it. After dinner I throw myself on a plank, on which has been spread a mat of rushes, having my habit for a pillow, and on this bed I sleep, very soundly I assure you, for four or five hours. On rising I recite my office, then sup on such fare as chance may offer. After short evening prayers I give a familiar instruction, and then go back to the confessional.'

This mode of life of course had its interruptions; there were visits to the sick, and sometimes it might be a journey of three or four days, and at the end of it there might be the disappointment of finding the sick person dead, and of being able to do no more than give burial.

The recovery of apostates was one of M. la Pavec's frequent employments. He heard of a village where the number of these was considerable, and he resolved to make an effort to reclaim them. He sent a catechist to visit them, but they showed no disposition at all to change; they had got accustomed to the superstitions of the other villagers, they had pagan wives, and their children were brought up pagans; they wished to be let alone.

M. la Pavec urged them to come and see him, and after a time two of the principal men of the village came. His words affected them, and they returned to the faith, with their wives and children. Then followed a visit to the village; a Mass, which drew together crowds of people; earnest preaching; and the result was the conversion of more than half the village.

Many pagans were converted, some from being present at a Mass, some from the view of a procession; but what especially touched their heart was the washing of the feet on Holy Thursday. Processions chime in with the feelings and the habits of the Tonkinese. 'It is their custom,' says M. la Pavec, 'when they have to be present at any civil or religious ceremony, to dress themselves in a long robe, black or white, something like that of our judges in Europe, having on their heads a tall round cap, the hair hanging down over the shoulders; and they go through their ceremonies with an admirable gravity. I have been much struck at seeing them in procession in this costume, walking at a measured pace in two lines, silent and composed, and never turning their eyes one side or the other.'

In two years his converts, he says, amounted to about eight hundred. Some of them were young females, and they had a great deal to put up with from their pagan relatives. One who had all her little property taken away submitted to the loss contentedly. 'Take it,' she said to her parents; 'it is yours; but my heart is my own, and I have given that to God.' Another—very young, only fourteen —had to suffer a great deal of ill usage because she would not join in the pagan rites of the household; but she bore all patiently, and her quiet docile ways so won upon her parents that in the end they also were converted.

In 1793 M. la Pavec made his way into some of the mountainous districts, through dense forests and wild rugged paths, urged on by his charity; for those whom he went to see had for years been without any ministry, even that of native priests. Tigers prowled about, and were constantly making a prey of some one. But his trouble was well repaid. He brought back six hundred to the faith, and baptised three hundred more. His presence when he came amongst these strangers was hailed with delight. They flocked to him to listen to his preaching. All business was for the time suspended. They feasted him with their best, killing fowls and an ox for his entertainment. The Feast of All Saints was distinguished. It was made a great festivity. 'It was kept with all the pomp possible in such a place. Musical instruments, flags, cannon, were lent us by the mandarin of the district, though a pagan. The Christians came to conduct me to the church; two and two in front of me, each holding a lighted taper; they marched along a path covered with tapestry, with music and the firing of cannon. The five weeks I stayed in this place was a constant festival. Pagans came in crowds to witness the ceremonies, and in their wonder said they had never seen anything so edifying; the mandarins too paid me a visit, and brought me a present. But what most consoled me was the return of a number of stray Christians to their duties, with great earnestness and signs of sorrow. A man who professed magic was so moved by what he saw, that, breaking his altar and idols, he came and asked for baptism. A young man of twenty came to me and entreated me to teach him the truth. "How can you tell," said I, "that I am able to teach it?" "I asked the Christians," he replied, "who you were, why you had come, and where you came from. They told me; and I cannot believe that a man like you would expose himself to such fatigue and danger, and receive nothing, but rather give to the poor, and not be a teacher of the truth. I want you therefore to instruct me in a religion that teaches in this way to do good to men. The masters of our temples are not like this. They care for nothing but their own interests. They have nothing to give to others, and you cannot give them too much."

'One evening, when I was preparing to hear confessions, a stranger came to me, and requested that I would go with him to give the sacraments to his mother. "Is your mother a Christian?" I asked. "No," he replied; "but she is very anxious that you should visit her." In consequence I went, and several Christians with me. I found a very old woman, exceedingly ill, and unfortunately so deaf that she could hear neither me nor the catechist. She could understand no one but her own son, to whose voice she was accustomed. I asked him to be my interpreter, and to inquire of his mother what it was she wanted. "Give me your blessing," she said. "There are terrors after death which make me afraid." I asked her who it was that created the heaven and the earth and all things, and she said she did not know. I gave her some instruction on the principal truths of religion, and she learnt all with an ease that surprised me, and replied to my questions in a way I should not have thought possible in one so old, whose instruction had been so small. The Christians assured me that she had always lived among pagans, and that they had never conversed with her on religion, and they added that her life, so far as they knew, had been blameless. When I went on with my questions, she stopped me, saying sorrowfully, "There is no more time for questions, my father; do not delay to wash me from my sins; the gates of eternity are opening on me." Without many more words I baptised her. It was then midnight, and in the morning she was dead. During her last moments she pressed the crucifix to her lips, and with her eyes flooded with tears she asked pardon of Jesus Christ for having so often offended Him, repeating over the words, "My God, why have I known Thee so late?" I returned to the church, admiring the goodness of God, who, when He pleases, knows how to change stones into children of Abraham. Both Christians and pagans were much affected by this event.'

While M. la Pavec was in this place, a pagan

woman took a journey of many days to visit him. Her husband was a Christian, but a careless one; she had, however, noticed him at times saying his prayers, and had picked up a little Christian knowledge; so her curiosity had been excited, and she took the trouble to come and see the new missionary, in the hope of being made a Christian. And her zeal was rewarded by baptism.

A woman was sick who had been an apostate for twenty years, and M. la Pavec went to visit her. She pretended to be deaf, and he went away without, as it seemed, having made any impression on her. But it was not so. The prayer which he had offered for her and the word he had spoken had not been in vain. Her heart had been really touched; her conscience had been roused, and she was full of trouble and remorse; nor could she find rest till at her own entreaty M. la Pavec had returned and heard her confession. She did not, however, die, but lived long enough to prove the sincerity of her conversion. Such were the employments of M. la Pavec during the happy days spent amongst the simple people of that rude district. The five weeks of his stay came to an end, and all were full of grief. On his going, there was a repetition of the same demonstrations with which his approach had been welcomed—the torches, the music, the cannon—but there was missing the burst of joy that then thrilled through the multitude. There was now a gloom, and the sad parting words told of the sorrow with which they saw him depart. 'My father, my father, are you going to leave us, and must we again be without a pastor?' But stay was impossible; already it had been too long; the fatal effects of the damp heavy air of the mountains had not been escaped, and even the strong frame of M. la Pavec for weeks afterwards could not throw off the mischief of that poisonous influence. As the stream bore away his boat the earnest people ran along the banks; but it was too rapid for them, and soon they could only follow him with their eyes.

The inhabitants of these mountains consider themselves the original inhabitants of the country, and look upon the Tonkinese as colonists from China. They have a language of their own. They are strict as to truth, and honest in their dealings. They are very hospitable, and not at all willing to receive a recompense for kindness done to a stranger. They worship the devil, fear and not love being the principle of their worship; still they are simple in their manners, and well disposed to receive Christianity.

The next year M. la Pavec was again at similar work, but on another range of the mountains. He shall recount his own story: 'Having been told that there were still on the mountains Christians who had not seen a priest for a number of years, I looked out for a way of procuring them some spiritual help. One of my catechists, a young man full of zeal, and who had no fear when God's glory or the salvation of souls was the question, as soon as he understood my purpose, asked to be allowed to go on before me. Hardly had he gone before he fell sick; but he did not desist for that—he went on to the boundaries of the kingdom preaching and instructing with much fruit. Some days after (October 1795) I set out myself, taking with me two Christians who used to serve my Mass. On entering the province of Hang, the last towards the west, I fell in with a village of about twenty houses, all Christian except two. Although they had seen no priest for a long time, they observed their religion, and assembled morning and evening in church. I remained with them ten days, to instruct them and give them the sacraments; the younger server teaching the children their catechism, the elder presiding at prayer and reading. I sent him to preach to the two pagan families, and after two days one was converted and came to hear my instructions. They learnt their prayers and catechism very eagerly. As they hoped to see us on our return, they let us go the more willingly. Then followed a fatiguing journey of ups and downs by paths over-run with thorns and briers, and at the end of the day we came upon some Christians living by the water, as they were fishers. They had not seen a priest for fifteen years, and were in consequence very ignorant. A day's journey higher up the mountains we found three Christian families. After this we got into a boat provided by the Christians at the extreme end of the kingdom. Three nights we slept in the open air; around us were steep mountains rising to a great height, and the still silence was relieved by the cries of the tigers and elephants. On the fourth day we reached a small village, where I met some Christians so utterly ignorant that they could not even baptise their children. I stayed with them some time, and then directed a Christian, who had come there to cut wood, to teach them, so that on my return I might admit them to the sacrament on their better preparation. After leaving them, I met my catechist quite hoarse with his preaching. We were now on the frontiers of China, and the Christians whom we found had seen no priest for twenty-five years. The man who had kept most of his religion had a pagan wife and pagan children; sometimes he said prayers with them. Their sad state only moved our compassion and zeal. We visited them house by house, speaking to them earnestly; and in a few days, to our consolation, eight of these families were converted; a third had been baptised—the rest were pagans—of the number an old sorcerer, who had carried on his arts for forty years. The mandarin of the place, a rich man, and an oracle with the people, had warned them not to attend our ceremonies. "If the master of the Christians," said he, "only sprinkle a drop of water on you, you will not be able to help becoming Christians." He compared our holy water to the superstitious charms in use amongst them. Notwithstanding this prohibition, they came to our ceremonies; but seeing me approach with the holy water, they hurried off. Some stayed, however, and said audibly, "When we are in hell, will the mandarin come and take us out? He will not be able to get out himself. The master teaches us the truth, and things that agree with sound reason. Who shall hinder us from believing and following his doctrine?" When we had stayed here a sufficient time to instruct and establish these Christians, we began to prepare to depart. Three days before we left there were continual tears and laments. I could not myself refrain from tears; but go we must. On our return we visited all the places through which we had before passed, and everywhere there was the same sorrow at our going.

'After the Epiphany I went down into the southern province, and joined MM. Bissachère and Eyot. We gave a retreat first to the priests, catechists, and religious, and afterwards to the Christians, who flocked to us in crowds. Lastly, we made one ourselves. As I went homewards I met Mgr. la Mothe, Bishop of Castoria. We would have liked to have remained together a little while; but that very day came news of persecution, and the danger was too great, for we were near the royal city. So we each went our way.'

Another year (1797) he took the range of mountains in the direction of Laos. The fatigues of the journey were very great. He was left at length with only one companion, his catechist; all the rest having fallen ill. It is better to take his own description: 'I was buried in the woods that border on Laos. The country is exceedingly mountainous. After journeying for two or three days on the heights, we descended into valleys, narrow but productive. The plains are watered by two large rivers, which rise in these mountains. Toil as we might, the utmost we could effect from morning to noon was to get over one range of these steeps; we might accomplish another by evening. Our path was simply such passage as the waters had formed, full of sharp rocks which wounded our feet. The branches overhanging these gullies furnished a support as we went up and down; but we had to cut our way through them, using the sword we carried as a defence against tigers. We found Christians who had been left to themselves for years, young persons of fifteen still unbaptised; yet they all observed their religion, and had their morning and evening prayers. They wept for joy on our coming, and again from grief at our going away. They would willingly have provided for us, could we have stayed with them; that was not possible, for we had other Christians to visit.

'These mountain regions touch upon China towards the north-west, and the kingdom of Laos on the south-west. They are inhabited by three separate races, all distinct in language and customs.

'1. The *Tonkinese*, who come there for traffic and other employments. These are not many.

'2. The *Mois*, who inhabit the valleys. They cultivate rice, cotton, and indigo. They keep bees and silk-worms. They manufacture silk and cotton, and from their rice make a liquor something like beer. Their letters are the same as those of the people of Laos, and there is much similarity between the two people.

'The Mois worship spirits, but out of fear. "They

will hurt us," they say, "if we do not appease them by sacrifices." They have some idols, but they come from Tonking. They give divine honour to their ancestors. Though superstitious, they are less so than the Tonkinese. They are simple and truthful; they detest theft, and are honest in paying their debts. They have each their own wife, but are not chaste. They love drink.

'3. The inhabitants of the mountains. After felling the forest trees, they sow a kind of rice that does not require water. At the foot of the mountains they sow cotton, and plant a peculiar kind of mulberry-tree. They have gardens too, fixing their houses in the mountain valleys. They close the entrances to their valleys, and make circuitous roads to them, in fear that the Tonkinese mandarins might trouble them with a visit. One from each district goes to pay the king's tribute, which they discharge punctually. The others never go down from their hills. They are even more simple and faithful than the Mois. They are exact in paying their debts, and never touch each other's property. They are more sober than the Mois; but though they have but one wife, they are not faithful. Their own story is that their ancestors came from a great kingdom, very likely Thibet. Their language is unlike both that of Tonking and Laos. Their worship is like that of their neighbours, but they are less superstitious.'

The Bishop of Gortyna made a visit to M. la Pavec in 1779, and he speaks of it in a letter: 'M. la Pavec has consoled me much. He has been with me over the three districts of his province. We gave a retreat together, which brought much fruit. I administered confirmation to over 3000 adults. I had to go up and down, in passing from one district to the other; sometimes in the midst of forests, tigers howling all around; sometimes on the rivers in a traffic boat. Once I was nearly overset, once quite. Two persons kept me from sinking, holding me up. I had an attack of fever. I lost one of my pupils, who went with me; several were sick. M. la Pavec alone was free from illness; but he has courage enough to do what is required of him, even though he be sick.'

CHAPTER VII.

M. GUERARD.

THERE was another missionary of these times no less busy than M. la Pavec, and who has left records of himself. This was M. Guérard. He was another of the five who came out to Tonking in 1790. His first act on landing in the country to which he had come to devote himself was significant: 'As soon as I set foot on land, I threw myself on the ground, and embraced it, and bedewed it with my tears. We went at once to return thanks to God for the favour granted us. It was the 29th of October. We celebrated the Feast of All Saints at the house of the Spanish Dominicans. Then we went to our own college, where we found M. le Roy; I formed a warm friendship with him. He is learned and holy. I wish I was like him. We stayed with him some time; but it seemed short, so great was the pleasure I took in the company of this holy priest.'

M. le Roy was an old missionary, and for some years his duties had been in the college of Ke-vinh. After a month's sojourn at Ke-vinh, M. Guérard started for his duties in the most southern province. His first business was to learn the language, and by the middle of the summer he had acquired a tolerable proficiency. Then he went to Thoki, a large village, inhabited partly by Christians, partly by pagans. He got there on the eve of the Assumption, and on the Feast he preached his first sermon. His health, which up to that time had been feeble, suddenly rallied; but in October he was so ill that his life was despaired of.

We may recount an incident he has related which happened during his stay at Thoki: 'Towards the end of August I thought it would recruit my health to take a walk out in the open country. This I had not yet done. So in the evening I went with some of the children. My tall figure, my long thick beard, my pale thin face—in short, my completely unusual appearance—failed not to draw around me a large retinue of pagans. I thought I ought to preach to them; they listened to me for the most part with attention and respect. But there was one who put to me rude questions unfit for modest ears. On my gently reproving him he got angry, and not only abused me, but began to threaten, and make a show of striking with his knife. Then I took up another tone, assuming the master, and soundly rated him for his scandalous conduct, and for daring to utter obscene words before a servant of God and the children of the village. Then the fellow went off quite intimidated. So ended my first sermon to the pagans. The next evening I went out in the direction of a temple of idols; a crowd collected around me, but I walked on without a word till I reached the gate of the temple. Then I preached to them of God, and of the rewards He will bestow on the good, and of the terrible punishment He will inflict on those who leave Him to worship idols of wood and stone. What I said of the pains of hell frightened them all away, even the guardian of the temple, and one only remained with me, a youth from sixteen to eighteen, who listened attentively throughout. I did not go out again, and during the three months I was in this village all the adults I baptised were ten. One of these was an old woman of eighty. Curiosity brought her to me one day, and I made an attempt to teach her; she would not listen, but hastily retired. I found out where she lived, and sent a catechist to her; but she could not be persuaded to give me a hearing. I went on sending messages, and at length, on my tenth application, she yielded, listened, and was converted. She had little memory left, but diligently set herself to learning her prayers. On leaving Thoki I made a journey into the interior to visit and instruct the Christians. I have reached the foot of the chain of mountains that divide Tonking from Laos. I find numerous Christians, and devote to them my principal attention. I can preach but little to the pagans. The Christians whom I meet are so little more than in name, so long have they been deprived of spiritual aid. It is hard work to instruct them, but consoling from the sight of the good that is done. They are very docile; only tell them a thing is wrong, and they do it no more. They are very diligent in prayer; young and old, men and women, rich and poor. In the evening after prayer the more fervent assemble together, and pass a great part of the night in going over their catechism and the instructions I have been giving to them.

'The order of my own proceeding is as follows: At sunset the Christians assemble in the place where I say Mass, which we call the church. For this purpose I choose the largest and most convenient room I can find. When they are assembled, I instruct them for an hour and a half or two hours, explaining the creed, the commandments, and their prayers. But before anything else, my first care is to teach them how to pray and make a meditation. While I am teaching the elder ones, my catechist is at the catechism with the younger. The instructions over, they say their prayers and retire to rest, the men by themselves, and the women and their daughters together; for a return home by night is not possible from the number of tigers in these parts. My own remaining time I spend in converse with my good Master. In the morning at three, for about three quarters of an hour, as far as we can tell without clock or watch, we have our prayer; then while they are reciting vocal prayers I am making my own preparation for Mass. Before Mass I preach for half an hour or an hour. After Mass they go to their work, those excepted who remain for confession. These poor people often continue without eating, for I have nothing to give them. Their confessions are, in fact, general confessions, sometimes of fifty or sixty years; most of them have never made a confession, and do not know how to make it. When I have completed the work of one village, I go on to another, and there is the same over again. You may suppose when I leave them there are tears. I was prepared for this in France, or rather my Lord prepared me, who gave me courage to see tears flow that went even more deeply to my heart. What a thrill even now when I think of them! My God, Thou art my God! All for Thee, all for Thee, my dear Master! I would sacrifice all, that I may find all.

'The pagans of this district are not at all unfriendly to our religion; indeed, they respect and like it. They allow it is the only true one; but the greater part have not the courage required in order to embrace it. I have, nevertheless, destroyed many columns erected in front of their houses, where three or four times in the month they burn incense, with the view of becoming rich. They all hold me in high respect; they come to consult me about what will happen, as if I could foresee it; they call me a saint; so putting me to shame, and forcing me to reprove them, but to no purpose. I have baptised a good number, and every day fresh persons are coming to me for instruction. I put them under as long a trial as I can manage. I preach to them on the sacrament they are seeking; I exhort the Christians who are present to pray for them; I teach them to make acts of faith, hope, and charity, and require a renunciation of Satan and all the superstition of paganism. Afterwards, with two catechists, I sing the *Veni Creator* and the *Monstra te esse matrem*, and read to them the Gospel for the Ascension, placing the stole on their heads as we do in France. This ceremony animates them, and stimulates their ardour and watchfulness. The Christians are told to observe their conduct, so as to be faithful witnesses when the time comes to baptise them. In this way they are impressed with a high idea of the purity demanded of a child of God. So after baptism they live like angels. I generally give them communion on the day after baptism, and this greatly supports them. The faith of these new Christians is mostly greater than that of the older ones, and their charity more warm; but when I say this I do not mean to disparage the others.'

Speaking of the ravages of the tigers, he says: 'Feb. 5th, I saw one very near me. He laid hold of three men close by my side, one not eight feet off. This last was a Christian, the others were pagans. Happily for them, the whole village had assembled to give chase. By timely succour the men are not dead; they got off with some strokes of the paws, but each grip caused a wound as large as a fowl's egg. The Christian had three wounds: one on his side, one on his back, and a third on his leg; the one on the side was a frightful gash. The two other men were dangerously wounded. The tiger was about the size of a young colt. The night before, as I was going to see a sick man, I twice passed the bushes where this tiger had his lair, but we saw nothing of him.

'On the 15th of February I was called to visit a sick person. In going I passed through a village hostile to our religion, where they had laid a plot to seize me. All the inhabitants had come out, and were ranged in two rows; but they did not venture to say a word. I knew nothing of their purpose then, but my catechist, who followed shortly after, learnt it, and met with some ill-treatment. As I came back, just as I had passed through a village, I three times saw a sword raised as if to cut off my head. I was saying my rosary, and my good Mother obtained for me the grace to have no fear; but my stupidity was such, that till the third time I did not think of making the offering of my life for my sins. This is how it happened: some twenty soldiers were running in little troops, looking for the chief of the village we had just passed, and intending to kill him. They were mad with rage, and when in this state they will kill any one who comes in their way, enemy or not, and think nothing of it. I came upon one of these parties just as I left the village, and before I was aware he had raised his sword to kill me. He was but two feet off when I stopped, and looked at him fixedly. Infuriated as he was, he lowered his head, and would not look me in the face. Still he kept his sword raised. Our Lord granted me the favour of retaining my self-possession, and I asked the soldier what he was about and what it was he wanted. "Whence do you come? Where are you going? Where do you live?" he cried out, in reply. "I come from visiting a sick person; I am going to visit another. As for home, I have none, for I go wherever the needs of my neighbour require." At these words he left me, and I went on my way. A little farther on I met six, and the same questions and answers were repeated. Then came another party of six full of rage, with naked swords, offering to cut off my head. It was then it came into my head to offer my life to the good Jesus, and to recommend myself to the holy Virgin and my guardian angel. The soldiers were only a step from me, crying out, "Where are you going? Whence do you come?" And I replied quietly, as I had done before, still walking on. Their arms fell at once. The road was muddy, with a narrow path in the middle. They all left the path, and went out into the mud, and let me go by. As I passed they looked at me with an air of amazement.

'After escaping this danger, I said a *Te Deum* and continued my rosary, as an act of thanksgiving. By evening I arrived at the house of the sick. These soldiers are not dangerous, except when out on quests like this. They hardly notice me when I meet them. They may pass a remark about my appearance, especially my beard. "What a fine beard! What a size it is!" Sometimes they salute me with politeness, saying to one another, "It's a European priest."

'I celebrated Easter with much solemnity, amidst large numbers of Christians and pagans. On Palm Sunday a young pagan girl, who came half-a-day's journey to see us, after hearing my sermon, was so touched in her heart by grace, that on her return to her master, who was also a pagan, she did what I had told her, that she might fit herself for embracing the faith. Her master beat her so as to draw blood; but she persisted, saying, "Beat me if you please, but

I will be a Christian; I would rather die than worship idols any more." The next day she fled to another village, where a good Christian took her in, and gave her food and instruction.

'I went through the office of the Holy Week as we do in France, crowds attending. On Holy Thursday I had the washing of feet; on Saturday, the benediction of the fire, of the font, &c. These poor people, who had never seen anything like it, were vastly struck. I was careful to instruct them in the meaning, and they were full of devotion. Although thousands were present, there was complete silence.

'On Easter-eve all the Christians, with candles in their hands, came to me, that we might go in procession to sing matins. For music they had two pieces of stick, which they beat in time. The men walked in front, two and two, with much order and propriety; then the women, singing a hymn in honour of the blessed Virgin. The pagans were in two rows, keeping perfectly silent. After matins they brought me back in just the same way. I was vested in surplice, stole, and biretta. The next day they came again to conduct me to and from Mass, which I celebrated with solemnities. I preached to the pagans three times that day, and my catechist spent the whole night in instructing them. God gave them the grace to profit. Great numbers asked to be received as catechumens, but I made them go through a trial. The temper of the people is very yielding, and you must see the fruits, and not count the blossom. But very many have persevered.

'At length the day came for my return. I intended to go to the river and take a boat, which was to convey me to the next village; but when I reached the river there was no one to take me, for every one had fled to escape the soldiers, who were pressing them into their service. A band of these soldiers occupied our path about a mile and a half in front. What were we to do? The sun was setting, and we dared not go back for the tigers. The river was on one side, the mountains on the other. My catechist was full of terror. "Come, my child," I said, reassuring him, "this is the time to show our confidence in God. Take courage; He will not abandon us." We went on, and in about half an hour we encountered the soldiers encamped in our very path. They were all asleep but two, and these had their backs towards us, and we passed through without being noticed. After this passage my catechist was full of wonder; we returned thanks to God for the deliverance He had granted us. But in allowing us to pursue our journey God had His own purposes, for I was but just in time to calm the sorrow of a poor woman in despair, who, close on the banks of the river, was on the point of throwing herself into the water. What caused her trouble was that the people of the village wanted to compel her daughter to marry contrary to her wishes. For by an order lately issued, in all villages where a sufficient number of men were not supplied for the public works the unmarried women were to fill the vacancies, and carry stores to the fortifications. And as the villages had to maintain all so employed, they wanted as much as they could to keep down the number, and were consequently forcing the young women to marry. What the Christians will do, I do not know, if God does not help them. They are often obliged to take pagan husbands, yet many, I know, would rather die than do so.'

Writing to his brother the following year, 1793, he says: 'I speak the Annamite tongue with as much ease as French, perhaps more. The language is not at all easy; there is some difference of language in every village, and some difference of accent. They have no notion of writing, except with an endless number of letters.

'The religion of the Annamites is marked by a number of ridiculous fancies that might appear incredible. There are a host of diviners, who make the ignorant people believe that when they are sick it is some devil who is tormenting their body. And to ease the dying man they set up a noise round him to frighten the imaginary devil away; sometimes they strike the sick man so as almost to kill him; sometimes they puncture his skin to let out the evil spirits. Only lately they cut the throat of a poor woman, who died a few days after. If during these practices the sick person cries out, they say it is the devil, who does not like to leave him. As they are naturally timid, the dread of injury is the only principle of their worship. The deities whom they call kind are poorly served. They adore all kinds of idols under the name of spirits. The dog and the tiger have also their altars. One superstition is general and deeply rooted, and on this you cannot undeceive them—the worship of parents. As soon as they are dead, they give them divine honours; and should any one refuse to join in this, he is accounted an unnatural child, who will not give his father and mother the honour which justly belongs to them, and he is ill-treated all kinds of ways, his property is taken from him, and his house is burnt. This custom is a great hindrance to religion.

'They believe in transmigration, and from this when a child dies his parents will sometimes cut up the body into small pieces, and then scatter the fragments in all directions, in fear that he should go back into the womb of his mother when she conceives again. And they fancy that if they give a good name to their child the devil will prize it the more, and take it away, which makes them give it the worst name they can. If any one were to say to them that their infant was pretty, it would displease them, out of the persuasion that the devil, hearing the compliment, would take their child away.

'The Tonkinese are polite, and ready to do kindness. The Christians especially will not spare anything in the service of the priest. About this I often blame them, but it is of no use. I cannot vex them more than by refusing to take the vegetables and fruits they bring me. Since I have been here I eat nothing else, and I am very well. The pagans will also occasionally bring me these kind of presents. It is the way an Annamite pays his respects, and to omit it is a breach of civility. It is an effort to me to take these presents, but not to do so would give offence. I cannot do more than insist that the gifts shall be of small value, and not like the presents to the mandarins; that they should treat me as the poor, who are the friends of Jesus Christ. If I wished to be rich, it would only depend on myself. But God preserve me from this! I am poor, and wish to be poor. I hope that by God's grace I shall be poor to my last hour. My colleagues have heard stories of my way of life, and blame me; but what is told them is an exaggeration, and they say that my appearance is hardly human. I am much better since I adopted this mode of life. I am only moderate about fastings, for I cannot practise severities: I only keep to my own rule as exactly as I can: that is all. But what I propose, in a burning climate like this, is much to a European, who everywhere has his cross. As I came back from my late expedition, for instance, I had something to suffer for the glory of my good Master. May His name be ever blessed! The sand on which I walked was so intensely hot, that in some places, where it was hottest, I might say with truth that you could have cooked an egg. But the pain was nothing to what I afterwards felt at meeting with hearts as hard as marble. They stopped their ears, and would not hear me. It was in a village half pagan, half Christian. The Christians were so only in name; the pagans, more determined, made the Christians contribute to their sacrifices. I went there to exhort the Christians to cease joining in these abominations, and to urge the others to acknowledge the true God. When I accosted them they were assembled at a place where they had rebuilt an idol temple. At first they received me well, but as soon as I began to speak to them on religion, one by one the Christians slunk away, partly through shame, partly through dread of the infidels. These last assailed me in the most insulting manner; I thought they would have killed me. But I did not desist. In spite of their outcries I went on preaching, and several were moved, and dared openly to take my part, and say aloud that what I taught was reasonable, and that the religion I preached was holy. What will come of it I know not.'

Again in 1794 he writes: 'The propriety of the behaviour of the women towards me would surprise you. They never approach me within a dozen feet, and then only when some necessary business requires. Otherwise my catechist speaks to them, conveying to them my instructions. My constant occupation is preaching and the administration of the sacraments—Penance, Baptism, Marriage, and Extreme Unction. There is no possibility of visiting the sick more than once; there are not priests enough. I am seldom alone, and that has its advantage as well as disadvantage. I try to make a retreat in the depths of my heart, and amidst my employment am busy about my poor soul's salvation, and lift it up to my adorable Master. He has given me the grace to have no attachment to anything on earth. Whatever happens to me, it is the same; praise and ridicule are all alike. The Bishop has given me a priest, who is always with me wherever I go; so whenever I wish I have the means of confession. He is a man of rare piety, and I am not ashamed to take him for an example; he is much attached to me, and I love him equally; he helps me, and is of great use to me. I have also three young persons who go about with me. They look on me as their father, and I treat them as my children. When I have time, I teach them Latin. They serve my Mass, and help me much in instructing the children, and grown persons too. If I was alone, I could not possibly do all I have to do.

'The missionary who brought my letters passed through this province to go into Cochin China. It was a great treat to me to see him, for it was long since I had seen a European. We were a fortnight together, and then I went with him to the river where he was to embark, and was of some use to him. We met fifty soldiers with a mandarin. As he did not know the language, it might have been an embarrassment. I made him keep silence, that they might not know he had lately arrived, and took all the speaking. My air of confidence imposed on them; they only put a question or two and asked for medicine. "I am not a physician," I said quietly. The mandarin did not even look me in the face. We separated at a village where there were some Christians and a church. There I stopped a month for the administration of the sacraments. While there, the Bishop passed on his way into Cochin China, in order to consecrate Mgr. La Bartette, the coadjutor of the Bishop of Adran. He stopped with me a week. What a consolation to me!

'After visiting some villages, a few days before the Assumption I arrived at a large Christian village where there was a church. These poor people were overjoyed to see me, and without saying a word to me about it had built a house for me. I remained with them two months, and had the consolation of celebrating with all the pomp possible the two feasts of our good Mother. I gave them a retreat, and God blessed it abundantly.

'While I was with these good Christians I heard of an old woman some distance off, who had long left the faith, and wished to return, and who was now near her end. I went to her; she lived in a pagan village, and was quite forsaken, even by her children. A pagan neighbour, when at leisure, came to cook her rice. As she was likely to live some time, and was very ignorant, I proposed that she should leave her house, and go to a village where she might have some spiritual help; and she agreed to it gladly. I hired pagans to carry her to the place where I was making the retreat, satisfied that the charity of these good people would supply all her wants. The pagans came in crowds to witness a thing so strange to them. "We never saw anything like it," they said. " The Christian religion must be true." So you see we can preach without uttering a word. After that I preached to them, and made an impression. I have since learnt that the whole village, two or three chief persons excepted, is in the way to be Christian. When the sick woman arrived, all the Christians vied who should take her in. I settled the dispute by assigning her to no one; but I made them place her in a corner of the church, and told them to show their charity by taking care of her. Not a person in Tonking was better cared for. I instructed her, heard her confession, and gave her communion, and when I left I put her in charge of a religious female; and after six or seven weeks she died the death of the just.

'These poor people come to the church in troops of twenty or thirty, all armed with clubs, pikes, or weapons of some sort. They do this because they come in the evening, and have to return at night, and the country is infested with tigers. If they find me engaged saying my office or prayers, they range themselves on the two sides of my doorway, and, without uttering a word, keep their eyes fixed on me, resting on their clubs, or having them on their shoulders; quite a picture, men, women, boys, and girls indiscriminately mixed. As soon as I close my book and turn towards them, joy lights their countenances. I tell them little stories, or oftentimes preach to them. They are satisfied, listening with full attention. They would like to be always with me, and are quite sad when they have to go. It is painful to be obliged to leave people so hopeful, but it must be—missionaries are so few.

'I have given a retreat. I preached four times a day, and when not preaching heard confessions. To my consolation many sinners were converted. In our seminary retreats I never witnessed such silence, and the numbers were very great—men, women, and children, Christians and pagans. They came from distances over sixty miles. The two Annamite priests who helped me did not close their eyes for a fortnight, and it was the same with me. The ease which our Lord gives me in expressing myself in the Annamite tongues is a great help. I can speak in this grave and musical language with more ease than I could ever do in French. But yet I am not understood as well as I was in France; but this is owing to my auditors, and not to myself. It is from the novelty of the things I say to them, and from their not grasping the meaning of the terms, being Christians in name only. After much patience and labour they begin to understand you.

'While I was in this country, a grand mandarin, the brother of the governor of the province, heard of me and wished to see me. He sent me a message to say that if I would go, he would send a boat, and an escort of soldiers to conduct me. I replied that it was not my habit to travel in such a fashion; that if he wished to see me, I would come on foot in my own way, and that he need not be at any trouble about sending for me. So I went with my catechist, and some Christians who chose to be my companions, though I did not wish it. After a walk of two hours, we reached the house of the mandarin, where preparation had been made for receiving me. He was delighted to see me, and entertained me with great politeness. I could not induce him to sit on the same mat with myself. He was a learned man of note. I spoke to him on religion with much freedom. He was much struck, and would certainly have been converted, if it were not that he shrank from the sacrifices required. Several times he said that he would like to be a Christian, but he could not face the thought of giving up his high dignities, and becoming a poor man: so hard is it for the rich to enter the kingdom of heaven. He wanted to make me a present, but I told him that I never received any, which made him admire our religion more. At my request he gave strict orders that the Christians should not be asked for contributions for temples, idols, or other superstitions.

'The same evening, as I was returning, I was bitten by a small insect about the size of my little finger, and about three inches long. I never in my whole life suffered such pain as I did the night afterwards. My limbs were convulsed; I could not keep myself still. I used the occasion as a meditation on the pains of hell. Great God, if the bite of a little insect caused pain so acute and insupportable, what must be that to which the sinner is doomed in that dread abyss!

'As I was passing through a village, I was told of a Christian family not far off that had abandoned the faith. I turned out of my path to go to them, and press them to repent. It was God's will that I should lose my way, and for the advantage of a fortune-teller, who daily practised at the markets. He ran up to me on perceiving me, thinking that I dealt in charms as he did. He asked me to his house, and offered me refreshment. I availed myself of the opportunity to give him some instructions; and the result was he was won to the faith.'

In 1797 M. Guérard took a very fatiguing journey, which he describes in a letter: 'At times the sands which I trod were so hot, that I was forced to run to ease somewhat of the pain, and make it bearable. Again, the mountains I had to climb were steeper than the roof of a house, and the natives dug steps for us; and then we had to walk through ravines where the water rose to our knees, while our feet were cut by the stones in these mountain torrents. In these ravines, hemmed in by mountains, shaded with trees, thickly set with brambles and thorns, we might fancy ourselves going down to the shades below. We could not move on without bending down low to escape the branches stretching over on each side. If we were thirsty, we could drink indeed; but for eating it was not so. We had absolutely nothing. When there was no water, we were bitten by little insects like caterpillars. They were very numerous, and we could not advance many steps without dozens swarming up our legs and thighs. We were all over blood, for a great flow of blood followed the bites. It quite weakened us, and was the worst suffering we had. It is not in complaint I speak of this; for I was never more happy. At the place I stopped there were some

Christians who had come there for traffic, who were mightily pleased to see me. They gave me cordial welcome, and in a short time had improvised a chapel, making use of the oars of their boat, which they covered with branches, and to ornament the altar they contrived an arch of bamboos twined together with all the skill they could. I stayed with them two days and a half, recruiting myself from my fatigues. My mattress was sharp stones, such as we had felt in the ravines. As for sheets or covering, it was useless to trouble ourselves about them. Our arrival was soon noised abroad. The chief of the district came to see me. I discoursed to him, and he listened with pleasure. I went with him to his house, and he showed me much attention. Afterwards I preached publicly.'

The effect of his preaching was considerable, but he was obliged to leave, and could not gather in the fruits. In Jan. 1796 he set out on a new journey, but he was ill of dysentery, and had been two months; and for months afterwards the illness lingered on him, but it did not stop his work. 'By direction of the Bishop I set off for a visit to the northern mountains. I travelled in a boat, so the fatigue was not great, or my strength would not have been equal to the journey. The river is very rapid, but still it is more suited to navigation than the one separating Tonking from Cochin China, on which I made a voyage the year before, and was in much danger. I was in a little boat not more than a foot and a half broad, larger ones being unfit for use in consequence of the frequent falls, some of them not less than fifteen or twenty feet, and in three days only we had to leap a hundred of them.

'We journeyed on steadily without a pause for ten days, and then reached the dwellings of some poor Christians, many of whom had never before seen a priest, and the others not for thirty years. You may imagine their joy, and mine was no less when I saw that they clung to their religion, though through their ignorance some superstitions were mixed up with it. I was so ill that I could scarcely speak. Nothing could exceed the care they took of me. And though they could do little, yet it increased the interior joy I felt, and somewhat checked the disorder; so that I set to work instructing them and administering the sacraments. I stayed with these people about three weeks; I baptised several adults and children of Christians, set right several marriages, and celebrated one with the rites of the Church. I never witnessed greater piety and devotion. It seemed as if our Lord had preserved these poor outcasts by a special providence. They were indefatigable in their studies; my catechist and myself had not a moment's rest. O my God, truly art Thou named the God of all consolation and mercy. Thou who givest us consolation in all our troubles, Thou only knowest what was their joy, what is that of a missionary, who has left all for Thy glory and the salvation of souls, when he finds himself in a situation like this.

'The devil could not see all this without being stirred to rage. He had an instrument in a petty mandarin. Some of his concubines had in childhood been baptised, and I did my utmost to convert them, and urged them to go away into the inner provinces, from which they had been brought. They foolishly asked his leave to go, and he flew into a fury, and said he would have my head off. I had to retreat to another village, and keep out of the way for a time; but the man calmed, and a slight beating inflicted on the head of the village ended the matter. But the poor concubines suffered from their imprudence. They lost their chance, and had not courage again to make the venture to escape from their miserable state.

'The rumour spread that an extraordinary master of religion had come from a strange country. It brought crowds around me from the whole mountain region; men, women, children, rich and poor, wanted to see me. Unfortunately, I knew but a few words of their language, which is quite different from that of the Tonkinese. I preached as well as I could by interpreters and by signs; they were so pleased that some of them wept for joy. They wondered at my coming so far to teach them, and for no reward, their own bonzes being so grasping. These mountaineers are ignorant, but full of candour, apt for religion, just, and loving truth. I can say that I had never anywhere seen pagans better disposed to receive the light of the Gospel. They wished to take me with them, that I might learn their language and instruct them; but I was so ill that it seemed I should not live many months. And besides, I had not the Bishop's permission, and he had sent me to visit the Christians on the borders of the kingdom, and not farther. My refusal caused much grief to these poor people, and made them bitterly complain; but my own sorrow was no less. But what could I do? It was not just to leave the poor Christians whose condition was so miserable, and go away to preach to the heathen.

'Since my return I have frequently asked the vicar-apostolic to send me into this kingdom, and he would really have sent me, though my strength is not equal to so hard a task, had he a new priest to replace me. The language is not difficult to learn, and the pronunciation is more easy than the Tonkinese. It is musical, and pleasing to the ear. Although I studied it only imperfectly, yet in three weeks I learnt sufficient to hold a sort of conversation with those who came to see me. And with some help from a Christian who spoke the language, I made something of a translation of the Lord's Prayer and the Commandments. O, how pleased they were when I read this to them! They admired it greatly, and their hearts were inflamed with love of our holy religion.

'It reached the ears of the bonzes that I was in the country, and they sent me a message to ask me to go and see them. I went with my two catechists, and a Christian who could speak the language. We had seven steeps of a mountain to climb, so perpendicular that it might seem like mounting the steps of a ladder. Several times I had to rest to get breath before I reached the cady, or monastery as it may be called. The chief came to receive me with much civility. He invited me to eat; but as we were in the temple I refused, fearing there might be some superstitious meaning. The whole neighbourhood was collected. They showed me their idols, and everything they thought would please me. But I had not come for that. I asked the chief to read me something out of his book. He read the commandments of his false religion. The whole was reduced to this, that by making large alms one could get to heaven. As I had a pen and paper, I wrote as he read, and then I read it off to them fluently; they were much surprised, thinking all writing ought to be in their own letters. Then I read to them my own translation of the commandments of God, which they perfectly understood. They could not help allowing that my doctrine was better than their own. I seized the occasion to speak to them of the true God. I explained the origin of their idol, and they admitted before all the people that they had been in error. I dictated to them my translations of the Commandments and the Lord's Prayer, and they wrote them out. They wanted me to stay with them one day at least, but I was too ill, and it was with much sorrow they saw me go. But to stay was impossible. The dysentery allowed me no rest.

'These people worship two principles, like the Manichees: the devil, out of fear of the injuries he may inflict, and their idol, of whom they expect reward in the next life. They teach that the heaven is sixty miles away from the earth, and that the highest place will be the lot of the most virtuous. They observe continence, or, if they break it, they must leave the cady. The people hold them in great respect, but I do not think it would be difficult to break the tie, were the true religion preached to them. They seem much less superstitious and more upright than the Annamites.'

CHAPTER IX.

DISAPPOINTMENTS IN THE REIGN OF GIA-LAONG.

It is plain, from the letters of MM. Guérard and la Pavec, that during the first years of their residence in Tonking, 1791-1797, they could pursue their labours without opposition. Neither the people, nor the mandarins, nor the supreme government, showed them any ill-will. The Taysons were then masters of Tonking, and till political reasons altered their minds they were more favourable than otherwise to the Christians. But the progress of Gialaong and the renown of the Bishop of Adran produced a very considerable change in their conduct. The Christians were supposed to wish well to the cause of their rival, in whose court a Christian bishop was in such high esteem, and in consequence they became the objects of serious jealousy. So a persecution arose, which for a time quite stopped the missionary work. Much alarm was excited, and a great deal of harm was done. The college was broken up. The missionaries dared no longer appear in public, but were obliged to hide closely. M. Bissachère spent seven months on a desert island upward of twenty miles from land. He had with him four students of the seminary. His retreat was found out, and he was pursued; but he eluded the search of his enemies by hiding himself in heights so steep and inaccessible, that it was thought no one could live in them. Christian fishermen brought him a little food, and so he sustained himself.

Mgr. Longer was once taken, and owed his release to the interference of the Christians, who rescued him. For two months before his capture he had been wandering about, now on the mountains, now secreted in the dwelling of some Christian. He tells us in a letter some of his adventures. His Christian friends were very anxious about him, and in their alarm hurried him off to the mountains, where he was quite wearied out with fatigue. After labouring over rugged paths and dense thickets, he lay down in the open air, with nothing to shelter him, without even a covering, in a spot so wild, that, in his own words, it was a mere haunt for tigers. The horrors of that frightful place were worse to him than the dangers from which he had escaped; and after a week spent in the savage mountain wilds, where he could find no better refuge than some old ruins or a deserted hut, he went down to the plains, and hid himself in a Christian hamlet. But in no place could he stop long. He had to change from hills to village, and from village to hills. At length, as it was approaching Christmas, he rested more permanently in a village, and even dared one night to hold an ordination; but he was immediately after frightened away, and this time the enemy were on his track, and followed him up closely. Wearied out by the fatigues of three sleepless nights, on Christmas morning he sought a short repose. He was roused by the tidings that the soldiers were close by, and he knew that he was himself the object of their search. He was off at once; he got up, and made his way out by a back entrance. But it was a strange place, and he did not know in what direction to go; soon he got plunged in a slough, and he could not extricate himself, and the soldiers came up and made him prisoner. They treated him with civility, and lent him a hat, as his head was bare, and were willing to release him if he would pay for it. But that was not necessary. Soon the Christians thronged round, the women first, then men armed with clubs; and the soldiers, finding themselves overpowered, released their captive and fled. These men had acted without orders, and the mandarin of the district had no wish to have the Bishop on his hands; so the pursuit ceased. The Christians who came to the rescue were let off with a small fine.

Mgr. Longer, the Vicar-Apostolic of Tonking, and the successor of Mgr. Davoust, had previously been a missionary in Upper Cochin China. His first approach to the shores of Cochin China, in 1777, was eventful. The ship, in which he was, was boarded by pirates, and he was struck down and severely wounded; and it is a memorable fact that he and M. la Bartette, who both became bishops, and both lived on in this country to an extreme old age, were in those early days of the missionary life lying side by side on beds of sickness; M. la Bartette in a state so dangerous that he received the last sacraments from his wounded friend beside him. M. Longer, on his nomination to the episcopate, looked round in vain for the means of consecration. In the whole country there was no other bishop alive but the Bishop of Adran, and to get at him he must pass through the lines of the Tayson armies, or attempt the dangerous passage of the seas. So he resolved to go to Macao; and as the means were not at hand for a voyage, he set out on foot, reached Macao safely, and returning gave consecration, first to the Vicar-Apostolic of Eastern Tonking, and then going on to his old friend M. la Bartette in Cochin China, conferred it on him.

The Tayson persecution had relaxed before these usurpers had to yield up the kingdom to Gia-laong. Gia-laong's success was immediate and full on his advancing into Tonking, and his adversaries were entirely prostrated. The Christians viewed the change with particular satisfaction, and large expectations were formed from the transfer of the rule into the hands of one in whose favour the Bishop of Adran was known to have stood so high. Mgr. Longer presented himself before the new king, and a kind and favourable audience was granted to him. But Gia-laong was not now what he had been, and he soon showed it. All the old ties that bound him to the Christians had been broken. Not only had the Bishop of Adran passed away, but those Christians whom he had known, and whose word he might have respected, were also gone. The missionaries of Tonking were entirely strangers to him, and Mgr. la Bartette, who lived near the court, was also unknown. And it soon was made evident that whatever had been his previous feelings, the Christian religion was now in no way acceptable to this prince. For the religions of the country he had not indeed any taste. That of Phat, the popular superstition, he despised; that of Confucius, which was the religion of the learned, was more favoured by him, but apparently rather from motives of policy than anything else. Whether or not the Christian religion had ever made any impression on him is altogether uncertain; it might have done in his earlier days; but ambition was his ruling principle, and stifled any such sentiments, if ever felt. But in later years his words and acts made plain that his feelings towards the Christian religion were hostile. He could not bear the idea of the restraints it imposed—the giving up his wives, and the denial of his sensual desires; and to be told of hell and the punishment of sin stirred up an amount of indignation that pushed him on to opposition.

The missionaries and Christians of Tonking had no doubt at all but that Gia-laong would prove their friend. They were pleasing themselves with the hope that now all those stern decrees that gave their enemies such an advantage over them would be at once revoked. They were looking for some open declaration of favour on the part of the monarch that would protect them from the caprices of mandarins or the unfriendliness of pagan neighbours; but they looked in vain. Gia-laong was altogether silent; no sign of any intention of moving in their favour was visible on his part. Disappointed and troubled, they made an effort on their own behalf. A deputation went to the king to supplicate him to issue a decree which would secure them from wrong, and especially exempt them from the dreaded call for contribution towards the village sacrifices. The king's reception was not ungracious, but he made no promise, and no advantage was gained. What his intentions were, however, were very soon revealed. A decree came out, but not such a one as the missionaries desired; it was one that startled them, and filled them with grief. It professed to deal with religion generally, and only indirectly affected the Christians; but the Christian religion was mentioned, and in terms of much contempt, and it was expressly ordered that no more Christian churches were to be built. The reference to the Christian religion was as follows: 'The religion of the Portuguese, one of foreign origin, has found its way into the kingdom, and established itself. The hell with which this religion threatens us is a word calculated to excite alarm, and the heaven of which it makes promise is a grand term, which may serve to cajole. There are persons so grossly ignorant, that they have allowed themselves to be misled by this doctrine, and cling to it with a senseless folly. Very many of our subjects have been infected by it, and are used to the observance of its laws and practices, following them like persons intoxicated and unable to think, or as if they had lost their sight, and could not get back to the path from which they had strayed.' Such is the description that Gia-laong gives of the religion of the Bishop of Adran, and then follows the order: 'Henceforth it is our command, that in the districts or villages where the Christians have a church no repairs be made unless first leave be asked of the governor; and in all places where there is no church the building one is strictly forbidden.'

Here was a blight to all the missionary's high hopes. Nothing was to be expected from Gia-laong. But, after all, the time of Gia-laong were quiet days in comparison with what came after. This decree was the worst thing he ever did to the Christians. He was not their friend, but he would not allow them to be ill-treated. What their state was during this reign is pretty fairly represented by these words of M. Guérard: 'With respect to religion, we are not troubled by the government, but the pagans vent their ill-will, knowing that the mandarins and the king are careless about protecting us. To seek redress from the law is but useless expense, for the pagans in such cases always get the best of it; and this is the reward of all the Bishop of Adran's services.' Another missionary makes the picture more favourable, but it was drawn at a later period: 'As far as religion is concerned, we are let alone. We are as free as ever. The king seems favourable to us, and those mandarins who are hostile do not venture to touch us.' The same missionary repeats this persuasion of the king's kind feeling: 'The king seems well disposed towards us. He says that of the five religions known here, *i. e.* that of Confucius,

Phat, sorcery, Bhudda, and the God of heaven, the last is the only one agreeable to reason; but that it is too strict in respect to plurality of wives, and that he has not strength to observe its rules.'

But though the Christians were free from persecution, they were during this reign exposed to another very serious evil. Their missionaries were gradually dying off one by one; that little band of fervent earnest labourers who had been doing their work so successfully were gradually dropping away, and as their ranks thinned no fresh recruit came to fill the vacant space. Many of these missionaries were veterans in the service. One who died in 1805, M. Sérard, had been in Tonking for thirty years. He was one of the first who came to the help of Mgr. Reydellet, after whose death, for some years, till the arrival of Mgr. Davoust, he had administered the vicariate. Lately he had been living in Ke-vinh, and had seen the gradual and successful progress of that institution of Mgr. Reydellet. M. le Roy, also one of the oldest priests, who had been living with him in the college, mournfully refers to his loss. 'I have lost one of my best friends, our dear dean, M. Philip Sérard,' he writes, May 1805. In the August of the same year his own career had closed.

The few who remained were worn out with age or fatigues, and it is pathetic to hear their calls for help and to read their descriptions of the mournful state to which they were reduced. In 1808 Mgr. Longer writes to Europe: 'Try to send us some help. Fifteen years have passed since a missionary has come out here, and within the last two years we have lost four—two by death, two by return to Europe.' Mgr. la Mothe, the same year, writes in the same tone of sadness: 'My health is but feeble, but God enables me to visit the most unhealthy spots without prejudice, and yet the priests, and others with me who are natives, are often laid down in their beds. As for my dear colleagues, the Bishop of Gortyna, in spite of his infirmities, seems likely yet to live long. I cannot hope this for M. Guérard, so greatly does he tax his strength. M. Tessier was sick, but is well again. M. Eyot I may say lives, but he is more feeble than myself. I totter along day by day, but hardly dare to look on to-morrow. But M. la Pavec, though his head and beard are bleached, has a constitution of iron.'

In 1810 we have a representation from M. Eyot. He shows the little band of missionaries at their several duties: 'M. la Pavec is at the general college (Ke-vinh), which is very numerous; M. Guérard presides at another, with fifty scholars. I have over sixty, twenty-five of them studying theology. The Bishop of Castoria, though his health is weak, is indefatigable, and always busy; the Bishop of Gortyna is afflicted with hernia, but he will not rest—all he can do is to hear some confessions; M. Tessier is working over his strength. Send us help, two missionaries at least.'

Then we have an earnest appeal from M. Tessier in 1811: 'What strong reasons have we for calling for relief! For twenty years this call has been repeated, and no one has come. So indeed God wills! But there must be priests in Europe who are free to come, and what good might they do! May God pity us, and cause some one to come out to the help of these millions of souls, that so much want them.'

Mgr. la Mothe supplements this appeal by again bringing out into view the actual state of the mission: 'Six Europeans, two bishops and four missionaries, are all we are. Not many for the 150,000 or 200,000 Christians under our care. Not one of us, M. la Pavec only excepted, is without his infirmities, and at times even on the verge of death. In spite of my sixty years, my weak stomach, and my many other duties, I am daily in the confessional almost up to midnight. It is the same with the others, all almost as old as myself. Judge whether it is not fit that we should look out for successors.'

And M. Guérard, the same year, writes just the same, though he cannot help speaking cheerfully: 'Thank God, I am well enough, but old. You would smile, I daresay, if you saw my gray beard and my whitening hairs. White is indeed the chosen colour with us all in Tonking. You know what I mean. Do what you can, then, to send us missionaries.'

In 1814 the stout M. la Pavec dies. We have heard nothing of his illness; all we are told is that June 22, 1814, he has fallen under his last sickness. In 1816 two more are taken away—Mgr. Mothe in May, M. Tessier in November. Only three Europeans then remained, all old, all long worn by sickness and labour. M. Guérard was chosen to be the successor of the Bishop of Castoria. The busy active labours of his earlier missionary life had been much reduced. He, like the other few Europeans in Tonking, had to give up much of his journeying. They had enough to do in their homes, hearing confessions, watching over their students. Still his earnest zeal must satisfy itself; he must, if he can, make converts; he must preach; and he tells us that in 1811 he baptised nearly as many as he used to do. He gives us a pleasing picture of a village where he had been at work: 'You will be surprised perhaps at what I now tell you, that in the space of a month I have taught a whole village to sing hymns and psalms in Latin, as they do in France. The little boys and girls at Mass sing the Psalm *Credidi*, with the refrain *Quid retribuam*, and the *Tantum ergo* at the elevation. When I walk out in the village the children of four or five, the young and old women, and men also, all together will sing *Quid retribuam*, and sing with an ardour and delight that would astonish you, and often it makes me weep.'

The consecration of Mgr. Guérard was at Kevinh. The two Bishops of Eastern Tonking were called in to give splendour to the ceremony. It was on the Feast of St. James, his own patron. His feeble frame, almost worn out, had soon after to sustain the attack of a new illness, and it seemed for a time that he must die. The illness was stone. The Tonkinese priests who were by him were talking over the arrangements of his funeral when he was suddenly relieved. 'Weak as he is,' says M. Eyot, 'he never rests, nor spares himself at all.' He had yet a life of several years before him, and up to the very last he worked on. In 1818 he journeyed into the mountains, and employed himself with all the ardour of former years. 'I made a long arduous journey,' he writes, 'into the mountains and forests, where tigers and robbers were rife. As for robbers, you may suppose that I need not dread them, for in truth I can say with St. Peter, "Silver and gold have I none." It was great consolation to witness the faith and piety of these mountaineers; some of them came distances of two, three, and even four days' journey, that they might receive the Sacrament of Confirmation. I had three priests with me, and still these poor people had to wait days, even eight or ten, before they could get to confession. We worked day and night, but it was not enough. O my good friend, what would have been your consolation to see the faith and earnestness of these poor Christians! A great many of them wanted food and clothing. They willingly forgot all. Our Lord was their only care. To my utmost I helped them with alms, but those who gave them had but little themselves; it was not much I could do. I have frequently seen persons who had had no food for three days caring for nothing but the making their confession.'

Poor as he was, this holy Bishop loved to be poor. His brother in France sent him a contribution, and thus he replies to him : 'Thank you for your generous gift. I must again say, what I have said before, that

I wonder that you, out of your poverty, should have a thought of enriching me, when my wish is to be like my Divine Master, and not to have where to lay my head. O my kind brother, what I say to you I think before God is true—that I have no desire at all for the goods of this world; and if I had, I should think myself unworthy the name of a missionary. I am but a poor workman; but I labour in my Lord's vineyard as well as I can; and in that is my consolation and my happiness. So, my very dear friend, content yourself with remembering me in your prayers and at the altar, as I also will do for you.'

In 1820 there was a terrible visitation of cholera, appalling every one by its novelty and severity. Mgr. Guérard speaks of it: 'This year there has been a frightful mortality in the country. Death is instant, or in two or three hours. To hold out a day is the very utmost. In this province alone, according to lists that have been prepared by the king's orders, twenty-two thousand have perished. It is the same in the other provinces. The whole kingdom was in consternation. The king shut himself up in his palace, and mandarins and nobles went into seclusion, as if to fly from God's judgments. It was noticeable that for every hundred pagans who died there was hardly one Christian. It was a general remark, and the pagans wondered at it, and confessed it to be the hand of God. They hasten to the churches, and ask for holy water, and, prostrating themselves outside, pray with earnestness. A hundred European priests might now find employment in preaching the Gospel; and we are but four.'

Yes, there were four priests now in Tonking. At length, after that long interval of years, a fresh priest had arrived. Those three aged infirm men were not to be left to themselves. Things had changed in Europe, and the missionary work could again become an object of attention; and from this date there gradually set in a stream of new priests, who would take up the work that these few old men were no longer able to cope with. Tonking too had drawn to itself some special interest, and the beauty of the virtues of Mgr. Guérard was one of the causes that had fixed attention on it. That very year, 1820, there arrived in Cochin China a young priest of the name of Magdinier, whose heart warmed at the thought of this holy bishop, and who some years earlier had expressed his admiration. 'What Almighty God wishes to do with me,' says this young man, in 1817, 'I do not know. On consideration, the wants of Tonking seem to be the most pressing. There a bishop, Mgr. Guérard, has lately been elected, whom I do not know, but whom I respect so much that I would go to the end of the earth to kiss his feet.' In 1820 Magdinier arrived in Cochin China, with the purpose of passing on to Tonking. But he never reached his destination; he fell sick and died; but his short holy career had made its impression. Soon after, his tomb was sought by M. Tabert, who had once been his companion, and knew his virtues, and he has told us the feelings with which he approached it. 'Like those warriors who go and whet their swords on the tombs of the brave leaders who have guided them to victory, so I would go in person and prostrate myself on the ashes of this holy missionary, that I might rise replenished with the zeal and ardour with which he burned.'

But though M. Magdinier never arrived in Tonking, there were two priests who came that same year. One was M. Ollivier, who succeeded Mgr. Guérard as coadjutor, but who lived only a year or two afterwards; the other was M. Jeantet, whose own history would be eventful, stretching on through a long series of years, and amidst scenes even more memorable than any that have been recorded. In 1821, at the request of Mgr. Guérard, M. Jeantet was sent to assist him. And this is the way the young priest speaks of him: 'The Bishop gave a retreat, in part to satisfy his zeal, and partly also to stir up in me a love for an exercise which to him had been a cause of so many triumphs. His first two sermons were such as might give me an idea of what he had been in former years. But his body was exhausted by labour and care, and the fatigue was too much for him; and after his second sermon he was obliged to desist, overpowered by the violence of his sickness. It was too great exertion; his pains were very great, and in all parts of his body; in particular, there was an ulcer in his left thigh, which had troubled him for fifteen years; a great aggravation of his sufferings, for it caused intense agony. I was just going to give him Extreme Unction, when God granted him some relief. As soon as he gained a little strength he was at work in another parish. Neither age nor sickness could quench his apostolic zeal. He kept on this work for two months, and did much good. He baptised above forty adults. He was ready to go off again to another place, but his infirmities would not allow him; he deferred from day to day, then gave it up altogether. From April 1822 to June 1823 he could not go out at all; his sufferings during these fourteen months were so extreme that it seemed like one long martyrdom, yet they did not oblige him to give up his duties. He went on with his administration as far as was possible, and almost up to his death his thoughts were occupied on it. As long as the illness lasted, I could not go far away from his residence. I visited the neighbouring parishes to give the sacraments, but did not stay away above three weeks. It was a consolation to both of us to meet again. I told him my difficulties, he spoke of his own sufferings; and in this converse we found a pleasure, renewing our strength and giving ease to our pains. I would remain with him four or five days, and then go away again to my visitations.

'The venerable prelate suffered from frequent giddiness, and he had a constant violent pain reaching from the right breast to the lower ribs of the left side, causing great difficulty of breathing. The ulcer got worse and worse. The twitches of pain were sometimes very violent. "A troop of mad dogs tearing me to pieces," he said, "would not give me such excruciating torments." These pains would come on nine or ten times a day, and so by night. No remedy could be found for them, and at length the wound began to mortify. Throughout this illness he had little rest day or night, and this especially when he was preparing to celebrate the Holy Sacrifice, or, in the last two months, to receive Holy Communion. Once he got to the church with great difficulty, but was immediately obliged to lie down; he raised himself for Holy Communion, but had quickly to lie down again. Once, for a whole fortnight, he could not lie down without extreme difficulty and pain. In the end, three months before he died five more ulcers formed in the joints of his thigh, as painful as the first, and which could not be cured. Mortification at length came on, and terminated a life spent in labour, fatigue, and sickness, and full of virtues and good works. Often did I look with admiration on that lofty soul, always in peace under a weight of so much pain, unshaken and invincible, raising his hopes to God, who had ever been the object of his love.'

From his sick-bed, a few months before his death, he wrote to a friend in France, director of the Seminary of Foreign Missions, and these are the last words of his we have: 'There is no more oil in my lamp; soon it will be out. I have only one trouble, the exceedingly wretched state to which our mission has been reduced. The Bishop of Gortyna is at the last gasp. M. Eyot, a little younger than myself, from his many infirmities can hardly long survive me. The only missionaries who can work are M. Jeantet, whose health is bad, and M. Ollivier. But they are both inexperienced, and just beginning to speak the language. They are both good and zealous. But more is wanted for the government of a mission like Tonking.'

Mgr. Ollivier, who succeeded him, as he afterwards travelled over the province of Xu-nghe had ample proof of the great work Mgr. Guérard had done. 'He has left on all sides,' he says, 'memorials of his piety, and his zeal for the salvation of the souls of this dear people; and the missionaries who pass over the same ground must find their zeal animated in turn. When I entered a village a week ago the people came round me and said, "Twelve years ago M. Guérard came to visit us; he planted a cross above our village." I was curious to see it, and asked to be led to it. The village was at the foot of a high hill, and on the top M. Guérard had erected his cross. Preaching was the great business of this good bishop, and he tried to urge it on the young missionaries. "Preach," he said to me, "preach; it is the only way of doing good in this country." Up to the very end he kept to the practice he so strongly recommended, never giving it up till his strength was gone. I have seen him many times sink down with exhaustion as soon as he came back to his chamber after preaching; and when, seeing he was so weak, I earnestly asked him to preach no more, he would reply, "I know that I have no strength left; but when this poor people is asking for some one to break to them the bread of the word, and there is no one, how can I be silent?"'

In his love for the pulpit, he asked to be buried under it, as M. Jeantet tells us, that he might preach when he was dead, and remind the labourers who came after him that the first of their duties was to preach the word of God. 'But,' says M. Jeantet, 'through his whole life, to pagans, Christians, religious, and priests, and to his brother missionaries too, he preached much more by his example than by his words.'

CHAPTER X.

MINH-MENH'S PERSECUTION.

BEFORE Bishop Guérard died, the days of King Gia-laong had come to an end. He was in some respects a great and successful monarch, but his reign was not a happy one for his subjects. In his latter days there were many matters of complaint; the people were sadly oppressed; those who suffered wrong sought in vain for redress, for the mandarins were more anxious to fill their coffers than to deal out justice. There was a wide-spreading poverty, owing to repeated failure of harvests, and the helpless poor, instead of meeting with commiseration, were the more abused. Troops of robbers roamed over the country, and were so strong and daring that they would attack villages, and burn and ransack them, and the villagers were unable to defend themselves. The mandarins shrank from leading the soldiers against them, and would avoid the conflict if they could, and as long as the marauders themselves did not force them into an encounter. But the worst of all the evils in Gia-laong's reign, and which began at an early date, arose out of his passion for building, and for other great public works, which required an immense amount of labour. It is true that the works in which he was engaged were useful, important, and striking to the eye. Hue had become quite a grand city. The European stranger was astonished at the unexpected sight in what he had considered a barbarous country. He beheld a town with walls stretching along a circuit of five miles, glacis, covert way, ditch, bastions, all on approved principles, with hardly anything to be detected as slovenly, barbarous, or incomplete in design. Inside these were buildings that astonished him no less; enormous granaries; barracks with arrangements so excellent that they would not disgrace the best troops of Europe; but more surprising still, an arsenal, with brass ordnance, balls and shells, manufactured in Cochin China by native workmen, from materials furnished from Tonking, and of approved make, the cannon of all sizes from four to sixty-eight pounders, and even larger still; gun-carriages, painted and beautifully finished off, with shot and shell piled up and arranged with an order quite admirable. And outside the city, in a country where roads had been unknown, and where the royal road, as it was called, was up to that time the single path that could pretend to the name, he would pass along straight, broad, well-laid roads, branching in from different points to the city. He would see well-constructed bridges of stone and wood, high embankments keeping back the water of the sea and river, and reclaiming from waste large tracts of country that were now rich with crops and fruits; while a canal, penetrating miles inland, and entering into the town, and communicating with the principal public edifices, would be a ready means of traffic, and of carrying in easily the produce of the country.* All this was well, but the cost was tremendous; a mighty sacrifice of life, an infliction of incalculable misery.

To take a single instance of the prodigality of labour in which this king indulged—he provided a burial-place for himself and his favourite queen. It was in a picturesque part of the mountains thirty miles from Hue. There a splendid mausoleum was raised in the midst of extensive gardens; and the formation of these gardens was the great work: hills were levelled, hollows were filled up, water was brought in by canals and stored in tanks. The gardens were elaborately laid out, and adorned with walks and terraces, interspersed with numerous trees. Thousands of persons were employed for years in this one business.

The successor of Gia-laong was his son Minh-Menh. This prince had never shown himself favourable to the Christians. It had long been rumoured that he had said, that when he came to the throne he would not spare them as his father had done; and his accession was viewed with considerable dread. But in the first years of his reign he betrayed no symptoms of any such ill-will. There was no alteration at all in the state of the Christians. It was not till his jealousy was aroused by learning that new missionaries were finding their way into the country that any indication was given that the Christians were in his thoughts. For a long series of years the

* Crawford's *Embassy to Siam and Cochin China*.

number of the missionaries had been decreasing, without any noticeable additions from Europe; so that he might have flattered himself that the few old men that were left would soon be gone, and that he might leave them alone. But in 1825 he became aware that a French priest, M. Regereau, had landed in Cochin China. There was an instant stir. M. Regereau, who had really landed at Touron, was not able to find a place of concealment; the Christians were all in alarm, and dared not take him in. M. Tabert, the pro-vicar and administrator of the vicariate, soon after the vicar-apostolic, himself little more than a novice, and wholly unprepared to find himself in such hard circumstances, frightened at the risks of the presence of this new priest, ordered him to retire; so M. Regereau, who had already faced the dangers of the sea and the dangers of landing, was obliged to go through a fresh round of wanderings and dangers before he could fix himself in the country, and commence his work as a missionary. But the jealousy of Minh-Menh was not lulled. Shortly after there appeared the first intimation of that hostile spirit which was in the end to spread such wide havoc and misery. There came out a decree, plain and decisive in its language, and most threatening to the Christians. It bore date Feb. 11, 1826, and ran as follows: 'The false religion of the Europeans corrupts and perverts the mind and heart of man. The European vessels that visit this kingdom for commercial purposes have constantly introduced masters of this religion, who lead our people

astray, destroying our customs and usages; and have thus thwarted us in our plans for correcting their errors and inclining their hearts to right. We command, therefore, that whenever French ships appear on our coasts, the mandarins cause them to be carefully watched, and take the most strict precautions in guarding every part; so that no European master of religion may stealthily find his way in, day or night, by land or by water, to spread errors in our kingdom.'
But although the Christians were much disturbed by this appearance of vigour, it was but a temporary panic. All the mandarins were not hostile to the Christians, and there was one that very resolutely took their part. This was the powerful governor of Saigon, the uncle of the king, one of Gia-laong's old captains, one who remembered the Bishop of Adran, who thought it ill-advised to adopt the harsh measures contemplated; so the king paused for the time. For some years things went on smoothly enough. Quietly there came in a new race of missionaries; in Tonking and Cochin China their numbers kept increasing. Watchful as the mandarins were, the Europeans still got ashore; and how many, and where they were, was not known to the authorities of Hue.

M. Tabert was one of the earliest of the new influx of missionaries, arriving in Cochin China before the death of the aged Bishop la Bartette. That bishop's life, however, was close at its end; he reached his seventy-seventh year, and the forty-ninth of his residence in Cochin China, and then, the same year as Mgr. Guérard, leaving only two young missionaries to take up the work, he died. Those priests who had been his expected successors were already removed. M. Jarot, an experienced priest, had died a month or two before; Mgr. Andemar, his coadjutor, had fallen still earlier. M. Gazelin and M. Tabert, very late arrivals, were immediately brought into prominence, and Mgr. Tabert became vicar-apostolic. It was not long before he found himself in difficulties. A troublesome apostate was his first anxiety, and, just at the moment when the jealousy of Minh-Menh was exciting apprehension, there was the constant dread that this evil-disposed fellow would be making revelations pernicious to the mission. But Mgr. Tabert soon left the neighbourhood of Hue, and went down to the more safe and quiet quarters of the governor of Saigon. There for a few years he was at peace. The grand mandarin was cordial towards him, and offered him special civilities. But Mgr. Tabert's troubles were not at an end. The governor died. The lower provinces were thrown into commotion. A rebellion arose, and the Christians were supposed to have a share in it. The troops of Minh-Menh came down, and were victorious, and the cause of the Christians was desperate. In this new alarm there was a general flight of the missionaries. Mgr. Tabert, and all who could get away, took refuge in Siam. Two, M. Jacquart and M. Gazelin, remained, and were taken. M. Gazelin voluntarily gave himself up, and was strangled. M. Jacquart was wanted by the king for purposes of his own, and for some years was detained a prisoner, employed with certain learned men of the kingdom on the business of the king. The missionary work of Mgr. Tabert in Cochin China was now over. He never came back again. In his place, a year or two after, in 1835, came Mgr. Cuenot, who was made coadjutor, and who had before been a missionary from the year 1829, and who for a long series of years actively and successfully administered the affairs of the vicariate, standing firm amidst dangers greater than had ever yet been known, and not terminating his career till enfeebled by old age, and then almost a martyr. When Mgr. Cuenot came back to Cochin China, there was an interval of quiet. He could move about if he went silently, and other missionaries entered the country as well as himself. But a real storm was approaching. Already, in 1833, Minh-Menh had issued a fresh decree, in language more alarming than the former. The words were as follows: "I the king Minh-Menh thus order: For these many years there have been in this kingdom men from the West, who preach the religion of Jesus, and delude the common people, teaching that there is a place of supreme happiness and a prison of the most frightful misery. The God Phat they hold in no reverence, nor do they worship their ancestors; so entirely are they opposed to the religion of the country. Besides, they build houses for religious worship, and collect in them large numbers of people, that they may seduce the women and young girls; also they tear out the eyes of the dying. What can be more opposite to reason and to our customs? Last year we punished two villages ... for having embraced this doctrine, thus to make known our will that every one should turn away from this crime, and come back to the right way. Let all, then, know what our will is. Although from ignorance very many have gone away to this religion, they have still sense enough to discern what is proper and what is not, and so it will be easy to reclaim them by instruction; so the first thing to be done is to let them well understand that if they do not comply they will have to suffer chastisement or death.

'Wherefore we command all who profess this religion, from the mandarin down to the lowest of the people, to renounce it entirely, if they acknowledge and fear our power; and we direct all mandarins to ascertain by careful inquiry whether the Christians within their district are submitting themselves to our decree, and to compel them to trample on the cross in their presence. On doing so they may be pardoned. As for the churches and houses of the priests, the mandarins must take care that they be razed to the ground; for should any one henceforth be accused of entering a church or of practising these abominable ceremonies, he shall be punished with the utmost rigour, that this religion may be utterly rooted out.'

The publication of this decree caused immense consternation. Everywhere in Cochin China and Tonking the Christians were in great trepidation. For some months the missionaries could hardly find a resting-place, so afraid was every one to harbour them; but the mandarins were not at once stirred into activity, and the terror was as yet more than the reality of the danger. There was, however, one priest who was the particular object of Minh-Menh's animosity. This was M. Marchand, and although he was innocent, a good case could be got up against him. He was at Saigon at the time of the rebellion, and was in the midst of the rebels when the city was captured. What added to the suspicion against him was, that the Christians were not wholly exempt from complicity. Then afterwards, in the war that sprang up between Cochin China and Siam, the Christians were again involved, and the presence of Mgr. Tabert and other missionaries in Siam at the time increased the idea of their disaffection and guilt. So M. Marchand was put down as an arch-rebel, and the king would make an example of him. In 1835 he was caught, and no mercy was shown him. He proved himself innocent of the charges laid against him, but it was of no use. He was pressed to give information that would compromise his brethren and the Christians, but he would not; he was pressed to own the truth of certain calumnious fabrications disgraceful to Christian morals, and he indignantly refused. The tortures he had to undergo were barbarous; his flesh was torn with hot pincers, pieces of flesh were cut away while he was yet living. The horrors which were in reserve for him were worse than any that he suffered; but he did not live to undergo them: he sank exhausted beforehand, and the king's malice and cruelty were disappointed.

Up to 1833 the missionary work in Tonking made

very good progress. By that time there had arisen a considerable staff of missionaries. Mgr. Longer, decrepit and aged as he was, lingered on for years. He did not die till 1831, eighty years of age, fifty-six years a resident in Annam. His coadjutor, Mgr. Ollivier, did not last out that time, for in 1827 his short term was closed. In 1830 a fourth coadjutor was consecrated, Mgr. Havard, who commenced his single episcopate just before the serious trials of Minh-Menh's reign set in. Mgr. Havard had around him several young missionaries, some of whom became conspicuous in the annals of the mission; these were M. Jeantet, M. Masson, M. Retort, M. Borie, all afterwards bishops, one a martyr, the others famous for the severities of their hard trials, and M. Jeantet living through them all, up almost to the present date. There was M. Corney, also a martyr; and some others less noted, M. Suat, who fell sick and died a few months after landing, and M. Rouge, who died in the forest wilds, unequal to the earliest troubles of the persecution.

The decree of 1833 brought a change in the state of things in Tonking. The Tonkinese, naturally timid, so long left in peace, were quite stunned when they became aware of the orders of the king. Before any real danger had arisen they were utterly overwhelmed. Before a mandarin had stirred or a soldier had approached they were in confusion, and were pressing the missionaries to fly away and conceal themselves, dreading the frightful punishment that would fall upon themselves should a missionary be found in their dwelling or in their village. M. Masson has given us a somewhat humorous picture of this trouble and alarm, contrasted as it was with the quiet easy way in which the missionaries themselves bore the shock. M. Borie and he were at this time together. 'We had just sat down to our meal,' he says, 'but they would allow us no time for eating. They carried us off to conceal us in a secluded house, where we remained till midnight, and then we each provided ourselves with what shelter we could. Rumours were flying about; they were worse and worse; every one was in alarm; the least sound created apprehension; in imagination it was the mandarin come to arrest us. Under the influence of these fears, the churches had already been torn down, and our houses too. What the consequences of this edict had been can hardly be told. And the fears were groundless. The mandarins had not been thinking about us, and were not in any hurry to execute the decree. About midnight we separated, and went each to his own hiding-place. The Christians did not know where to put us; they received us trembling with fear, forcing us into some dark corner of the house, making us promise that we would not speak or stir, lest our presence should be betrayed to a neighbour. M. Borie's host, at the third day, would keep him no longer, so he came to me; but my host, on seeing two Europeans in his house, was almost beside himself with fear. Without a word he went away and hid himself, leaving us alone in his house. Though we had to bear every sort of privation both as to food and lodging, and had no fresh air, and were shut out from all communication with the outside world, for the most part it did not make me uneasy. Even the close retreat had its pleasures, but I could not help feeling some concern at the trouble I was giving to others. There was nothing that at the time I felt more than this. But with M. Borie it was not so. He was altogether undisturbed, quite gay and joyous. When I spoke to him of the anxieties of our Christians, and seemed vexed at it, he only laughed and said, "What do you wish that we should do? For my part I am at ease. We are suffering for God, and they also are suffering for God."'

For the next six months, or till the latter end of the year 1833, the missionaries had to keep in close hiding. They were ever on the move, for wherever they went they were received with dread, and very shortly some new concealment was sought. M. Borie, after he parted from M. Masson, changed his dwelling twenty times before he found a resting-place or an opportunity of resuming duty. M. Retort, writing of this period, says: 'You would feel for me were I to go over to you the various homes in which I have been lodging.' The Christians themselves, in their perplexity, wandered in great numbers in various directions, seeking safety in the mountains or on the rivers, anywhere to save themselves from the dreadful trial of the abjuring of their religion.

But by the end of the year there was an amelioration. The missionaries cautiously got back to their work, and up to 1838, in different places, a good deal of work was done.

In 1837 there were intimations of the approaching storm. In that year there were two martyrdoms; one a European priest, the other a native catechist. But neither of these instances indicated any fixed purpose on the part of the mandarins to act up to the decree, but from their circumstances might be regarded as casualties. It was really a simple accident that led to the first of these martyrdoms; indeed it may be said to have been a series of accidents. There was a missionary in Tonking of the name of Cornay. China, not Tonking, was the destination arranged for him; but to reach Su-Tchuen, which was his province, it was thought most convenient to go through Tonking, where he was to be met by Chinese couriers, who were to guide him to his station; but the couriers were late, and when they came they fell sick and died; and so the project failed. This led to M. Cornay's remaining in Tonking. He was in a mountain district out of the way, and not exposed to danger as much as others. But a bandit chief who had been captured by some soldiers, out of some spite he had against the village where M. Cornay was, gave information that there was a European resident in it; and, to add value to his information, he coined the lie that this European was a great captain, and had taken part in a recent rebellion. So one morning the village was surrounded by soldiers. M. Cornay made an attempt at flight, but it was ineffectual. He hid himself under some thick bushes, but the soldiers came round pricking him with their long spears, and the missionary thought it best to come forth and surrender. He was lodged in a cage and mounted on the shoulders of eight bearers, and thus, under a guard of soldiers, conveyed to the provincial town. Little severity was used towards him in the first instance, and M. Cornay imagined that, as there was no truth at all in the accusation made against him, he should soon recover his liberty. But the local judges, who had to decide the case, considered their own credit involved in maintaining the charge they had once admitted, and were resolved not to retract the reports they had sent up to the king. So M. Cornay's case was lost, and whatever he could say, he could not free himself from the odium of being a leader of rebels. It was not till he had been a month in prison that he could open his eyes to the fatal truth; but when the day of his examination came, July 20th, then it became plain to him that it was settled in the minds of his judges that he should be brought in guilty. How much he felt the proceedings of that day is plainly marked in a letter, in which he tells us what passed: 'On that day—not to be recollected without the most bitter sorrow—I was brought up before my judges for examination. Alone I had to contend with an accuser who hoped to secure his own pardon at the price of my blood; two miserable Christians, captives with me, whom the arts of the mandarins had seduced, and who told a story, which had no truth in it at all, about my being a leader in the late revolt; a whole host of inferior mandarins, each pressing some artful question, to force an admission on my part of having been in league with the rebels; three bribed witnesses, who persisted in their monstrous lying; and a judge, too, who threatened me with hot pincers, and who said that my body should be cut up piecemeal if I continued to deny the facts laid to my charge. I had nothing to oppose to this but my own innocence. With eager vehemence the questions were constantly repeated. I could say nothing but that the whole story was false, and that I would rather bear any torture than confess what was not true, nor would I lie to save my life. But what they wanted was not a defence, but a confession of guilt. I knew that I was exposing myself to the danger of torture. I saw before me my unfortunate companions, who were being flogged, and bleeding, and whose cries wrung my heart. Threats were made to me during the examination of similar treatment. I was expecting the moment when my cage would be opened; and when I saw my catechist stretched on the ground, I thought that my own turn had come. The soldiers were already around my cage; I prayed to Jesus bound to the pillar, and took off my coat. But my examination was over, and it was to bear me back to prison that the soldiers had come. When I got there my strength was all gone.'

M. Cornay did not now doubt what his fate was to be.

He had to appear before his judges again on Aug. 11.

'I was taken out of my cage; a large cangue, newly ironed, was put on me, and when some questions had been asked me in reference to the rebellion, I was stripped, stretched on the ground, and bound. Every time, in answer to their questions, I said, "The accusation brought against me is false," it renewed their lashes. I was told that they would not cease till evening; that they would be repeated the next day if I did not confess. I was promised full pardon if only my guilt was first proved; but no admission was drawn from me, so after receiving fifty lashes I was untied. Painful as these examinations were, the most acute pain I felt was in my arms, tied by the wrists, and benumbed by the cangue. I was at last dragged back to my cage, and on reaching my prison could sing the *Salve Regina*.'

In singing M. Cornay seemed to take a remarkable pleasure. Throughout his captivity he never ceased to sing. He sang not only to please himself, but his singing attracted notice, and he was constantly pestered with applications to sing, for the amusement of his gaoler, or of a curious mandarin, or of the crowds who came to look on the European stranger. His person was small, his temper was mild and gentle, and there was nothing about him that inspired awe, as was the case with missionaries of grand imposing aspect, like M. la Pavec or M. Borie. They importuned him without fear, and he mildly yielded to their importunities. One day, the captain who was set over him said to him that he would certainly have to die if he did not confess his crime, and he asked him if he would then be able to sing. At once M. Cornay began the canticle, 'Religion calls us; let us conquer, let us die.' After his examination, M. Cornay wrote the following letter to his parents:

'My dear Father and Mother,—My blood has already begun to flow under torture, and it will flow again twice or thrice before I am quartered and beheaded. Tears sometimes come in my eyes when I think of the pain you will feel on receiving these accounts; but then comes the consolation of the thought, that when you shall read this letter, I shall be in heaven to intercede for you. Mourn not, then, the day of my death, the happiest indeed of my life; for then happiness begins, and all suffering is at an end. I might have to go through torturings still more cruel: my wounds will be healed before I am scourged again; I shall not be tortured with the pincers, nor will my body be racked as M. Marchand's was; and if my four limbs are to be cut off, four men will do it at once, and a fifth will at the same moment cut off my head; so my sufferings will not be so very much. Console yourselves, then. All will soon be over, and I will await you in heaven. I am, my dear father and mother, with all filial affection,

'Your son,
'J. C. CORNAY.

'In Cage, August 18, 1837.'

On the 29th of August there was a third examination:

'They tried to make me trample on the cross, but I threw myself on my face, raised it up and put it to my lips, when they snatched it from me.' Then he received sixty-five lashes. After that, again they attempted to force him to place his foot on the cross. 'They made me put my foot out of the cage. I thought it was to tear off the flesh with pincers, and as I stretched it out I made an offering of it to my Saviour; but they took hold of it, and put the cross under, and asked if I consented. "No!" I cried. "Never!"'

M. Cornay received in all one hundred and fifteen lashes, the torture of which is excessive. For this punishment bamboos are used, about three feet long, with leaden weights at the end, to add force to the blow. The executioner is sometimes bribed to moderate his strokes; but should he exert his full skill and force, the wretched victim is terribly mangled, the bamboos not only cutting, but taking off pieces of flesh.

On the feast of the Exaltation of the Cross, six days before his death, he wrote the following letter to his brethren:

'Farewell, dearly beloved; farewell, my brethren and my honoured bishop. If against my will I have ever given him pain, I ask his forgiveness. It was never in malice. I am anxious that you should procure me absolution; but if it cannot be, I say, as I have often done before, "My God, let contrition stand for confession, and my blood be instead of Extreme Unction." I am not conscious, indeed, of any grievous sin; but I am not by that justified. But Mary will obtain contrition for me, and the sword will gain for me the holy Unction. I before wrote out my confession for Father Thé; but to leave nothing undone I have rewritten it. Entrust it to whomever you depute. Tell him when he has made the concerted sign to follow me, step by step, till all is over. I shall give absolution to my companions if they die with me. Farewell, farewell! Pray for me, and offer up the Holy Sacrifice, that I may obtain a happy death. —J. C. CORNAY, unworthy soldier of Jesus Christ.'

'Such was the martyr's last will,' says M. Marette, to whom the letter was written, ' but it reached me only with the news of his death.'

Six days after this letter was written was the day of his death, the 20th of September. The order for his execution came suddenly. An hour after he heard it, M. Cornay was carried forth from his prison in his cage. There was the usual procession: three hundred soldiers in front; by his side the executioners with naked swords and axes; behind, a cymbal, at intervals, sent forth its mournful sounds. Then came on horseback the presiding mandarin. The spectacle was a novel one, and had collected a vast crowd; for in that part of the country a European had never before been put to death. The martyr, as he was borne along, continued to sing, or if he did not sing he was in silent prayer. Before the execution the sentence was read out aloud: ' The so-called Tan, whose real name is Cornay, coming in disguise from the kingdom of France, and from the city of London, is guilty as chief of a false sect and as a leader of rebels. The king's order is that he be cut in pieces, and that his head, after exposure for three days, be thrown into the river. Let this sentence be an example to warn every one.'

He was to die as a State criminal. In this case the arms and legs are first cut off, and then the head. It is a horrid mutilation; but M. Cornay was spared the full rigour of this sentence. The mandarin, on his own authority, and with some risk to himself, spared him, and ordered the head to be cut off first. M. Cornay was taken out of his cage, stripped to his shirt, and laid on the ground; his hands and feet were tied to four stakes, and his head was fastened to two others. Four executioners stood round with their swords ready to strike. At the sound of the cymbal the head was cut off at a blow; and then came the mangling of the body, a fearful spectacle. Arms and legs were cut off, the body quartered, and, most horrid of all, the executioner plucked out the liver, and cut off a piece of it and ate it. Brutal as it seems, it was not done out of simple brutality, but out of a popular superstition, that by eating the liver of a great criminal one may acquire courage. An old nun, who had been on the watch, had placed mats and an old altar-cloth under the martyr. And now the crowd eagerly pressed in to possess themselves of some relic. Christians and pagans too mingled in the throng; anything stained by his blood was a precious prize.

M. Cornay was in his twenty-ninth year. The cage in which he lived three months has been described by himself: 'It is sufficiently high and wide to enable me easily to change my posture, but it is not long enough for me to stretch myself at night. It rests upon four feet, raising it six inches from the ground, and has four handles in the middle, by which it is carried. All round are wooden bars crossed, six inches apart. Its height inside is four feet, with a length of five and a breadth of four feet.' Shut up in this cage, he had round his neck a ring, with a chain attached to it, branching off at the middle, and fastened by rings to both his feet. The rings were riveted, and not removed till the day of execution. During his imprisonment the nun who attended his execution constantly visited him, and was the means of his communicating with his friends.

On November 20th, two months after M. Cornay's martyrdom, died Xavier Can, a catechist. He had been brought up from childhood in the college of the missions, and in 1832, when M. Retort came to Tonking, he was attached to his service. He had been a prisoner for twenty months, and would have been set at liberty if he could only have been induced to trample on the cross; but he remained firm against all importunities. On the day of his execution he was assailed afresh. A cross, without any figure, was presented to him, and he was asked to put his foot on it. 'The crosses of the Christians,' said the mandarin, 'are blessed; so they honour them, and do not like to see them profaned. This one has no virtue; it is only two pieces of wood, and represents the number ten. Can will not refuse to tread upon it.' But the young man knew better than to be deceived in this way. 'Tread on the number ten,' urged the mandarin, 'and be free.' 'I am ready to die,' replied the young catechist, 'but I cannot trample on the object of my worship. I would rather die than trample on the head of my fathers, by profaning the symbol of the religion they have taught me.' 'Shut your eyes, and tread on it; you can then go to the priest and be absolved.' 'A crime does not become less by shutting your eyes,' said Xavier. Then he was asked whether he had seen the king's edict pronouncing his sentence, and they showed it him: 'As to the culprit Tien-Truat,' Can's Annamite name, 'if he submit, he may live; but if he refuses to obey, he is to be strangled at once.' Can looked at the edict, and returned it, saying: 'Lead me to punishment; I would rather die than listen to your deceiving words.' This angered the mandarins, and one of them said: 'He fancies there is a heaven, to which he shall go when he is dead. Well, let him die; it is his own business.' 'Mandarin,' said Can, 'you believe neither in heaven nor hell, but ere long you will know better. Do not pity me because I am to die by the hands of men, nor think yourselves happy if your last breath is on a bed of ease. What really distinguishes a good from a bad death is the reward or the punishment that follows good and bad actions.' They went on endeavouring to seduce the martyr, but it was in vain.

'This is no common man,' said one of the mandarins; 'his faith is not to be shaken: he does not serve two kings.' As he went to execution the people made their comments. 'The man thinks little of death; the Master of heaven must have come down on him.' Or again, 'The Christians have an enchanted bread; those who eat it fear nothing, and will never abandon their religion.' Some, pitying him, went up to him and said: 'Why are you resolved to die? Your hair is not yet gray, your countenance is fresh and youthful. Animals with no reason value life; a man, then, should surely have it in regard.' Others murmured, 'He is a fool.' Still the general feeling of the crowd was admiration at conduct which was unintelligible. While he was seated with the cord round his neck, just before it was drawn, again the mandarin came up to him and tempted him for the last time. 'O Tien Truat, it is yet in your power to save your life; your sentence is not irrevocable. Only put your foot on the number *ten*.' 'My mind is fixed,' said Xavier. 'Do your business.' Then the signal was given; the soldiers on each side gave a sudden pull, the neck of the martyr was broken, and his soul went to heaven.

But these martyrdoms were only preliminaries. The persecution did not commence in its full severity till 1838. Then the missionaries were no longer able to work on in the secret desultory manner which had been the case during the last six years. The work was suddenly and entirely stopped. There was a universal flight and a general hiding. The intimations of the change to take place commenced in Cochin China. M. Candalh, a young missionary, very lately come to Cochin China, was stationed at Diloam. There, in secret, he had formed a small college, over which he presided. Suddenly the village was surrounded by the military, and this little nest of supposed conspirators was discovered. The unpardonable offence stimulated the rage of the king and mandarins, and the search for M. Candalh created a stir, which soon spread itself over Tonking, as well as Cochin China. M. Jacquart felt the consequences in a more rigorous captivity, M. Borie in the active search which led to his capture. M. Candalh himself had just time to make off in company with the native priest, Father Joachim. Wandering from village to village, they could not find a resting-place or a concealment. They betook themselves to the mountain forest; and there, in a very short time, in the month of July, M. Candalh sank under the influences of fever. His fate, later in the year, was that of M. Vialle, another Cochin-China missionary.

By the beginning of June the missionaries became aware that flight was the only means of safety. Mgr. Havard also fled to the mountains, and with a fatal result. He first sought out the village of Bach-Bat, close under the mountain range of Sanh, in the province of Ninh-Binh. Not thinking it safe to remain, he left it for the mountains; but a fortnight's stay on the hills, amidst the unwholesome damps, lodging in a cavern, and with no food but cold rice, wore him out; and when he got back to

Bach-Bat he was too weak to throw off the fever that attacked him, and died.

The other missionaries who fled, except M. Borie, although they had their share of suffering, escaped. M. Charrier, fearless for his own safety, and knowing the value of his life to his people, sought an asylum in all directions. He passed from place to place. When he rested, it was in some comfortless dark den; hunted as he was, he eluded all search till, after some years, in more easy times, his own turn came to be taken. M. Guarthier penetrated into a dense solitude, far away from all companions, and at the end of four months was, as his brother missionary said, 'like one risen from the grave.' M. Jeantet, at much hazard, secured a refuge comparatively easy and safe; and there, after a while, he was joined by M. Retort, who had been roaming and hiding as he could, and then the two lived together in some peace and happiness.

One of the first to feel the effect of the severe measures which marked this year of 1838 was M. Jacquart. For several years he had now been a captive, but, except that he was detained, a good deal of freedom had been allowed. The king employed him in superintending certain works, in maps and translations, and he taught French to young Cochin-Chinese of distinction. But this year it all came to an end. First, March 7, he was called up before the chief mandarin of the province to undergo an examination. It was, in this instance, simply a few questions and answers. He was asked to abandon his religion, but of course he would not. M. Jacquart has given us the dialogue: 'The profession of this religion is not allowed; the king has proscribed it, and the orders of the king are the orders of Heaven. If you persist in following it, you must die. It is a happy thing for you that you have escaped so long.' 'I wish to die, and the sooner the better; my chief desire will be thus fulfilled.' 'What can make you so blind?' 'I am not blind. Religion teaches the truth; that is why I love and obey it.' 'What advantage can you hope to obtain by dying for it?' 'When one dies for the sake of religion, he is sure of going to heaven. If, then, the king wishes quickly to bring me to that glorious happiness, he has only to give the order that I be beheaded. A moment's suffering will lead to perfect happiness, and I shall have what I wish.' 'How can one who is dead go to heaven? Has any one ever been seen going to heaven after he has been beheaded? Then it is all over with him.' 'It is only after death that the soul, by being separated from the body, can go to heaven. And this is why I do not desire to live, but would wish the king to give the order at once for me to be beheaded.' 'Well, this is indeed great blindness!' 'It is no blindness; the great mandarin will permit me to say the religion I profess is agreeable to right reason.' And then he goes on to explain how it is so, but the mandarin interrupts him: 'Enough, enough! He speaks to us of heaven, and says that there is a sovereign Lord of all things. Who can comprehend this doctrine? He is a fanatic. Enough! Lead him away.' So the examination was over, to be repeated some months after in more stern fashion. Yet after this examination he was not at once entirely deprived of his freedom; that was not till July 13. Then he was loaded with the cangue and chains, and thrown into a damp unwholesome prison. He was sick at the time, but that was no plea for mitigation. After a second preparatory examination came the real contest. What the mandarins wanted was to force M. Jacquart to give certain information, which he would not do; so for hours he had to lie bound before them, bearing stroke after stroke, coming down at slow intervals, according to their custom, they proceeding with their questions, and he firm in refusing to answer. This went on for three hours. He received forty-five strokes, and every blow brought blood, and ten rattans were broken; but M. Jacquart uttered not a sigh, no sound passed his lips. 'When he was loosened,' we are told, 'and had put on his clothes, he remained some instants in prayer.'

During the last days of his imprisonment M. Jacquart had the consolation of a companion, an heroic young Christian, named Thomas Thien, who, having bravely sustained the most cruel tortures—seven beatings, and the tearing of his flesh with cold and hot pincers—was lodged in the prison to await his execution. He was but a lad, being no more than eighteen. After a few days spent together they both willingly gave up their lives for the faith; joyfully they walked to the place where they were to suffer. It is the custom of the country to pause on their walk and to take some refreshments; and when they reached the place where this was usually done, the boy, turning to M. Jacquart, innocently asked whether he would take anything. 'No, my child,' he replied. 'Then I will not,' said Thomas. 'To heaven, my father!' A little farther on was the place of execution. There the rope was placed round their necks, and they were strangled. The day of these martyrdoms was September 20th.

Mgr. Borie was the next victim. He had just succeeded to the vacant throne of Mgr. Havard, when by his own death the throne was again empty. He was a young missionary, but active and enterprising. He had entered Tonking shortly before the edict of 1833, and had then given proof of his high qualities. After some months of wandering, and some narrow escapes, he had been established in Binh-Chinh, the southern province adjoining Cochin China. There were numerous Christians there—computed at 20,000. Quietly he did a good deal of work, collected fresh scholars, got around him several ecclesiastical students, built two colleges, two houses for nuns. He went about amongst the Christians, visiting their villages, and in one year he heard as many as 3000 confessions. Sometimes, in places near the sea, he ventured on a more open display of religion, sang a Mass, had an occasional procession. This went on for five years; but that fatal surprise of M. Candalh was a signal for all to stop. M. Borie had now to go into retirement. He had himself no wish to fly; his own wish had been—but it had been restrained by his brother missionaries—to go boldly before Minh-Menh, and plead for the Christian faith. But though he concealed himself, he was discovered. Those who were out in pursuit laid hold of a certain Father Diem. The man was old—seventy-five years of age—and not equal to the terrors of his situation. When he was thrown on the ground, and his clothes were stripped off, his hands and feet bound, and all was ready for the scourging, his courage failed. He answered every question, and gave information that led to the pursuit and capture of M. Borie. It was a momentary weakness of the poor old man; he bitterly bewailed what he had done, and eventually courageously sacrificed his life for the faith.

Instant search was made for M. Borie. A house, where he was reported to have been, was entered at midnight, but he was not there. The master of the house was importuned for his secret, but fifty blows failed to extract any intelligence. Blows were tried with one and another, but no one proved faithless. One had sixty blows, and it was got out of him that M. Borie was gone in the direction of the sea. The pursuit then was eager, and a man was caught who was said to have been the guide who had last directed him. This man had seventy blows, but nothing could induce the bold fellow to betray the father. A young girl of sixteen was well beaten, but revealed nothing. At length they fell in with the very man who had guided M. Borie to his last concealment. They had only just parted. And this man's heart failed. The sight of the dreaded bamboo was too much for him, and he acknowledged that he had seen not far off a tall man with a fair complexion and a long beard. That was enough. A strict search was at once made, and after it had been some time continued, M. Borie, who had been lying concealed in a sand-hole, conscious that he must be discovered, came forth of his own accord, and delivered himself up. 'Whom are you seeking?' he asked the astonished soldiers; and possibly, under the alarm of his sudden appearance and lofty stature, he might have escaped, but he did not attempt it, and quietly allowed them to make him their prisoner.

A young native named Peter Tu, one of M. Borie's students, seeing his master in chains, drew attention by his cries of grief, and was arrested. He might have recovered his liberty, but he was not willing to be separated from M. Borie. 'No, my father,' he said, 'I will follow you to death; by the grace of God I will be firm.' Then M. Borie, taking off his turban, tore off two pieces, and gave them to Peter, saying, 'Keep this in remembrance of your promise;' so to confirm his courage. M. Borie and his companion were then conducted to the principal town of the province for examination. The unfortunate Father Diem was added to the party. The poor old man was now repentant, and the words of M. Borie confirmed him in his resolution.

In the provincial town the prisoners were brought up for examination. Peter Tu kept his promise, and did not flinch under his trial; he took his twenty strokes, and no persuasion or intimidation could induce him to put his foot on the cross. Then came M. Borie's turn. The mandarin addressed him. 'Cao,' said he, using the Annamite name, 'the king has strictly forbidden your religion, but if you will consent to trample on the cross I will at once set you at liberty.' 'I would rather die a hundred times,' was the indignant reply. Father Diem, on the same demand, made a like response.

After a few questions came the torture. M. Borie was made to lie down, and his hands and feet were bound, a brick was placed under his stomach, another under his chin, and thirty strokes were ordered. For the first twenty he moved not, nor showed any signs of pain; but during the last ten some groans were heard, and it was noticed that he had his handkerchief in his mouth throughout. 'That will do,' said the mandarin. 'It is only lost time to scourge him.' Then he asked M. Borie if he had felt much pain. 'I cannot but feel,' he said, 'but I am content.'

M. Borie's imprisonment lasted some months. He was taken July 31, and the order for his execution was not received before November 24. During this time he was not badly treated. The mandarins showed him respect, and even indulgence. He was not confined in the common prison, but kept under guard in a large room, having with him Fathers Diem and Koa, and Anthony Nam and Peter Tu; and persons were allowed to come and see them with a good deal of freedom. During this interval he wrote the following letter to his mother and family, dated October 1838:

'Dearest Mother and beloved Brothers and Sisters,—It is to-day twelve years since, on returning from a walk with my brother Augustin, I told you the purpose which the Lord had inspired of renouncing the follies of the world, and giving myself to the priesthood. You will still remember the tears we shed, while we adored the will of Divine Providence. On the 1st of October 1829, we made a sacrifice yet more painful than the first. Then I parted from you without the hope of ever seeing you again in this world, and your submission to the will of God supported my courage, and gave me the consolation of which I had need. I thank the Giver of all good for it. To-day I make known to you a third sacrifice which our Divine Master asks from us all, or rather I acquaint you with the decrees of His mercy, by which He vouchsafes to honour your son and brother. I know well that the voice of nature must be heard, but it is silenced by that of religion. In the midst of my sorrow I am full of consolation and joy. The feeling that I am not worthy of so great a favour will sometimes frighten me, but I am quieted by the thought of the goodness of God, and so encouraged that I sigh for the day when I shall have the happiness of shedding my blood for the faith which I have preached. The sword or the bow-string, whichever be the instrument of my death, neither has terror. I think of the happiness of being allowed to expiate my sins with my blood. Do not, then, grieve, my beloved ones, for what is a real cause of joy, but join me in thanking the Father of mercies for this grace.

Let us strive to live and die as good Christians. Our life is but a pilgrimage, which should conduct us to heaven. I urge my dear brother Augustin, as the eldest of the family, to be the support and comfort of our good mother, and to take a fatherly care of his brothers and sisters, and to be to them a pattern and guide. I love you all from the bottom of my heart.'

M. Borie had quite made up his mind to die. His sentence, indeed, had been already pronounced, but the confirmation was delayed. In a letter to M. Masson, with whom he kept up communication, and who had sent him the bulls raising him to the episcopal dignity, he shows the steady cheerful way in which he was awaiting his end:

'Since the year 1826, when the goodness of God drew me from the follies of the world, I have never ceased to wish to shed my blood in expiation of my sins. I would not exchange my cangue for the most glorious crown in the world. I do not wish it to be taken from my neck till it is removed that I may receive my death-blow. Last night our prison resounded with the chanting of the *Miserere*. Father Koa and my beloved Tu, after every verse, gave the refrain, "Parce, Domine, parce populo tuo." The guards wanted us to prolong our singing. The report is that I and the Fathers Koa and Diem are to be beheaded, and my boy Tu to be strangled. Our sentence is pronounced; it is only for the king to confirm it, and then we shall have the happiness of being for ever united in the Lord. Fiat! fiat!'

The confirmation came. M. Borie was to be beheaded. Without any delay, the same evening he was led out to execution. Fathers Koa and Diem were to die also, but to be strangled. Nam and Tu were not to die for the present, but their sentence was not cancelled. The mandarin, according to custom, ordered a fowl to be cooked, but M. Borie and his companions would eat nothing. In deference to the mandarin, they took a little wine. The mandarin would have been pleased if M. Borie's life had been spared, and said so; but M. Borie told him it was his wish to die, and that he thanked him for the favour; adding, 'I have never before from childhood knelt before any one, but I will now kneel to you, mandarin, to thank you for the kindness you are showing me.' But the mandarin would not permit it, and was moved to tears.

But he could not understand how any one could be grateful for being condemned to death. Peter Tu and the aged Nam were in grief that they were not to die with their beloved father. M. Borie committed Tu to the charge of the old man, saying: 'The youth is very dear to me; I must leave him behind, and his virtue may be tried by terrible dangers. Promise me that you will show him the same love you have shown to me. To your love and care I intrust him.'

As they were on the way to execution, a mandarin named Bo, who had no friendly feeling, accosting M. Borie, asked him if he was now afraid of death. 'I am not a rebel or a robber, that I should fear death,' replied M. Borie. 'I fear God alone. It is my turn to-day, it will be another's to-morrow.' 'Insolence!' said the mandarin, with a curse; 'give him a blow on the mouth.' Shortly after M. Borie sent a message to the mandarin, asking his pardon if he had offended him.

On the spot chosen for execution six mats had been laid for the three martyrs by a Christian. Reaching it, they all knelt down and prayed. Next a smith knocked off the irons that fastened the cangues. Then Fathers Diem and Koa were ordered to lie flat on the ground, and they were presently strangled. M. Borie's sufferings were not so short. The man was drunk who was to strike off his head. He struck again and again, making frightful gashes, breaking the jaw, cutting the shoulder, wounding the neck, but not till the seventh blow severing the head from the body, and ending the pains of the martyr.

In Eastern Tonking, the province of the Spanish Dominicans, the persecution was from the beginning more prompt and stringent than in other places. There presided in that province a mandarin who had made himself notorious for the excess of his brutality and vindictiveness; he hunted up the Christians with an eagerness that never tired, and had no pity in the punishments he inflicted. The two bishops of this vicariate were very aged: Mgr. Delgado, the

Vicar-Apostolic, was seventy-six, and had been forty years a bishop; and Mgr. Henares, the coadjutor, was seventy-three, and had been forty-nine years a missionary, and thirty-eight a bishop. They were hardly equal to meet the exceeding perils of the time. Early in June they had to seek concealment, like the other missionaries, but they did not succeed. Mgr. Delgado was discovered in the little village of Kien-Lao, where he was lying hid. There was an attempt at escape. His faithful Christians carried him off in a basket, but they were pursued and overtaken, and the old man was made prisoner. Age, sickness, and privation, the summer heats, and the confinement of the prison, were too much for him, and in a few days he was dead, just anticipating the sentence which had already been pronounced on him. A few days after, his colleague and successor became the prey of his enemies. He had hid himself in a boat, and, if he had not been betrayed by a pagan, might have managed to have made off to some more safe spot; but, information having been given, the soldiers quickly appeared, and he was borne off in a cage to receive the sentence of the cruel Trinh-Quanh-Khanh. He had not long to wait for it; before June was over (June 25) he was a martyr. His catechist, Francis Chien, was his partner in suffering. As they proceeded to execution it was proclaimed aloud: 'Hearken, O people, and know that this man is a European come amongst us to preach the false religion of Christ. It is for this crime that the king has condemned him to death. Avoid this doctrine if you would escape a like fate.' The next month the priest F. Joseph Fernandez was added to the list of martyrs.

The Tonkinese character is timid, and ill calculated to face dangers such as they had to encounter in these dreadful times. But we have instances in which they showed remarkable heroism; and of all those who distinguished themselves by their courage, Michael Mi stands out conspicuous. Michael was the principal man in his own village. He was taken on the first outbreak of the persecution in this year, and at the same time Anthony Dich, his father-in-law, a rich man, and James Nam, a priest. All alike resisted the importunities to abandon their faith. Anthony Dich, who was an old man of sixty-nine, seemed to shrink from the terrible ordeal through which he knew he must pass. The feebleness of age, the horrors of a violent death, attachment to his family and friends, his comfortable easy state in the world, were all so many influences holding him back, and he had none of the fervour of his bold son-in-law or the calm courage of the priest. But from their companionship he gained strength, and their example revived his drooping spirits. 'Think, father,' said Michael Mi; 'from your great age you cannot live long. There are two ways in which you may die: one is natural, and to what it may lead you do not know; the other that which you will suffer from your persecutors, and it will be followed by an eternity of happiness. Can you hesitate in your choice? Is it not easy to see which is best?

If in our mutual circumstances it were allowable to regret life, it is I, who am young and strong, that might be excused for doing so; but you see how joyfully I give up my life for the sake of God. Your children are all grown and settled in the world; by living you cannot benefit them, but by dying a martyr you will give them matter for instruction and glory. I shall leave behind a young widow, with four infant children not yet able to maintain themselves; but God, who has given them to me, will not fail to provide for their wants, and from that heaven where we shall soon be we shall protect them by our prayers.' And then he promised the old man that he would himself bear the stripes that his persecutors might wish to inflict on him, concluding with these words: 'Let us be content and firm. It is now we must prove ourselves true Christians, and show that we can die for Jesus Christ, as He was pleased to die for us.'

And he kept his promise; for rising up after he had received his own beating, he would approach the mandarin, and say: 'My father is old and infirm; pity him, and let me be flogged in his stead.' And then anew he would lie down, and with steady courage endure a second flogging, and while the blood flowed down from his wounds, and his flesh was torn, no cry nor sigh was heard to escape him. He was indeed a hero. And his family were like him. His wife and his children partook of the same spirit. His wife came to visit him, but it was not to take from him his firm courage. She told him not to fear for her or for her young children; for with the grace of God she would not fail on her part. His little boy and girl were trained to think and feel like their parents. His boy, only nine, sent a message to his father in prison not to renounce his religion, but to be a martyr, and go straight to heaven. His daughter—a little older, she was only eleven—escaped one day from the house, and went to see her father in prison. She had miles to walk. She made her way in, fearlessly, through the guards, and urged her father rather to die than trample on the cross. The mandarins were very anxious to subdue the spirit of this bold confessor. His position in his village, as well as his high character, made the conquest important. They flogged him without mercy. Five hundred lashes in forty days was the sum of his heavy punishment.

'Fool,' they said to him, 'why do you choose to die? Your wife and children want your protection. You are young, you have learning, you may expect to acquire riches, and you might live a long and happy life. Trample on the cross, and we will let you go. Many other Christians have done so. Why do you not imitate them? When you are at home you may follow the religion of Jesus; you will be perfectly free to do so.' But all their words made no impression on the heart of Mi. 'Mandarins,' he replied, 'I will never abandon the religion I have been taught, and which I know to be true. If you were asked to trample on the head of the king, from whom you hold your dignities and places, would you dare to do it? And do you think that I would dare to profane the image of the King of Heaven, whom I adore? I grant that my wife and children bind me to life; but I shall not fear to leave them; for I am certain that He who gave them to me will watch over them, and unite us in heaven. Those who have trampled on the cross are no example to me, no more than that of deserters would have on soldiers who were brave and loyal to their king.' This indomitable fearlessness continued to the end. On the day of his death the executioner said to him, 'Give me five bands, and I will sever your head at a single blow, so that you will not suffer much.' 'Cut it into a hundred pieces, if you please,' he answered; 'so that you cut it off, that is all I want; as to bands, though I have plenty at home, I will give you none; I would rather give them to the poor.'

The day of the execution was indeed more of a festival day than anything else. The boldness of the holy martyrs stirred up an extraordinary interest. The enthusiasm was general. There were no signs of sorrow on the countenances of the three men as they walked to death; they were joyous, they talked together of their happiness. The Christians crowded round; multitudes were collected; and as they moved on they were objects of respect and honour. No sooner did their blood begin to flow than the anxious crowds pressed in; all wanted a relic, some memorial of these glorious Christians, who had given such testimony to their faith. The funeral rites were magnificent: sixteen hundred guests sat down at the tables spread for their entertainment by the children of Anthony Dich.

There is a long list of the principal martyrs of Annam. The names recorded for this year are twenty-six. Besides the five Europeans, there were six native priests and six catechists. Of the number were three soldiers. They failed at first, but soon recovered. It was but a short weakness; and when they saw their fault, they went, of their own accord, and acknowledged it, and submitted themselves to the king's vengeance. They are honourable names, and not to be omitted—Augustin Huy, Nicholas Thé, and Dominc Dat. The two first were sawn asunder; the last was strangled.

Three of the catechists were the catechists of M. Cornay—Paul Mi, Peter Duong, and Peter Truat. They suffered a great deal, and never showed any weakness. After an imprisonment of eighteen months they were strangled November 24.

The next year there was a repetition of similar scenes. In Eastern Tonking six bold and fervent Christians gave proof of their fidelity, and conspicuous amongst them was one Francis Xavier Mau. The judge, struck by his demeanour, tried to win him, offering him honours if he would walk on the cross. 'I will never trample on the cross!' was his only reply. Some mandarins attempted force, pushing him towards the crucifix. 'Take one step at least,' they said, 'that you may escape death.' 'It is the image of my Lord,' he replied. 'We cannot honour Him enough. I will never dishonour Him.'

So they left him alone. In the prison his fervour was no less marked; he converted many of his fellow-prisoners, and brought them over to the faith. He was in prison a year, but his courage did not flag, and at the end he walked firmly to his execution, his countenance beaming with joy. 'I am going to heaven,' he said to his Christian friends. 'It matters not that the way is strewn with thorns. In a moment they will be forgotten in an eternity of joy.' The six were beheaded.

We may mention also two priests who suffered this year. Father Thi and Father Andrew Luc were two old patriarchs; their memories would go back to scenes which we have long since recorded. Peter Thi, at eleven years of age, in the days of Bishop Reydellet, had entered a house of God. He was a catechist when the Taysons were supreme in Tonking, and, early in the reign of Gia-laong, had been ordained priest. He was mild and prudent, but his timidity was excessive. Mgr. Havard valued him highly. Andrew Luc was the son of pagan parents. When a boy of twelve he was brought to M. le Roy at Ke-vinh, and after his baptism trained as a catechist, and in 1823 he was raised to the priesthood by the Bishop of Gortyna, Mgr. Longer. He was held in much esteem for his many virtues, but, like F. Thi, he had much of the Tonkinese timidity. These two fathers were great friends. On November 10th, 1839, F. Luc made a visit to Ke-song to see F. Thi. He stayed with him the night. But the stay was dangerous. In the middle of the night the house was beset, and the two fathers were made prisoners. They were bought off by their Christians, but to no purpose, for soon they fell into the hands of a fresh party, who would not part with them, and, amidst the tears and lamentations of numerous Christians, they were carried away to Kecho. Their sufferings were not aggravated nor long. They were of course asked to apostatise, but they were not beaten nor tortured. Sentence was soon passed on them, and about five weeks after their capture the day for execution arrived. The night before a priest found his way into their prison, and gave them Communion. So fortified, the two fathers proceeded to the place of execution. A tinge of paleness was observed on F. Luc's countenance, but he smiled, and his step, as he moved on, was firm. F. Thi was weak, and advanced feebly, and, impeded by his chain, he fell from exhaustion; so a soldier took him on his back and carried him. They suffered with composure and firmness.

A prominent martyr of the next year, 1840, was F. Paul Khoan. He was sixty-nine years of age. The treachery of a pagan caused him to fall into the hands of his enemies, and he was taken with two scholars, Peter Kien and John Baptist Thanh. They were pressed to trample on the cross, and a long conference on the subject ensued. F. Khoan said that the request was not reasonable. 'Why not reasonable,' he was asked, 'when by doing so you will preserve your life, which you will lose if you do not?' 'Mandarin,' said F. Khoan, 'suppose that you, who

o

receive your honours and appointments from the king, were to desert him in the day of battle, under pretext that you would so risk your life, would it not be cowardice, ingratitude, and base infidelity? This is my case. From my birth I have received graces and favours from the God of heaven; He has raised me to dignity in His religion, and you wish me to abandon Him in the day of trial. It is by death, as the Chinese books say, that we prove our truth. I have now the opportunity of proving mine, and I must embrace it.' To this the mandarin could make no reply. Twelve lashes were ordered to F. Khoan. John Baptist Thanh and his companion were next tried, but they would not yield, and were in their turn beaten. All three were then thrown into prison, and importuned to give up their religion. They were told that their faith was absurd; they were enticed by promises, they were threatened with torture, they were dragged over the cross, and their feet were forcibly placed on the sacred image. Then again followed the lash. But they were not to be shaken. Sentence of death was passed, but execution was delayed. F. Khoan lingered out a year in prison, but never wavered, although the endeavours to induce him to apostatise were repeated. The mandarin, by kind words, tried all he could to persuade him to change his mind. He invited him to sit down on the mat by his side, offered him tea and betel, and renewed his solicitations. But F. Khoan plainly told him that he had well thought over what he was doing, and that the more he thought the stronger was his resolution. And the mandarin, disappointed, said to those around, 'You hear what he says! What hope can we have to conquer a man like this?' Then said he to F. Khoan, 'Why is it you do not wish to live?' The father said that he should be thankful if his life was spared; but still, that when a Christian died for God, he would obtain a better reward in heaven than anything he could possess in this world. The mandarin, on this, inquired how he knew there was a Paradise, and how he knew there was a Master of heaven; and F. Khoan's replies made such impression that he ceased his opposition, and said that it was very plain that F. Khoan himself believed there was a Paradise. He told Father Khoan that he pitied him, and wished he could save him, but that unless he would trample on the cross he could not. Then he referred to an apostate priest named Duyet, and asked F. Khoan whether he had any resentment against him. 'No,' replied F. Khoan; 'our religion forbids all anger and hatred.' Such a precept of religion seemed strange to the mandarin; and he next wanted to know whether this fallen priest, Duyet, might still get into heaven. 'He might,' said F. Khoan, 'if he was converted, and did penance.' But the mandarin would not believe that it was possible, and said that, should he reach the door, F. Khoan would push him back and prevent his entering. 'No,' said F. Khoan, 'we should not; we could not do it, if we wished.'

F. Khoan's day at length came. For the last time he was called up before the tribunal to make his choice. But his mind was fixed. On the 28th of April, 1840, the father and his two pupils proceeded to their execution, singing a *Te Deum* by the way. Crowds were around, and he spoke to them. He told them not to pity him, for he and his companions were suffering for no crime, but for the religion of Jesus Christ, which was the true one. And, just before the execution, he said out aloud, 'Glory, honour, and praise to the Lord of heaven and earth, for the love of whom we die. We pray for the king that he may prosper, that he may live long, and cease to persecute our holy religion, the only one that can make men happy.' Then the cangues were sawn off, the chains broken, and the sword quickly severed the heads of the three martyrs.

F. Luke Loan was a very old priest, eighty years of age. He was well known for his charity. Once, when he was sick in bed, he was called to visit a dying person. He got up at once, and, as he was not able to walk, he was carried to the house. He fainted away on reaching it, but revived in time to administer the sacraments. Old as he was, the last year of his life he is said, even in those difficult times, to have heard sixteen hundred confessions. The mandarin who conducted him to execution showed him remarkable honour. He wished him to be carried in a net, and offered him his own parasol; but the old man declined; and so, with the aid of two men supporting him, one on each side, and holding fans, he tottered along, every one wondering at the condescension of the mandarin, and at the unusual mode in which the criminal was proceeding to his execution. For the execution no one could be found who was willing to undertake the office. Six soldiers were successively called up in vain. At length a Cochin-Chinese soldier was bribed to do the work, and even he excused himself to the priest, saying the king must be obeyed, and asking the father to pray for him in Paradise.

The same summer died Anthony Nam and Peter Tu. From the day they had parted with Mgr. Borie, when he consigned Peter to the care of Nam, these two had remained in prison. They had been captives nearly two years, and would listen to nothing that was said to induce them to apostatise. Nam was a man of some distinction—a physician—known and esteemed by the mandarins, and they were anxious to force from him some testimony of abandoning his faith. On the day of execution they repeated their efforts, using some amount of violence; but the old man drew back, exclaiming that if he touched the cross it was not by his own will, and it would mean nothing. The place where they suffered was the very spot where Mgr. Borie had been beheaded. Peter Tu reverently knelt down there and said his last prayer. Both the martyrs rejoiced in the prospect before them. 'This is a favour that comes from God alone,' said Tu. 'We must indeed thank God,' responded Nam. Then, standing in the place where his former companions in prison had yielded up their lives, he said, ' I thank Thee, O my God, that Thou hast granted me the grace and happiness that they had.' Seeing his relations and friends about him in tears, he asked them why they wept. 'You ought to rejoice with me,' he said, 'for my heart is full of consolation.' His parting words were, 'Live in peace and united in charity, my brethren; love one another; praise and glorify our Lord Jesus Christ.' Then at the order of the mandarin they had to lie down and extend their arms. 'Thus it was,' said Nam, ' that my God and Saviour once stretched out His to receive the nails.'

The most memorable martyrdoms of the year took place in Nam-Dinh, the province of the cruel Trinh-Quanh-Khanh. Keen in his pursuit after the Christians, he one morning surrounded a small village and carried off a body of captives. There were three priests in the number. F. Nghi was saying Mass when the tidings came that the soldiers were at hand. He had time to conceal himself, but he was hunted up by the next day. His curate, F. Ngan, was taken also, and an old priest, F. Thinh. F. Ngan, as they put the cangue on his neck, whispered a *Deo gratias*, and 'his heart,' as he said, 'beat with joy.' F. Thinh was eighty years of age, and sick in bed. It was not known at first that he was a priest, but the truth got out, and he had to appear with the others before Trinh-Quanh-Khanh. The three priests and seven Christians were conveyed to the provincial town, Vi-Hoang, and imprisoned. There they had to stand a severe trial, for elaborate means were used to compel them to submit to the demand of treading on the cross. The Christians, all at first, made a show of resolution, but the majority could not hold out; of the seven only two persevered. But these two were resolute, and one of them, Martin Tho, was another of those heroes that here and there appear in these annals. He was a man of good position in his village, fifty-two years of age, an earnest Christian, always ready to afford shelter to a priest. When he had been in prison some weeks, an attempt was made to break his spirit. As he would not yield to promise or intimidation, he was tested with punishment. The formidable governor himself presided, bent upon subjugating to his will one who seemed so stubborn. Tho was stretched on a pole and tied, and then by means of his cangue held up by the soldiers, so as to be raised a foot from the ground; and thus suspended, he was beaten without mercy; several striking at once on hands and feet, on the whole body, others at the same time tearing his hair, or pricking him with lances, and irritating the bleeding wounds. 'Now will you apostatise?' said Trinh-Quanh-Khanh, in tones of mockery and insult. 'Renounce Christ, and you shall be free. Do you consent?' 'Great mandarin,' replied the sufferer, 'let me live, and I will thank you; if you order me to die, I will submit cheerfully; but my faith I will not abjure. Never!' 'Then you do not wish to live?' 'Mandarin, the God of heaven and earth, when He created us, implanted in us all a love of life; but it is better to give up life than to preserve it by sin.' 'Obey, or I will cut off your head.' 'If, because I will not deny my religion, the great mandarin please to strike it off, he can do so; but when it falls my happiness will be complete.' 'If I bring your wife and children, and put them to death before your eyes, will you not compassionate them, and apostatise to save them?' 'I thought my own blood would have been enough, but, if you mingle with it that of my wife and children, that would be no reason for apostatising. Though a father and a husband, I prefer death to perjury. My family is very dear, but God is still dearer.' 'You desire, then, to go to heaven? How will you get there? In what way will you ascend?' 'Heaven! Yes, it is the hope of heaven that makes me persevere in fidelity to my religion; when my head falls under the sword of the executioner, my soul will fly towards the Christian's home.' 'Must you not have wings to fly?' 'This cangue and the rods that have bruised my body are the wings on which I shall soar towards my God.' No words, however noble, could soften the heart of the hard Trinh-Quanh-Khanh. Martin Tho, after this examination, was ordered out to be exposed under the burning sun. Afterwards he was shut up in a noisome filthy hole, and for days kept without food. All sorts of methods were adopted to conquer him. He had not always been so perfectly imperturbable; he had at the beginning, as he has confessed, some shrinkings of heart. When first seized he had shuddered at the prospect before him. He could hardly trust himself, and be sure that he should not fall under the dreadful trial; but he raised his heart to God and prayed for strength, and God heard him. The scene just narrated was not the first stage of the process; he and his brother prisoners had before passed through a long series of cruelties. Brave and confirmed as we have seen him here, the original trial had been keen and real.

The sight of the instruments of cruelty, the red-hot irons, the burning coals, and then the executioner approaching to throw him on the ground and tie him to the stake—the first stroke, too, which seemed to cut him in two,—as far as this it was all anguish. There was the full resolution to suffer for God to the end; but there was the human fear—the dread of pain; but after that first stroke the fear and dread was gone, and the pain seemed to have ceased. When he returned to his prison, and saw the blood flowing from his wounds, his wonder was that when he had felt so little there should be signs of such severity of punishment. And then he perceived how great had been God's mercy, and he called to mind the miracles of which he had heard, and which he now understood. What is here told is his own story, the sum of what he stated to a native subdeacon whom M. Jeantet sent into the prison to confer with these champions of the faith, and to carry to them the Holy Eucharist. 'Our torn bodies,' said Martin Tho, as they were conversing, 'were, after the examination and tortures, objects of compassion to every one; they thought us wretched, and at the time our hearts were overflowing with joy. O, what a happiness that a vile creature, a sinner like me, should have been granted consolations like that!'

This man had a wife and eight children, all animated with his own faith. Their one thought and desire was that he might not fall in the trial. His son wanted in the first instance to go to the prison to see his father; but the prudent mother dissuaded him. 'No, my son,' she said; 'your father is now on the field of battle; we do not know whether he will be so happy as to confess the gospel; the idea of the torments prepared for him is quite trial enough without adding to it, and the greatness of his affection to you might draw his thoughts from the glory awaiting him.' But afterwards, when his triumph was known, she gave her consent, and his son and daughter and other children went to visit their father. 'My children,' said the Christian hero, as he embraced them, 'your father is soon to die. My last counsel to you is that you remember you have one soul. Pray God to give you grace to be faithful to your religion; above all, keep yourselves pure from the contagion of the world.'

These prisoners, though one has been singled out, were all severely tried, and were all strong in their constancy. They were many months in prison, from May to November. Towards the end, when the idea of forcing them to apostatise was relinquished, their treatment was more lenient. November 6 the confirmation of the sentence of death arrived, and the five prisoners were led out to punishment. Still the figure of Martin Tho was conspicuous. He walked with an air of gravity and recollection. There was something solemn and majestic in his countenance, something the Christians of his village had never noticed before. Soon the conflict was over. A single stroke severed the heads of all except the aged Father Thinh. His sufferings were more prolonged, for it was the fourth or fifth stroke before his head fell.

M. Jeantet is authority for this account, and everything that is narrated respecting all these martyrdoms is derived from the letters of one or other of the missionaries, who were watching with earnest interest the prolonged trials of the Christians. Of course they heard many a sad story, as well as these glorious triumphs of the faith. There was many a grievous fall in those terrible contests. But some who fell rose up again almost as soon as they had fallen, to contend with the more hardihood, to compensate for a momentary weakness. And here is an instance from the pen of a Dominican father. An old catechist, seventy-four years of age, yielded under torture and gave up his faith. A few days after Trinh-Quanh-Khanh sent for him, and said, 'Since you have listened to reason, the king has pardoned you, and you may go.' But the catechist was now full of sorrow for the sin which he had committed, and said so to the governor. He was beaten, and then shut up in a filthy sewer, and having been left there for two days, was again called before the governor for a fresh trial. As he showed no disposition to yield, the governor adopted the following plan to force him: He shut him up in a prison with some renegades, who had the commission to work upon him. Their own safety was to depend upon their success, and if they did not induce him to comply, they were to die together. So these wretches used all their arts to bring him down to their own degradation. They vied with each other in their ill-usage; they spit upon him, they cursed him, they entreated him. This went on for four days, when he was again called before Trinh-Quanh-Khanh. But he had in no degree relented. On this he was put to the torture, and a second time the poor man failed. But a quick remorse followed, and he could not bear to think of what he had done. The praises of his fellow-prisoners fell heavily on his ear; he groaned in the depth of his anguish as he contemplated his folly. Fortunately, there was in that prison a native priest, and to him the unhappy catechist opened his heart; and rising up after his confession with renewed strength, he resolved to repair his act of weakness by enduring the worst for the future. He was again summoned before Trinh-Quanh-Khanh, that the tyrant might satisfy himself as to the sincerity of his apostasy. But he was disappointed. The catechist, instead of avowing his apostasy, boldly declared that he would bear anything, tortures or death, rather than repeat his sin. And instantly he was put to the proof. A round of blows followed, the satellites striking him furiously, the mandarin urging them on to greater extremities. But the catechist did not change his mind again. 'No,' he cried, 'I will never consent to trample on the cross.' He was sent back to his prison, loaded with the cangue, then brought out and exposed to the burning sun, his clothes stripped off, a crucifix tied to each foot, he himself

being bound to a pillar; and, while he was so left, the
soldiers insulted him, spit on him, struck him, plucked
his beard. So he remained five days and nights.
He went back into his prison, was brought out again
into the sun, was kept without food, led up afresh
before the judge, was beaten and tortured, thrown
into the sewers of the public prison. Nothing could
break the spirit of the humbled, repentant old man;
no more weakness, only patience and contrition for
his faults, till he sank under his sufferings, and gave
up his soul to God.

No European was put to death after Mgr. Borie
during Minh-Menh's reign; only one was made prisoner.
In April 1839 M. Delamotte was secreted in a village
near Huè. He knew that his enemies were
in search for him, and he resolved to secure a
new refuge. In the darkness of night he set out on
his journey, got into a boat, but was discovered and
chased, and bodies of pagans were active in their
endeavours to intercept him or cut him off. He left
his boat and tried swimming, thinking he might unobserved
land on the opposite bank of the river; but
when he reached the shore the pagans were there
and intercepted him, and he was made prisoner.
He was carried to Huè, but he was not put to death;
he was tortured, and he bore it calmly. It was not
mercy that caused Minh-Menh to spare his life, but
he wanted to use him, as he had used M. Jacquart,
on business of his own. Though he did not fall
under the sword, M. Delamotte could not stand the
rigours of his captivity, and after having been in

prison a year and a half, he died October 3, 1840, worn out by sickness.

All the other missionaries succeeded in eluding the search of their enemies. We know little about them, during that time, of their struggles or privations. Some chance has now and then revealed a scene or two, which makes us understand how hard and trying was their lot. M. Retort was selected to succeed to the government of the vicariate. His first business was to obtain consecration, and for that, as it was not attainable in Annam, the four bishops of Tonking being dead, and the single bishop in Cochin China unapproachable, he went to Manilla. He was absent about a year, but early in 1841 he again made his appearance in Tonking.

CHAPTER IX.

THE DUNGEONS OF HUE.

On the 17th of January 1841, after a year's absence, Mgr. Retort again set his foot on Annamite territory. With him there came to Tonking two Europeans, M. Berneux and M. Galy. He placed them for present safety in a Christian village some miles from the coast. Minh-Menh was dead. His death was almost the first news heard on landing in Tonking, for it had just occurred. His successor, Thieu-Tri, had not as yet indicated what his purpose was towards the Christians. But the edicts of the last reign were still in force, and things went on the same as if the old monarch was on the throne. The fierce Trinh-Quanh-Khanh was raging as usual in the province of Nam-Dinh, where these two missionaries were. He was bent on laying hands on Mgr. Hermosilla, and very diligent search was made for him. So it happened that the strange priests, whose presence was not even suspected, a month or two after their arrival, fell into the hands of their enemies. A large body of men, one morning, beset the village, ransacked it completely, and both M. Berneux and M. Galy became prisoners.

M. Berneux has written a long narrative of the incidents attending and following on his capture, and no picture could be more vivid or interesting than that which he has himself given:

'The Holy Week had been passed in meditating on the sufferings of our Saviour. On Saturday evening I heard some confessions; they were the first-fruits of my ministry in the Annamite land; they were also the last. The designs of God are impenetrable, but worthy always to be adored. The next day I distributed the Bread of Life to the little flock around me. I had hardly put off my vestments when the sound of the mandarin's speaking-trumpet was heard quite close, ordering the men of the village to repair to a specified spot, that the soldiers at will might search their houses. Once before I had been forced to fly from my residence, that I might escape the honours of a visit from the mandarin; this time retreat was impossible. I left the house which for two months had afforded me most generous hospitality, and took refuge in that of the nuns, by no means a suitable place of concealment. I had nothing better to do than place myself on some bamboos suspended from the wall; there, seated on a basket of onions, I awaited the soldiers without apprehension, adoring Jesus Christ, whom I had just received for the last time. Soon a dozen satellites burst into my retreat; long I listened, as, with pikes and guns, they went about searching, putting questions to the only nun that remained in the house, who replied with a few words and then turned aside and wept. At the same time, to keep me out of view, she burnt some straw under my resting-place, shrouding me in a thick cloud of smoke; and, urged on by her zeal or her fears, she warmed me somewhat more than was pleasant. More than once, as they were looking about, the pikes of the intruders raised the framework on which I was lying, yet without a suspicion of my presence. At length there came in some soldiers more sharp than the others, who drew me forth from this hiding-place, where I had been by no means at ease, laying hold of me with an eager delight, the greater from their surprise, and uttering shouts of victory; then, after searching my person and taking possession of whatever they fancied, they led me off to the mandarin. I felt a great joy while I was being dragged on by the satellites, as our adorable Saviour was formerly dragged from the Garden of Olives to Jerusalem. Their chief deprived me of my scapular, my beads, and the reliquary that hung from my neck. As I was covered with perspiration and soot, black too as a chimney-sweeper, they gave me some water to wash myself, and afterwards tied my hands behind my back. It was then that my dear colleague, M. Galy, was brought in. "Is not this a good day?" said he, as he embraced me. "Yes," I replied, "it is indeed the day that the Lord has made; let us rejoice!" M. Galy was preparing to say Mass when he heard of the coming of the mandarin. At once he had to hasten from the house where he had been sheltered, and was left quite alone. Driven back from every corner where he sought a retreat, and tracked like some wild animal, he flung himself into a ditch shaded by bamboos. Though children came to look at him, the soldiers passed by and did not perceive him. He recited his Breviary and then fell asleep, but at length he was discovered. Roused by a blow of a stick on the arm, his reliquary, hanging by a double cord of silk from his neck, was torn off and snatched from him; but he felt no grief, and when he came to join me he was singing a *Te Deum*. Then, led in by the soldiers, came seven native Christians, most of whom were catechists, with two nuns and another female. Recognising one of the nuns, I pointed to heaven, as a sign to her that she should trust in God; in return she smiled, so letting me understand that she was not insensible of the favour with which the Lord had honoured her. It might be two in the afternoon. M. Galy and myself were not allowed to converse; notwithstanding, as we were taking our repast, my dear companion managed to confess. We agreed, too, that we would seem to be entirely ignorant of the Annamite language, and, having so very lately come into the country, such a pretence, it may be well understood, was easy. So, on an officer accosting us and demanding our names, to carry out our resolution we let him for a good half hour perplex himself with endeavours to force upon our apprehension the meaning of the words, "Ten la gi？"— "What is your name？" At last we took pity on the poor scribe, and told him that in Europe we were called Galy and Berneux; but these names had to be written in Chinese letters, and then followed the attempts to reproduce in the language of the country the sounds which I had uttered, and it was curious indeed to witness their struggling efforts to accomplish the task.

'Several of the inhabitants of the village came in for a good beating; by the time that was over night was closing in, so the Christians arrested with us being dressed with a cangue, and my colleague and myself lodged in a cage so short that my long legs had scarce room to stow themselves, we set out on our journey. For an instant my heart felt a pang of grief. It was when, on arriving at the bank of a river which led to the chief town of the province, M. Galy was continuing his route by land, while I had just been placed in a boat, and I knew not whether the separation was to be final. But I was prepared for every sacrifice, and submitting myself to the will of God, my soul was again in peace. Though resigned, I was still not the less glad when the next morning, on awaking, I found that I had been mistaken, and that my colleague was following me in another boat only a little distant.

'The same day a good Christian prepared a meal for me; but, on its coming, my soldiers, thinking their own title better, laid claim to it; so my breakfast was simply imaginary, and it was the same with dinner.

'It was almost night when we arrived at Nam-Dinh. Crowds flocked to the river-side to witness our landing. I heard the people surrounding my cage eagerly exclaiming: "It is Father Vong. What a famous prize!" But it being mooted that I was no more than twenty-seven years of age, eventually the honours of the episcopate were made over to M. Galy. That we might stop the pursuit of Mgr. Hermosilla, we thought it best not to rectify the mistake. The mandarins also fell into it, and were confirmed in the idea, as well by our silence as by the false declarations of several Cochin-Chinese.

'At Nam-Dinh longer cages were given us, but not without the precaution of chaining us. Our irons might weigh some ten or eleven pounds; we could bear them without much fatigue, except when deprived of sleep. The mandarin was much amused at seeing us of our own accord helping the smith engaged in riveting the large rings to our feet. I kissed with great ardour this chain, which had become for me the source of great confidence in the mercy of the Lord; I offered it daily for the expiation of my sins to Him who on Calvary bore a more weighty instrument of punishment for the salvation of the world.

'Two Europeans are a sight inviting curiosity in this kingdom; so the mandarin considerately allowed his subordinates to grant access to our prison to all who might wish for a near view of us. From morning to evening we were beset with numerous visitors, full of wonder at our beards, our hair, and our ways. The Christians were not the last to come. It was difficult for me to moderate their testimonies of compassion, and to reject their charitable offerings. Pious mothers brought their children to me that I might bless them. Pagans, too, came asking for medicines, begging me to look at their features or at the lines on their hands, and to tell them whether they would have long life, or would one day be raised to the dignities at which they aimed.

'Then it became impossible for me to keep my resolution, and to remain any longer silent. Not having been able to preach Jesus Christ when I was free, I tried to do so from my cage for the instruction of my neophytes, and, further, that I might undeceive these idolaters, who only knew the gospel from the false reports of its enemies. By the help of some Annamite words that I knew, I attempted to explain to the pagans the motives of our joy in captivity, to them an inexplicable enigma. "Here," said they, "when a person is in chains, he is sad, but you appear happy." "It is because the Christians have a secret, which you do not know, by which their pains are changed into consolations. We are come to teach you the means of being always happy, because we love you; but, instead of profiting by it, you put to death those who bring you this inestimable advantage."

'For a week these conversations continued, when, for what reason I cannot tell, all approach to my cage was forbidden, and I became the object of the strictest watch—night and day, as I perceived, surrounded by numerous guards. Yet I could hear the confessions of some Christians, who by a bribe made their way into my prison. I must render this testimony to the mandarins of Nam-Dinh, that, if they were rigorous in the precautions they took with respect to me, they did their best by constant little attentions to make me forget this severity. They often came to visit me, and seemed to take a pleasure in putting questions to me about Christianity. One day, the mandarin who was more particularly charged with my safe keeping asked me why it was that by my religion a priest was forbidden to marry. I told him, in reply, that this discipline of the Church was altogether in the interest of the people; that if the priest had a family, he would live for it; that he would employ himself in amassing a fortune for it; and that he would leave the poor unassisted rather than deprive his own children of what he had; that, on the other hand, by not marrying, he had all men for his children, and the unfortunate more than others; and that, when a poor man wanted food, he would be sure to find in the priest a father who would share with him his last mess of rice.

'This man would repeat over my reply to the mandarins who visited him, and then they were not content without a second repetition from myself. "Here is one of your children," said a mandarin to me, one day, pointing to his little boy, and alluding to my former words. "Yes," I said, "but a child of sorrow." "How is that?" he asked. "Because I cannot feed him; that is, I cannot teach him the truth, which is the life of the soul. A man who calls himself his father will not allow it." "That is not so; I do not prevent his listening to or following your lessons." "Mandarin, you are not serious when you say this;

for, should I begin to instruct your child, I should soon cease to see him playing by the bars of my cage."

'I had then made friends of all our officers, who shared with me their tea and betel. They did the same with M. Galy, who was allowed more freedom than I, and was not kept so apart from others. My dear colleague often saw Christians; he even had with him a Christian family, captives for the faith; three children who had followed their parents into prison did him many little services, and used to watch for the times when the soldiers were asleep, that they might give him their daily tribute of homage. One day one of them said to him, as he kissed his hand: "The father suffers for Jesus Christ, but God aids and strengthens him."

'The time for examining us came at length. Several times the mandarin went to M. Galy, whom he mistook for Mgr. Hermosilla, and put questions to him, which he managed to evade. For my part, I was not equally fortunate; I could not avoid a reply; and, as far as I remember, the following are the principal points on which they pressed me for explanation:

'*First Examination.*—A mandarin, whom I shall style *my friend*, because he has shown an interest in me greater than others have done, came to me accompanied by two Annamite priests in chains for the faith; one of them an old man with gray hair, and blind. The purpose of the mandarin was to use them as interpreters in putting his questions to me; but on my request he consented to question me himself, and to take my own replies. "Your name?" he asked. "I have written it with my own hand on the report of my arrest; I must ask you to consult that paper." "Your age?" "Twenty-seven years." "How long have you been in this kingdom?" "To reply to this question would lead to other questions, and thus expose me to the danger of compromising some one else. Now, I wish to suffer alone. Let it suffice for me to say to you that in coming here my only object has been to be useful to the Annamites." "How long have you been living with the other European?" "I cannot answer." "What is the name of your companion?" "I must beg the mandarin himself to ask him." "Come, since you are not willing to speak, I must go. That will do."

'*Second Examination.*—This was six days after the preceding. *My friend* had with him on the commission another mandarin, and one of the two beforementioned priests accompanied them. The new mandarin: "Your name?" "Nhân." [This was his Annamite name.] "How long have you been in this country?" "I request permission not to answer." "From what ship were you put ashore?" "It was not a European ship." "Did it belong to the Chinese or to the Annamites?" (No answer.) "Did you set out from Macao or Canton?" "I must again ask the mandarin to allow me not to answer." "But I did not come here to let you say nothing. It is my duty to ask you these questions." "I know that; but these are things on which it is proper that the accused should be silent."

'The mandarin did not seem to relish my resolution. For a short time he kept silence as if offended; but in the end, to make his peace, he sent me some cups of tea and some betel. . *My friend* then took up the examination: "Do you know the Annamite priests that I will now name to you?" (And he named five or six.) "I do not know them." "Then this one?" "No more than the others. I must beg the mandarin not to ask me such questions; it might happen that out of a great many persons mentioned a name might be brought forward that I knew, and in that case my silence would be taken for a confession, an inconvenience which I ought to anticipate." "Do you compassionate this white-headed priest whom you see seated near your cage?" "Yes, mandarin." "Would you consent to bear his chain in his stead?" "Most readily; I have more strength than he has to bear it. I would still more readily bear it, if nothing more were required to procure your conversion." "And for myself," put in the old man, "I would not willingly give up this chain; it is my treasure." The mandarin: "If you do not answer, these two priests shall be beaten with rods." "I think that it is useless to remind a judge of the laws of justice; if any one should suffer for my silence, it is only myself." At these words the mandarins went away. I asked the old man to forgive me should he suffer any ill-treatment through me, and he replied that I need not fear.

'*Third Examination.*—To the two former mandarins a third judge was added. *My friend:* "Are you always happy?" "Always." "Can you eat the rice and the other food with which the mandarins supply you at their own expense?" "Yes, and I thank the mandarins for them." "Do you know Thang-Sanh?" This was the name taken by one of the clerks of M. Galy subsequent to the arrest, and I did not know of the change. "No, mandarin." Then they made him advance, removing a part of his dress to show me the marks of the rattan scarring his body. It was a fearful sight. At the same time the rods and stakes were brought forth. Then the mandarin questioned me again as to the place where I landed, the time of my arrival in Cochin China, and the names of our catechists; and seeing that I did not answer his questions, he went on: "Speak, or you shall be beaten." "I am in your hands; if you choose to beat me, you have the power; for myself, I am not at liberty to do what you ask." To say the truth, I was not sorry that I was not taken at my word. Yet I think I should have suffered less from the rattan than I did from the constraint under which I was to put on an appearance of cold indifference towards our catechists, those devoted men who had served us in so many ways, and who on our account had endured such a cruel beating. How painful to them must have been this seeming insensibility, if they did not understand that it was assumed, that they themselves might not be compromised!

'The examination continuing, my judges availed themselves for a time of a Cochin-Chinese clerk, as an interpreter to put to me their questions; but ere long they dispensed with his assistance, and managed the discussion themselves. "When you came here, did you bring a letter from the king of France?" "No, mandarin." "Did your king grant you money, or bestow on you any rank?" "None at all." "Does he know that you are here?" "I do not think so." "Who sent you to this kingdom?" "No one obliged me to come here; when I was fully resolved to preach the gospel to the heathen, I asked leave of my bishop to quit his diocese, but did not tell him to what mission I proposed to go." "What is this bishop's name?" "He is called Bouvier." "Where is the permission he gave you?" "It was a verbal permission." "Have you received letters from Europe since your arrival in Cochin China?" "I have not." "Have you written to your friends?" "I have written to my mother; but I have not been able to send the letter." "Do not missionaries sometimes return to Europe after having lived among the Annamites?" Just then *my friend* took it into his head to ask me if the word "Jacobi" was one I had heard pronounced in France. So, as if I had not heard the first question, I quickly passed to the second. "Yes," I said, "the name is common with many persons in my country." "Do France and Spain send missionaries to other countries?" "To a great many." "Tell us how long it is since you came here. We will not ask you the place where you landed, nor the names of the persons who have received you." "It is impossible."

'A catechist of the village where I was taken was then brought forward, and the mandarins asked me if I knew him. I would not look at the man, and replied: "You know that in this respect it is my resolve to maintain silence." "Come, will you not make an answer?" "Ask me other questions, and perhaps I may satisfy you; on this point I cannot." With these words the examination concluded. The three catechists then approached my cage, and told me that they had been cruelly beaten.

'*Fourth Examination.*—After some unimportant questions they commenced reading over to me my previous declarations, with the view to my signing them. But no sooner did I object to certain admissions which I was said to have made, and which I had been constant in refusing, than the mandarins made as if they scratched the *procès-verbal*, and read no more of it. "Well, we've got to an end," said *my friend* to me; "I am glad of it." "Does it matter to you that your religion should be persecuted in Cochin China?" "It does indeed, mandarin; it is to aid in maintaining it that I have come here at the risk of my life." "Stop," he interposed; "look at those men who are about to die;" and he pointed to the three Annamite clerks; "advise them to abjure your religion, if only for a month—they might afterwards practise it again—and their lives will be saved." "Mandarin, one would not urge a father to sacrifice his children; and you would wish that a priest should advise apostasy to his Christians." Then, addressing myself to the three confessors, "I have but one advice to give you," I said; "think that you have almost come to the end of your sufferings, while the happiness that awaits you in the other world is eternal. Be worthy of it by your constancy." This they promised.

'The mandarin: "What is that other life of which you speak?" "After death, the soul, when separated from the body which it has inhabited, goes to appear before the Master of heaven. He who has followed the true religion comes to the possession of eternal happiness; on the contrary, he who has rejected the gift of faith, or, having received it, has transgressed its duties, is condemned to punishments which have no end." "Have all Christians a soul?" "Most certainly, and the pagans too; and you also, mandarin, have a soul. And the desire of my heart is that you may one day be of the number of those that God will reward." "Where does this soul go when it is separated from the body?" And my interrogator began to laugh. "You laugh, mandarin, but a time will come when you will laugh no more."

'I was then told that my examinations were over, and I was taken back to prison. The fatigue had been very great, and I was glad to be dismissed. For not only in court, but during the interval between each sitting, I was surrounded by persons who tried to inveigle me, and to draw me unawares into admissions which I did not intend to make. I was also considerably pained at causing, by my repeated refusals, so much annoyance to the mandarins, who in so many ways gave proofs of their kind feeling. The mandarin under whose more especial charge I was showed a particular desire to know the precise time of my arrival in my mission, and promised that, if I would trust him, he would say nothing about it to the grand mandarin. "You cannot be in earnest," I replied, "in putting to me this question, nor can you wish that I should give you information which I have withholden from your superior. At any rate, it is for your advantage that I should not yield to your demand. The grand mandarin would be sure to ask you whether you have got at my secret, and, supposing that I had intrusted it to you, you would not like to tell a lie, and so I should be betrayed; or, should you say to him that you could not unfold what I had made known to you, your own disgrace would be the consequence."

'*My friend* came to see me some days later, accompanied by the three confessors of whom I have spoken. He gave me a paper written by my catechist, in which I was made to say that I had been in Tonking nine years, and that I had been taken with a Spaniard, a friend, whose name was Trum-Vong. The mandarin pressed me to adapt my answers to what was here said, when I made my appearance in the royal city; should I not do so, great indeed would be the trouble that would fall on my first judges and my neophytes. I replied that I would do my best to save the mandarins from disgrace, but that, as this paper contained statements that were false, I could not affirm their truth; that still they need not fear, for I hoped to keep clear of compromising any person.

'A little before our departure the same mandarin brought my catechist to me, to give me the pleasure of seeing him for the last time. I told him that I was going to the royal city, and that there I well knew I must expect suffering; then I again exhorted him to be constant. He answered me: "We think ourselves happy in following the two fathers, and in dying with them."

'The grand mandarin once more summoned M. Galy and myself before him; the two Annamite priests were also brought into court, one of them acting as interpreter to my colleague, who underwent the following examination: "Why did you come into this kingdom?" "To preach the Christian religion." "What does this religion teach?" "It teaches man to serve the true God, and to love others, and to obey the king." "Did you know that it was prohibited in this kingdom?" "I was well aware of it." "Why, then, did you come?" "Because it is the command of God that the blessing of the gospel should be borne to all men." "But when, on landing, you perceived that your religion was not accepted, and that the king forbade it to be preached, and would not allow his people to follow it, why did you not go away?" "I hoped that the persecution would cease." On each answer of M. Galy the good old man who acted as interpreter would turn towards the mandarins, and say with a simple-hearted complacency, "See, he has no fear of death." And a thing that might really surprise is that even the satellites took a satisfaction in his courage, and carried him back in triumph to his prison, exclaiming that M. Galy had no fear, but was full of joy. I did not witness the end of this examination; for the judge, having learnt that I had fever, ordered me to be taken back to my prison. The next day two men were sent at his instance to inquire how I was, and to ask if I could travel; and they assured me that the most ample precautions had been taken by the mandarin to lessen the fatigues of the journey, and that, in this view, he had paid from money of his own as much as six ligatures, or about twelve shillings. They then begged me to make the paper lately offered me for signature the basis of my depositions in the royal city. I replied that I was much touched by the kindness and attentions of the mandarin, but that, grateful as I was, I could not depart from the truth, and that the utmost I could do, when the judges should question me on the facts falsely alleged in the report, would be to preserve silence; and this I promised. "But it will be impossible for you to maintain silence," they said. "You should understand that even innocent persons, under the severity of their tortures, are compelled to make acknowledgments of guilt." "Those persons were not priests suffering for their religion. I hope, with the grace of God, to remain silent as the wood of my cage." The day of departure came. After having received the farewell of the mandarins and the soldiers of the prison, we set out on Sunday morning, May 9th, each of us carried by twelve Annamites. From a hundred and fifty to two hundred satellites, armed with pikes, and formed in two lines, made up our escort; in the midst of the detachment were our cages, and close by us were four or five mandarins, who did not leave us till we quitted the town. Our good neophytes did not fail to meet us in the way. What pleased me most was to notice the little children that used to come and see us in prison. They would hide themselves behind the soldiers to make their salutes; in return I smiled at them, and then, covering their faces with both their hands, they would turn away and weep, and still would come back again.

'Our progress was extremely irksome, especially in crossing Tonking. What is called the Royal Way is not in this part of the kingdom comparable with the worst road in France, constantly intercepted, as it is, by a succession of rivers or streams, which must be crossed by some bridge in ruins no wider than our cages. Even greater difficulties followed in our passage up the perpendicular mountain which separates Tonking from Cochin China; we were each carried by twenty men, and, with all their straining, it was as much as they could do to reach the top. But on the opposite side it was quite another thing; so steep was the descent that they were obliged to let down the cages by cords, and let them slide along over rocks and precipices. So we travelled for nineteen days, starting at one or two in the morning by torchlight; then, making a good halt about noon, we would proceed on again till night.

'The fatigues of such a journey were abundantly compensated, not only by the beauty of the prospects and richness of the country we were traversing, but by the enthusiasm of the Christians who flocked to visit the fathers imprisoned for the faith. I was ever admiring that divine Providence which, without stint, lavishes its blessings on good and bad, and does not refuse fertility to those places where His holy name is treated with dishonour and His worship is proscribed. And, again, the consolation which we drew from the expressions of attachment on the part of our neophytes was very soothing. You would think that I was exaggerating, were I to tell you with what religious ardour they pressed round our moving prison; with what touching obstinacy they clung to the bars of our cages; what heart-rending cries they uttered when they saw us about to leave them.

'It was when we first entered a province of Cochin China that we encountered the largest throng; there, more than any place, the people had no fear of showing themselves Christians. Hardly had we come out into the plain when they were crowding in haste towards our procession; they blocked up the road, the soldiers could not move onward, and the mandarin was constrained to order the cages to be placed on the ground, to allow time for these inconsolable neophytes to give expression to their sorrow and their veneration for us. Each of them brought us his money or his fruit; even the pagans were not content if they too did not present their offerings to us; but we steadily refused to take anything, saying that all we needed was prayers.

'When the satellites were about to take up our cages, the Christians were so importunate in their demands to bear so precious a burden, that there was no refusing them the permission of carrying us as far as the river. There more than two hundred of them were waiting for us. Coming in after us for one last look, for another parting word, they plunged up to the waist into the water; neither the threats of the soldiers nor the rattan coming down on their shoulders could make them let go the bars of our cages; and when we were on the other bank we still heard their lamentations. Then I became aware what had been the anxiety of the mandarin during the scene. "Do you know," said he to me, "that these people wanted to carry you off?" "If they had wished it nothing could have been more easy; but we would not have allowed it." "Why not?" "Because it would have cost you your life; and I do not think that you would have given your head as readily as we would surrender ours."

'I was deeply moved by all that had passed under our very eyes. What painful emotions thrilled through me as I looked on that scattered flock, without a pastor to collect them around the cross, and to nourish them with the Word of Life! Again and again I besought my Lord to put an end to the sorrows of His people, and to grant them at last some days of peace.

'In all the chief provincial towns we were visited by the mandarins, who were forward in displays of kind feeling towards us. I feel myself bound to mention two officials out of the leading dignitaries. The first, a good old man with white head and beard, congratulated us on our tranquillity, and urged us to keep up our calm bearing and resignation of mind; and then he made the sign of the cross. "Mandarin," I said to him, "you can make the sign of the cross, but that is not enough; you must also know and practise our religion. If the king and his officers knew it they would not dare to persecute it."

'At length, May 28th, we reached the royal city. Some miles from the town a cloud of grief, almost imperceptible, seemed to overshadow my soul. I was about to go, as it were, into the lair of the tiger; but the feeling did not last. Soon the walls of Huè came in sight, and my joy and confidence were greater than ever.

'On the very first day God gave us fresh matter of consolation. At Nam-Dinh the questions put to me made me dread that it was their purpose to sentence me as a rebel and not as a missionary; and here, scarcely had we come into the presence of the grand mandarin, when we were ordered to put our foot on the cross. I cannot bring back to mind the order of the questions to which we replied; I must content myself with stating them just as memory suggests them. They first addressed M. Galy. "How long have you been in Tonking?" "I left Cadiz, a city of Spain, four years ago." "If your chain was taken off, would you preach again?" "If I was able to preach, I would go on till death; yes, for ever."

'The mandarin asked me, too, my name, my age, and the time of my coming into the kingdom. Then taking a cross he presented it to my colleague, with the command to trample on it. "No, no!" cried M. Galy. "Death is better, far better." It was then my turn. I wished to take the cross and kiss it; as they would not let me, I said to the judges, "When you require me to die, I will offer my head to the soldier charged to cut it off; but when you command apostasy, I will resist to the utmost." At the bidding of the mandarin, a soldier trampled on the cross before us. "Is this a crime?" I made no reply. The mandarin: "He is angry." "No, mandarin, but I am grieved at an act so profane." "Is there harm, then, in walking on the cross?" "This crucifix is the image of God. If you were asked to insult the image of your father, would you do it? Now God is the Father of all men; He loves them as children: to trample on His image is an enormous crime. I would die rather than commit it." "Mandarin," said M. Galy, "I share in the answer you have just heard; and I request you, M. Berneux, to speak in my name every time you have similar answers to make."

'The mandarin went on with his questions: "What is God?" "God is an eternal Being, who created heaven and earth; His power is infinite; He holds in His hands the life and death of men." "If He has infinite power, why does He not destroy all who profane His cross?" Then a soldier anew trampled on it. "Because He is good, and wishes to give men, who are His children, time to amend." "Why does He not free you from your chains?" "Sometimes He permits that here on earth the wicked should triumph, but in the other life the wicked will be punished, and the just will have their reward." "Do you mean that men live again after death?" "I do; and he who has done good has an entrance into an eternity of joys; but he that has done evil begins a misery that will never cease." The mandarins smiled. "You laugh at my doctrine; but the time will come, perhaps is near, when you will know which of us is right." Again we were urged to tread on the cross. We refused; and our first examination ended. In the second the demand was repeated, and again refused; and then I was so happy as to take the cross in my hands, kiss it, and offer it to M. Galy, who did the same.

'We had three more examinations before we were put to the torture. The following are the principal questions of the mandarins, and our answers:

'The chief judge asked me if I knew the difference between mountains containing gold, silver, or sulphur; and whether I understood the construction of steam-boats, or the mechanism of watches. "I know nothing of any of these things; it is no use to count on my services." "O, we can do without them; we have Annamites who profess this knowledge." M. Galy added, "I know only one thing, which is the preaching of the Gospel." The Judges: "Obey the king, and you shall be mandarins." M. Galy: "I left my country, my relations and friends, to preach to you the true religion; and could I now abandon it in the face of those whom I have come to convert? No, never." A mandarin: "I know that your religion is good, and that it makes men good; for I also myself observe the religion of heaven." "How is it, then," I replied, "that you occupy that tribunal, while I, an apostle of this religion of which you call yourself a disciple, am loaded with chains and threatened with death?" Another mandarin: "What does this religion teach?" "To fly from vice and to practise virtue." "To practise virtue—to practise virtue!" repeated the mandarin impatiently; and going off to another subject, "You are lying," he said, "when you pretend that you do not know the names of those I ask you about." "Mandarin, if we wished to lie, what could be more easy? I might say, for instance, it was in this city that I had spent part of my time; that it was in your house, mandarin, that I received welcome, and was concealed." The mandarin looked uncomfortable. The interpreter advised me not to irritate the judge, for I would be beaten. I was again required to declare what Annamites I knew, but I steadily refused. Then my hands were bound, and the demand was repeated. Still I would not comply. Then a soldier brought a cross, and two others laying hold of me dragged me over the emblem of our salvation. Struggling with them I cried out, "I never will—I never will!" M. Galy was outside the enclosure, and pressing in eagerly towards me, repeated over the words, "We never will!" A cross was then offered to him; they wanted him to put his foot on it; he took it and kissed it, saying, "To die is a thousand times better than to profane it." On this I was stretched on the ground and bound to two stakes, my arms and legs being thus secured; and the mandarin proceeded: "Tell the truth, or you shall be beaten to death." "I have told it; strike if you will." For some time I remained in this posture; then it commenced raining, and we were sent back to prison.

'On the 13th of June they did more than threaten. After the questioning came flogging: M. Galy received twenty strokes of the rattan, I only seven. We had asked our Lord grace to suffer with firmness, and without uttering any cry; and we were heard: a stone could not have been more silent and more motionless. They beat slowly, and between the strokes they asked M. Galy whether he suffered. "A great deal," he replied. "See," said the mandarin; "the soldier is tired of beating, but he is not of suffering."

'The next day the same punishment was repeated; I received thirteen strokes on the wounds of the day before. On raising my head to answer the questions of the judges, they said one to another, "His countenance is not at all changed; it is like beating the ground." M. Galy was next treated to ten fresh blows. This rattan is a horrible affair. Every time it touched us it made a bloody gash five or six inches long. "Danh Dan! Strike hard!" cried the mandarin to the executioner; and he on his part did his work conscientiously. One might have taken his stick for a rod of red-hot iron. Soon will come the nails and the pincers; let be. The grace of God is our strength, and will be stronger than the tortures. Jesus be ever praised!

'During the early days of our imprisonment in the capital the people crowded round as we passed, not as they had done in the provinces, to express sympathy and respect, but to vent execrations and abuse; and the old man, or even the child, would count it a good thing if he could join in some insult, or get a blow at us with his stick. The enclosure of the prison was not always a protection from this hatred of the populace; and more than once, when we had come out into the courts of an evening for a little fresh air, we were driven back into our dungeon by the stones they threw at us. But it is only natural after the absurd stories invented by calumny, and current amongst these idolaters. They look upon us as beings full of mystery and ill-nature, who take delight in a mischievous use of powers which they imagine we possess. Can you credit it, that even when I was lying under the rod of the executioner they should ask me—and quite in earnest—whether I had really scooped out the eyes of children to make holy water? Poor people!

'I omitted to mention that in going from the prison to the judgment-hall the whole way was strewed with crosses, over which we had to pass. Blessed be our dearest Saviour, who in His love not only associates us in His humiliations, but even uses us for His own reproach! In return, we will glorify Him to our utmost by our sufferings.'

This letter of M. Berneux's was addressed to his brother missionaries, MM. Masson and Simonin. M. Galy adds his signature to confirm all its statements; and afterwards M. Berneux adds a postscript, in which he earnestly asks his brethren not to let the letter pass out of their own hands, as it is written only for themselves, and that they may know the exact truth about him. The date of the letter was August 1841.

We have also a short letter to his mother, informing her of the privilege granted him of suffering for his Lord: 'Dear mother, my good God has been pleased to crown the graces He has granted me in the course of my life by one more precious than all—that of suffering for His holy name. I write only a few words lest my keepers should surprise me. I am happy, more happy than ever! O, how sweet it is to suffer for our good God! Love Him, dearest mother; love Him, my good sister; and you too, my dear Frederick. Be good Christians, I entreat you by the chain I am bearing, by my sufferings which I offer to God for you. Live so that we may all be united in heaven for all eternity—that is the place of meeting. Farewell. I embrace you all affectionately.'

The prison* in which the two missionaries were confined was a large walled building covered with tiles. In appearance it was just like the other public buildings or the houses of the great mandarins. In France it might have passed for a fine stable. It had a frontage of a hundred and thirty feet, with a

* Letter of M. Miche.

depth of about forty. It was divided into three compartments, a captain with fifty soldiers being in charge of each. Each compartment had a further subdivision: one behind; which was confined and dark, and the smaller, which was the prison; the other, more large and commodious, with more light and air, in front, which was reserved for the gaolers and soldiers and such prisoners as could obtain the favour.

In the first days of their imprisonment MM. Berneux and Galy were exposed to various kinds of ill-treatment from the other prisoners and from the soldiers. Many of the inmates of the prison were the most abandoned characters, but the depth of their degradation could hardly be imagined by one who had not heard their words or seen their actions. The two missionaries were not together, which made their case worse.

'I was parted from my companion,' writes M. Galy, who takes up the thread of the story. 'He was in a part of the prison where the good *cai* (the principal gaoler) was present, and had the further protection of the companionship of two mandarins, one of the royal family, who were prisoners. But for myself I was left defenceless against the brutal annoyances of my gaolers: bawling out their rude questions and stirring one another on; burning tapers, after their superstitious usage, and fixing them close by my mat; covering the ground near me with crosses just for the purpose of vexing me; pestering me in fact in every way they could. Down to the *boi* (the raw recruit), there is not one who does not think that he has failed in his duty if he has not given his kick to the cruel *dá-tô* (Christian) who plucks out, as they say, the eyes of the little children.

'Some of the prisoners joined with them, and took pleasure in expressing by signs the horrors of the punishment which I was to expect. And by the people outside I was looked at as if I was some curious animal, and left exposed to their insults; and they would watch me, and make faces at me, and mutter their threats. But at the same time I was in their eyes an object of ridiculous dread; for no sooner did I make a move towards the door, though I did not even glance at them, than they were off, scampering away as if I were the *maqui* (the devil) himself at their heels.

'I must admit that I should not have been much troubled at the brutality of the soldiers, and should have been amused by the fears of the curious, were it not for another trial of a different and more painful nature. I was not only forced to live amongst persons with no human feelings, but I was shut up in a sink of vice.'

But there were moments of joy even in this foul prison; it was when some of their Christians came to make them a visit. The two missionaries received them together in M. Berneux's part of the prison. The friendly *cai* introduced them. 'One day two old men came to see us. They were deputies from their village to bear the respectful homage of their Christians, and the expression of their regret that they could not all come in a body to the prison of the fathers.

'One Christian woman deserves particular recollection; from her patriarchal appearance we gave her the name of the Good Rachel. She came to us every Sunday, under the pretext of visiting a relation who was a prisoner. Although she was seated only a few feet from M. Berneux, we could never exchange a word with her; but her looks and gestures were quite enough. All our intercourse was by means of the relative; it was from him we learned that she had come from a great distance to the capital to see the fathers; it was through him that from time to time we received her gifts of fruit and money. The other prisoners, too, and the soldiers came in for their share; she did not leave them out; to them all these visits were a piece of luck. As she looked at us eating, great drops would fall from her eyes; at times a deep sigh would escape her, which made us shudder lest she should betray herself. Once she was all but sobbing aloud; she hid herself, however, behind a pillar and concealed her emotion; still it would have been poor protection against the notice of the soldiers if by good chance they had not been occupied in doing honour to her presents.

'That she might have the pleasure of a last look, on her leaving, we would go out and take a turn in the court of the prison; and she would linger at the door, by her side the relative whom we have since called the *little brother*. One Sunday the Good Rachel failed to come; and then we learnt that the little brother had been transferred to another prison, and so, her means of introduction gone, she gave up the pilgrimage, and we saw her no more.'

But there was one interview more pleasing than any, one that created quite an enthusiasm. It was that with a brave young man named Philip Phê, distinguished as one of the three confessors of Quantri. These were three native Christians who had been made prisoners with M. Delamotte. M. Berneux and M. Galy were in the very prison where M. Delamotte had died. Philip Phê with Peter Duyen had been captured on the same day as M. Delamotte. They were his companions at the time, and were helping him to escape. Vincent Luah, the third confessor, was taken a few days after, betrayed by a pagan who had wormed himself into his confidence, and then informed against him. Philip Phê, who was a physician, was always a warm earnest Christian; the other two had never been so regarded; but in this day of trial there was no lack of firmness. Seven had been the original number of this party of captives, and Emmanuel Hoa had been the chief. Emmanuel was already a martyr. He was the man who had sheltered M. Delamotte, and the brunt of the punishment fell upon him. He had been tortured fearfully. The rattan and the pincers, hot and cold, had been used, and he had borne all his pain firmly and in silence, and then he was beheaded. Two more of the prisoners were dead. John Trang died in-prison from sickness. So did Magdalen Hoa, but not before she had suffered barbarous ill-treatment.

One of the refinements of cruelty practised was to place her feet in rice-water in which were a number of worms. Philip Phé and his two companions had been in the capital more than a year. All sorts of means had been used to induce them to apostatise, cajolery and threats by turns; but all in vain. They had been called up before their judges some twenty times, but had never flinched. Sentence of death had already been passed, but it had been deferred.

The introduction of Philip Phê to the two missionaries was a memorable event. 'One day,' says M. Galy, 'our *cai* made a sign to us that a Christian was waiting for us in a retired part of the prison. We went there at once. It was Philip Phê, the youngest of the three confessors of Quang-tri. The sight of this fine young man, whose manly figure forms a pleasing contrast with his mild tone, and the pious fervour of his language, came on us like an apparition. Under the plea of buying medicines, he had come out of his prison in company with a Christian soldier. It was inexpressible happiness to converse with this young confessor. Calm as he was, he could not hear of our arrest and our trials at the prefecture without some show of emotion. So it was also as he went through to us the story of M. Delamotte's sufferings; but when he spoke of what he had borne himself, it was all joy. "Heaven," he said, "is what we hope for, and it is well worth the little we have had to suffer for Christ our Master, in whose steps we would follow." It was not for us to give encouragement to one like this; we were encouraged ourselves by looking at him more than he could have been by our words.'

Philip Phê often afterwards made visits to the prison, the soldier Lorenzo always with him. One day he was the bearer of tidings that made their hearts beat. 'No words before,' writes M. Galy, 'had a sound so sweet.' 'You will die in three days,' he said; and as he spoke he shared the enthusiasm that was stirring the hearts of the missionaries. They talked it over amongst themselves as if it was a sure thing, and felt all the happiness of martyrdom in prospect; but after all it was a disappointment. The three days came to an end, and there was no summons for the execution. The two prisoners were every moment expecting the welcome call. They cut off each other's hair to prepare for the sword's stroke. The best clothes were all ready. M. Berneux with unnnecessary haste tied on his sandals. But no one came to lead them out. When Philip Phê came again, it was not with his former enthusiasm; it was to tell them they must still wait. 'The disappointment,' says M. Galy, 'was bitter; but the peace of our souls is the same.' It was God's will that they embraced; and those who embrace God's will are always content.

There was another visitor who frequented the prison, Philip Phê's sister. She would bring little gifts—fruit and other things—and sometimes she would take with her Philip's little daughter Agnes, and the child would play about near their mat, and take part in their meals. The three confessors were constantly sending to them, and, if they heard of any ailment, one of Philip's remedies was sure to arrive by the hand of some messenger or other. These were mitigations of their sorrows, these to their devout minds were so many marks of God's tender care. 'See,' says M. Galy, in his letter to the Bishop, 'see the care with which we are treated by a God who is never stinting in kindness. His goodness takes away our pains, and turns them into joys. Shall we not love a Master who is so good to us? Shall we not desire to shed our blood for His glory?'

Before the year had closed a third missionary was introduced into the prison, M. Peter Charrier, who had been living in Tonking for several years, and up to that time had passed uninjured through all the severities of Minh-Menh's persecution. His adventures had been various, and he had had many a hard trial. First, there were the days of close hiding, of which we have his own description as to what sort of life he led. 'It's a happy chance when I can find a night's lodging in a corner of some poor house, where, however, I must be constantly on my guard, taking care not to cough or to speak so as to be heard beyond the partition-wall, for often it is but a slight partition that separates from the next habitation. In this little corner I have my bed, and there I manage to construct my altar.' But in the great heats of the country, and the heavy atmosphere of this confined cell, where light and air could scarcely come in through the little hole contrived to give them entrance, it was a most comfortless situation.

And when he got outside it was only for labour and trial of a new kind, to hasten away to some other home no better than what he had left. Here, again, we may use his own words, which will picture to us his condition: 'I must run at night from village to village, across fields, water and mud up to my knees, carefully avoiding the common path, in dread of meeting some one of the numerous emissaries on the look-out for us. A large straw hat on head, a stout stick in hand, as well to grope in the dark as for a support, dress tucked up to the knees; such is the fashion of a missionary in flight.'

He was living in a dangerous district, that of the formidable Tranh-Quanh-Khan. Three out of four of the native priests under him were early in the list of martyrs. A catechist had the misfortune to fail in his fearful trial, and to became an apostate. He was a man well-esteemed, sincere in his faith, correct in his conduct. Three times he braved the torture and came out successful, and then he fell. The whole mission had been desolated; all its property was gone. What had escaped the spoiler and been hidden had rotted and perished; and the sum of the property left to M. Charrier was his Bible, his Missal, his Breviary, the clothes on his back, and a knapsack. That roaming fugitive life did at length come to an end. By the time Mgr. Retort returned to Tonking, M. Charrier had discovered a resting-place where he could remain more tranquilly. There, when he separated from MM. Berneux and Galy, Mgr. Retort joined him; and shortly after they both went together to the mountain retreat of M. Jeantet. In that quiet solitude important business was done. M. Hermosilla contrived to reach them, and was consecrated.

M. Charrier was then sent off in a new direction to the large village of Bauno, the place where M. Cornay was when he was taken. The journey to Bauno was safely effected, but shortly after, in passing from Bauno to another village, he was stopped and made prisoner. He was in a boat. They had to pass a pagan village, and were startled by the summons, 'Who goes there?' The captain lost his self-command, and by his flurried manner caused suspicion. Instantly the drums beat and the alarm was given and the whole village was in pursuit, some in boats, some on foot.

'We flung ourselves into the river,' says M. Charrier, writing to the Bishop; 'but soon I found the fatigue too much for me; three or four times I fell; I thought my last hour was come. Still I tried to walk in the water, now up to my waist, now as high as my neck, and at times even over my head; once I sank into a hole, and it was only by a strong effort that I succeeded in rising. For two hours this painful race went on, when, having no more strength and quite unable to move farther, and seeing myself pursued by above a hundred persons, as escape was impossible, I told those about me to fly and leave me alone.'

So he was taken, transferred to the principal town, and brought up for examination. He had to go through a beating, but not a severe one—only eight strokes. For the most part during his stay in the provincial town, which lasted nearly a month, from October 10th to the beginning of November, he was treated with consideration and mildness. He was in a roomy prison; he was not kept in a cage; he had no cangue, no fetters, only a slight chain; he had a mat under him; he could walk in the court and in the garden; his keepers left him much to himself, and they were mostly Christian soldiers. His companion at meals was a Christian mandarin, in prison for some misdemeanour. A native priest visited him and brought him messages and money from the Bishop. The mandarin over the prison was particularly complacent towards him. He was an old servant of Gia-laong's, and had a kind feeling towards the Christians. He never came into the prison without showing some attention to M. Charrier; and sometimes he would invite him to his house, and treat him with fruit and tea.

'In the beginning of November orders arrived that M. Charrier was to be taken to Huè. His journey was an ovation. The Christians crowded to see him, to show their respect, to bring him presents, and begged to be allowed to carry him in his net. In his journey he passed close to the spot where the Bishop was, M. Jeantet's retreat. They interchanged messages, but they could not see each other. November the 26th he arrived in Huè. There he was put to the trial. He was questioned; he was importuned to profane the cross; he was teased by having a crucifix tied to his foot, which he was urged to press, and he had to lie down and be beaten—to be beaten in that slow tedious manner which is customary in the country, one stroke coming down after the other at long intervals; and though it was only eleven strokes he had to bear, the strokes were severe, and he knew not how long they would continue. But he bore all with fortitude. 'He seemed to sleep,' said the mandarin of justice; but M. Charrier on his part thought the blows were hard enough to keep him awake.

M. Charrier was not beaten a second time. Sentence of death was passed on all three prisoners, but it was not executed, and they were left all together in prison.

In the spring of the next year, May 1842, two more captives entered the prison, M. Miche and M. Duclos. They came this time from Cochin China. The adventures of M. Miche were full of incident, and he has described them graphically in a series of letters. His voyage from Penang to Cochin China, the hazards of the passage and of the landing, his start in the missionary life in Cochin China and Laos, his arrest, his first and second sojourn in prison, his examinations and floggings, are all depicted in such lively colours that they fix our attention.

'At half-past one, after midnight,' writes M. Miche, 'on the 19th of June 1841, we set our feet on the land of martyrs, praying God to grant us the high favour of watering it with our blood.' His feelings were solemnised by the peculiarity of the crisis. On landing, the first news heard was the arrest of MM. Berneux and Galy. His own landing had been in the midst of perils, after sundry bafflings and delays. His account of his voyage and previous risks he has narrated with some detail, and we may take it as a specimen of the preliminary difficulties of a missionary going to labour in this country. 'We left Penang on the 1st of May, on board a small brig, having with us one hundred and twenty Chinese passengers. I can tell you that one could not anywhere undergo a better novitiate for martyrdom; we were stowed so thick together that we were kept constantly standing, and at night we thought ourselves well off if we could stretch ourselves on a barrel, the only bed to be had. But those discomforts we considered would be over in ten days, when we should reach Singapore; and besides, we were going to a land where other sufferings awaited us, and what was then undergone would be a preparation for them. But as to our short passage we were disappointed; twenty-two days instead of ten; the winds were contrary, we were driven back three times, and the pilot, carelessly going to sleep at a critical moment when the navigation was dangerous, we were nearly wrecked. A timely alarm from a Japanese sailor saved us; the ship was just aground, but was righted by a quick manœuvre, and we escaped.'

At Singapore, a vessel, despatched by Bishop Cuenot, awaited them, and the party, consisting of three missionaries and five students from the college at Penang, were transferred into her. The crew of the new ship were five Christians and three pagans. Everything was now done with strict secrecy. They entered the vessel by night. The landing also had to be effected under cover of darkness. Unfortunately, the winds did not favour them, and as they neared the Cochin-Chinese coast the light began to dawn. For a European to attempt to land under the circumstances would be madness, but the students and a catechist went ashore, and were to give notice the next night if the venture might be made. A torch was to be waved as a signal. The interval was one of uncertainty and fear. The missionaries were obliged to keep below, in a hiding-place prepared for them. Mandarin junks were moving to and fro, and the slightest ground of suspicion would cause a visit. The next night there was an anxious watch; no light, however, appeared till the early morning, and then it was not easy to ascertain the meaning. Two men were sent off in a boat to make sure. Their friends were on the look-out, but it was to warn not to invite. 'Fly, fly,' they cried; 'make off with the vessel. Hundreds of soldiers are surrounding the town.' The moment was critical. Observation was drawn to the boat, and to the vessel also, and chase was given. The wind failed, and they had to take to rowing, and every minute the barque of the missionaries was losing ground. Escape was thought impossible. The Cochin-Chinese were trembling with alarm, and anxiously calling to the fathers below to pray for deliverance. Fortunately, just in time, they fell in with their own boat, and the two men detached joining them, their extra strength enabled them to get away. But then it was a difficult question to decide what to do. Gothi, where the Bishop was, was the only other place of landing they knew, and there the Bishop had warned them not to make the attempt. To Gothi, however, they went, and a messenger was sent ashore to tell their mischance, and to learn the Bishop's will. It would take three days to get an answer, and meanwhile they must keep their distance and not venture to approach the land except by night. It was midday when their messenger again came in sight. They dared not take him on board. They crossed near to each other, and words were exchanged, and a place of meeting was fixed for the next night. But again they were baffled; a vessel bore down upon them just at the critical moment, and they were obliged to fly, and it was not till after a second night that the object·could be accomplished. Their messenger brought word that they were to land as they could. So, entering their little boat, and lying down at the bottom, the missionaries resolved on the venture, and after a few risks and fears succeeded in reaching the retreat of the Bishop. 'After many a turning and winding we stopped at the gate of a little garden surrounded with a thick hedge of bamboos. A Cochin-Chinese priest came to receive us, and led us to the episcopal palace; that is, to a little hut, into which I could not enter without stooping.'

For six months, in the seclusion of this Christian village, M. Miche remained with the Bishop, and then Mgr. Cuenot resolved to employ him in a business which for a long time he had had much at heart. He would send him to Laos. It was but a short journey, and the people seemed well disposed for conversion. Missionaries had at different periods penetrated into their country, and had brought favourable reports. The people were primitive, honest, generous, hospitable to strangers, and strict as to truth. They were not slaves of any particular superstition, there being no dominating religion amongst them, and yet they were open to religious impressions. M. Miche and M. Duclos were now therefore to go and commence the missionary work in Laos. Should they succeed, this spot would furnish a useful retreat in time of persecution, and possibly a college might be formed there. So the two missionaries set off. They passed beyond the bounds of Cochin China, and got amongst some of the native tribes. Travelling was then difficult. They were attempting to go up the stream in a boat, but the obstacles were too many for them, and they were forced to leave their boat, and, piling their luggage on horses, they made their way on foot. It was but a slow passage, and they were followed. The Annamites in pursuit came up, compelled the natives to join them, and the capture of the missionaries was effected. The two missionaries were then taken to Phuyen, and were at once brought up for trial. They were not alone. There were several Cochin-Chinese with them, implicated in the affair. It was Feb. 25th. The first two days there was a long battling between the prisoners and the mandarins, who wanted information about persons and places which could not be given without bringing others into danger. The first day it was only words, the second it came to blows. The controversies began at six in the morning, and very soon the mandarins showed that they were in earnest. Punishment began with the Cochin-Chinese. Ong-Quong, the chief person in the late expedition, was first questioned, and, not replying as was wished, the beating began. He received twenty blows. By his side was placed a cross, on which was a painted image of Jesus Christ, and he was asked to trample on it, which he firmly refused. Another was called up, a soldier named Thien. He was sick and weak. But he took his beating of thirty blows without giving way. It was not his first trial, for in 1838 he had proved his constancy. A third, Chu-Quon, on the twelfth blow failed and became an apostate; and then another, a boy of fifteen. The next was worse still. He was an old man, of seeming virtue, whose quick fall caused surprise and disappointment. The first word of the mandarin intimidated him, and he gave up before he had received a single blow. After these submissions, Ong-Quong was called again, and though he was firm up to the twentieth blow, his courage then failed, and he also, notwithstanding all the fervour and zeal he had displayed, now became an apostate. The next put to trial was a young man, named Chu-Ngai, twenty years of age. He took three beatings on that day, fifty strokes in all, but he came out of the trial victorious. M. Miche, too, was laid on the ground, and beaten. Ten strokes were all he had at that time, nor would he have had these, if it had not been for a lie of Ong-Quong's, which M. Miche would not corroborate, and they wanted to compel him to do so; but poor Ong-Quong, when he had once yielded, became quite faint-hearted, and said whatever the mandarins put in his mouth. That was a long weary day, five hours in the morning sitting, five more in the evening, and the next day the same. And next day the brave Ngai was overcome. Twelve more blows of the rattan on the wounds of the previous day were too much for him, and all the glories of his first heroism were tarnished.

On the second day of examination M. Miche was led into another court. The principal mandarin did not sit there, but the business was conducted by judges of inferior rank. There was quite a crowd of them; some twenty or thirty young Cochin-Chinese aspirants for fame, pretentious and self-sufficient, teasing M. Miche with their foolish questions, and offending him by their rude arrogance. There was no order or decency in their proceedings. They spoke in loud tones, they spoke several at once, they thought to frighten M. Miche by their airs of superiority. But he was not one to be frightened. He turned round on them when they pressed him hard, and once, when the president adopted this cavalier mode and proceeded to threats, M. Miche's patience seemed to be quite gone, and he took him by the beard, and made him understand that he did not fear him or regard him, and that he might spare his threats and promises. His colleagues were more amused than angry at the scene, and the man himself, after a short burst of anger, joined in the general merriment. They were six wearying hours to M. Miche (he had tasted nothing for the day), and when they were over he was not allowed repose. He was carried up then before a superior mandarin, who angrily reproved him for not answering the questions asked. Teased and worn out he said to the mandarin, 'What is the name of the King of France?' on which the mandarin stared, and seemed to wonder at such a question being put to him. 'Supposing I was a mandarin,' M. Miche then went on, 'and threatened to beat you till you told me the name, would the rattan help you? So no tortures will teach me what I do not know.'

M. Miche's situation this day was very harassing. After all his fatigues all the food he had was two or three spoonfuls of rice, and he lay down for rest on the rough dirty floor of his prison, his mind sad and troubled by the thought of the fall of the poor Christians who had been his companions.

The false testimony of Ong-Quong was a cause of more misery still. It implicated several other persons; and men and women, in consequence, from different villages were brought up before the tribunal, and beaten because they would not confess charges that were not true. At length, however, Ong-Quong was brought to a sense of his misconduct, and obliged to retract what he had said; but then it was too late; he could not undo what he had done, and he brought down vengeance on himself. Again he was bound to the stakes, and had to submit to twenty fresh strokes.

Neither M. Duclos nor M. Miche were beaten with the severity adopted towards the Cochin-Chinese Christians, but they were each beaten twice, M. Miche receiving twelve strokes in the second instance.

The pagans in Cochin China seemed to have more ill-feeling towards the Christians than was noticeable in Tonking. They showed positive pleasure in seeing them beaten. They were not satisfied if the blows were not dealt vigorously; they were pleased to hear the cries of pain that the blows extorted. Even the children shared in these feelings of animosity. They came round M. Miche, as he was sorrowfully looking on his suffering companions, and made game of him, pulling his dress, making mocking signs, one even presuming to touch his wounds, and ask him 'Is it cold here?' M. Miche confessed that he fretted under the indignities of the little urchins. 'My blood,' he says, 'was boiling in my veins, my patience was fast going; but happily the Lord sustained me.'

M. Miche much offended his judges by the dauntless bearing that he always maintained. In their view it was effrontery not to be borne. Once, to their great indignation, he warned them that the Emperor of France would avenge the wrongs he was suffering. This in no way answered the purpose for which he spoke it. It stirred their anger to hear one, who in their eyes was a miserable culprit, daring to threaten his judges. 'What bold insolence for one in chains!' said one of the mandarins; 'he wants to frighten us.' They would listen to no word of explanation: down he must go upon the ground, and submit to another beating. But they were content with making him understand that they were not afraid; and after three strokes of the bamboo, the beating stopped.

The prison life in this place was wretched. The heat of the prison was stifling; and the missionaries were in the midst of a crowd of prisoners of the worst description, who delighted to plague and annoy them in every way they could. But this life came to an end. In May the order arrived that they should be conducted to Huè. It was a mournful journey—one without any of those glad demonstrations that had met the missionaries from Tonking. They passed on, silently and unnoticed, under their guard of soldiers. One single incident is mentioned that interrupted the sad tediousness of the procession. It was the bold earnest affectionateness of a Christian woman, who, at one of the villages, would press forward to show her devotion to the fathers. She threw herself at their feet; she wept for their sorrows; she gave them all she had to give—a fowl and some bananas, which she was carrying in a basket to market. This was the one sign of care and interest that relieved them. 'How greatly this affection and devotion touched us,' says M. Miche, 'I cannot tell you.'

On the 13th May they reached Huè, after a journey

of eleven days. Having been presented to the grand mandarin of the Bo, and asked a few questions, they were freed from their cangues and led to their prison. Then at last a real joy awaited them: the meeting their three colleagues who had been so long shut up there. It was relief, indeed, to be in this prison, where everything was quite different from the misery of Phuyen, and where the missionaries had a great deal of freedom. Although they did not all live together, but were separated in three different compartments, yet they could pass from one to the other, and meet when they liked. M. Berneux's quarters were the usual place of assembling. There they would sit till late on in the evening, talking together of martyrs and confessors, or running back to the subjects of their several missions; or, in the cool of the evening, they would go out into the court, and, all five together, make their promenade; and even after the evening gun had sounded (the signal for retirement), they would have leave to go on with their walk, and continue it, perhaps, late into the night. The early rigours had ceased. They were known to their gaolers, and had become objects of regard and attention. They could read and write; they could repeat prayers together openly; and they had formed for themselves a little Office of the Blessed Virgin, which they constantly recited—sometimes it might be in their respective stations, sometimes in the public court-yard. It was to their gaolers, not to the king or the mandarins, that they owed their indulgences, for their gaolers viewed them with favour.

The gaolers are soldiers; for in Cochin China the soldiers have a variety of employments: they have to do whatever they are told to do; and soldiers are the ministers of the king's will, whatever it may be; but a principal business of the soldiers is to be gaolers and executioners. In the court of the prison, as the missionaries looked out, they would see the soldiers at their daily exercise. The exercise was confined to one single practice—the use of the rattan—so as to lay it on with dexterity. A stuffed figure was placed in the midst of the court, and one after the other the soldiers took their turn in elaborately thrashing it. The great art was to administer the blows so that they left but a single wheal. He who could hit best in this manner carried off the prize of skill. Soldiers, too, would be seen constantly passing out of the prison on their way to the Bo, and the arms in their hands were the never-failing rattan, with a rope, a mallet, and the stakes—the instruments of torture. In Cochin China, indeed, the rattan is the universal remedy; and the soldier feels it as often as he uses it. Each in his turn has to succumb, and so he is taught his duty. The common soldier who tortures the prisoners falls in his turn before the corporal; and the corporal before the sergeant. The same rattan is ever the instrument that enforces obedience: so fear is the influence that is working, so comes that cringing servility that results from the despotism passing down from the supreme tyrant on the throne, from rank to rank, even to the lowest.

Although he found his condition in the prisons of

Huè so much better than at Phuyen, still there was in the mind of M. Miche a subject of anxiety which he could not dismiss. He knew that he would have to stand an examination; he knew the embarrassment caused by questions that he could not answer without bringing down punishment on others; he knew the danger of silence; he knew the perplexity of the moment when he had to seek for some mode of evading the question without departing from truth. He honestly tells us that he had a dread of the bamboo, and would avoid it if he could; and when he found himself able he took advantage of the want of astuteness in the Annamite mind, and by his own subtlety of language sought to extricate himself from his difficulties. But the anxiety and the mental effort was great, and the thought of it was a trouble. 'I have a great dread of torture,' he says; 'for much as I desire to be a martyr, I know how weak I am, and how unworthy of such an honour. When I find myself bound hand and foot, stretched between two stakes, and the executioner is raising his hand to lacerate me, the voice of nature is heard shrinking back, and says, "*Transeat a me calix iste.*" But I turn my eyes to Jesus Christ bound at the pillar—yes, on the cross—and strengthened by grace the same voice will exclaim, "*Veruntamen, non sicut ego volo, sed sicut Tu.*" But then,' he goes on, 'the executioner's work over, and the cords again loosened, the feelings are quite changed; then it is real joy that is felt—an inebriation, a foretaste of heaven, so lively that all feeling of torture is quite lost.'

The missionaries remained together in their prison up to the autumn of 1842. Then an interruption occurred. MM. Galy and Berneux and Charrier were removed to what was called the Great Prison, and MM. Miche and Duclos were left by themselves. Up to that time these two missionaries had escaped the dreaded examination. They had only, in the first instance, been asked a few preliminary questions. A few days after they parted with their companions, October 22, they were again summoned into court. Witnesses had been brought up from Phuyen; of the number, two Christians who had apostatised. But happily they had regained their courage; and in this court, although they were heavily beaten, they would betray no sign at all of weakness. M. Miche conducted himself with his usual intrepidity. His air, if anything, might be considered too daring and contemptuous. It provoked him to be pestered with questions that had little meaning, and to listen to the idle suspicions of his judges. What moved his especial ridicule on this occasion was the vain fears with which they were troubling themselves about the dangerous character of a simple map: they could not make out at all what it meant, and were wonderfully puzzled by the variety of colours.

M. Miche, however, at this time had a protection which was a restraint on the mandarin. The power of the Europeans was really overawing them. The English and French ships were then numerous in those seas, and the war carried into China would be a warning not to provoke too far. So, though M.

Miche was called on to profane the cross, his refusal was not attended with the usual consequences. The missionaries were neither of them this time beaten. They went back to their prison, and the sentence of death was passed on them; the day came also on which they thought the sentence would be executed. On the third of December the sentence was ratified by the king, and on the seventh M. Miche and M. Duclos were also led off to the Great Prison, which was the prison of the condemned. The sentence was one which the missionary always hailed with joy; it would put an end to his griefs, it would bring him to the reward which had been ever in his thoughts.

'It was an inconceivable joy,' says M. Miche, 'with which the king's decision filled our souls. None could tell what it was who had not experienced it. And what must be the joy when the day of punishment really comes! What will it be when the executioner is heard knocking at the door, and saying, "Come away, Heaven is open for you!"'

The new prison into which M. Miche now entered was a very gloomy one. One solace, too, to which he had been looking forward was not granted. He did not then join his former companions as he had hoped. M. Berneux and the others were gone. M. Miche has himself given us an idea of the prison. A vast pile of buildings in the midst of marshes, shut in by walls, dykes, and an impenetrable hedge of prickly bamboos. This prison is a receptacle of the worst criminals; from all parts of the kingdom it takes in its inmates, who are those who have been sentenced to death. The misery to be here seen—poverty, hunger and thirst, and every wretchedness—is in the extreme pitiable. Once introduced into this prison there is little hope of coming out alive.

The five missionaries, however, were an exception. The king, Thien-Tri, had all along shrunk from putting the Christians to death. The bloody executions had stopped which had been so numerous in the previous reign. M. Berneux and his two companions were removed from the Great Prison about the time M. Miche entered it, and it was proposed to them by the king that they should do some of the same sort of work as had been done before by M. Jacquart and M. Delamotte. M. Berneux, however, was firm in insisting that he would do nothing unless he ceased to be treated as a prisoner. He was accordingly removed from the prison, and put into a commodious place enough, but his chain was not taken off, and so instead of work, as had been intended, the matter remained ever in suspense. M. Berneux was not sent back to prison, but the chain remained round his neck and feet.

What would have been the result to the missionaries cannot be said. But help came to them from without. A French ship of war, the Heroine (February 25, 1843), anchored off Touron, and the commander, M. Leveque, made a demand for the delivering up of the prisoners at Huè. The mandarin resolutely denied that there were any French prisoners at all. But M. Leveque was not to be so put off. He had exact information on the subject. So he placed in the hands of the mandarin a letter, which he required him to transmit to the king, formally demanding the five missionaries. The mandarin shuffled and tried to evade, but the French captain was pressing, so the letter went, and accomplished its purpose.

The missionaries, when they heard in their prison that they were to be free, could hardly believe the truth of what they were told; but the news once heard there was little delay. Their chains were really struck off, and on the 17th of March 1843 they found themselves off the port of Touron on board the Heroine.

They would have wished, if it had been allowed, again and at once to go back to the land in which they had already suffered for Christ; but it was not allowed; M. Leveque considered himself bound to take them away. He took M. Miche and M. Duclos to Singapore, and there he left them: M. Duclos because he was too ill to bear the fatigues of a longer voyage; M. Miche because he was to remain at Penang with charge of the college. M. Berneux, too, was permitted to remain behind, on the engagement that he would no more return to Cochin China; and, after some years' labour in Machouria, this missionary, so full of the martyr's spirit, went to a land even more dangerous to him than Annam, to Corea, and there he had the accomplishment of his ardent desire, and died a martyr.* M. Galy and M. Charrier went back to France, but they both returned to Tonking; each of them, notwithstanding, after more or less stay, had again to retire, and ended their days in France.

* This last stage of Mgr. Berneux's life is given in author's *Corean Martyrs*.

CHAPTER X.

BISHOP RETORT.

WITH the death of Minh-Menh the persecution relaxed. The great stimulus for it was removed. Thien-Tri never showed any strong interest in the matter. His policy was always a hesitating one, and as time went on causes arose to increase his hesitation. So the persecution gradually subsided. What persecution there was resulted rather from the dispositions of the local governors than from any impulse from the central authority, and local governors were more frequently checked than encouraged, if inclined to be meddlesome. In this way it happened that gradually the priests, European as well as native, began to resume their work, and as early as 1842 the work had become very considerable. Mgr. Retort tells us that in that year he himself heard three thousand confessions, and confirmed almost as many. When he travelled he took with him several priests, some of them European. Where he stopped, it was short work to extemporise a church, where, before daylight, there was Mass and a sermon. Through the night the Bishop and the priests were busy in the confessional, while the catechists collected around them numerous bands, preparing some for confession or first communion, or giving elementary instructions to pagans seeking admission to the faith; chosen young men all the while patrolled the village to guard against a sudden surprise. Hard as these duties were they were full of consolation to the missionary; so many were the proofs given by the Tonkinese of their ardent devotion—crowding the confessional, listening to instructions, their prayers and chants resounding in the church and outside it too. These duties in a large village would go on for days, sometimes for a fortnight or even more. A great inundation which occurred this year facilitated the Bishop's movements. Vast tracts of country were covered, and the water was so deep that ships of large burthen might have sailed on it. The Bishop, during this season, could go about freely in his little skiff by day, and without notice; and the beauty of the scene, as well as his independence, would add to the pleasure of his exertions. When Christmas came, and he counted over the work of his year, there had been one hundred and ten thousand communions, and as many as one hundred and eighty-one thousand confessions. And the Christmas ceremonies were on a magnificent scale. Six thousand Christians were present at them, and five priests were ordained with several in inferior orders.

Work like this continued for several years, and the missionary, if he was cautious, experienced very slight interruption. Now and then he was reminded that the edicts were still in force, and that the risk still existed of being thrown into prison, or perhaps of forfeiting his life. Mgr. Retort had at times his narrow escapes. Once, late in the evening, in a Christian village, he was sitting, and quietly conversing with M. Titaut, one of his missionaries, when news was brought that a mandarin was at hand at the head of a body of soldiers. His purpose was not known, but some precautions were taken; they conversed in a lower tone, but continued sipping their tea. Soon a knocking was heard, and the alarm was found to be real. Mgr. Retort slipped away out of the house, leapt a high wall, and got off; but M. Titaut fell into the hands of the soldiers. Nevertheless, after all, it was but a fright. The women crowded round, clamorous and threatening, and a sum of money compromised the matter. Another time, on the eve of St. Peter's, 1848, when numerous companies had collected for the next day's festival, tidings were brought that a surprise was contemplated. But relief came opportunely. A violent storm, with floods of rain, made the country impassable, and frustrated the plans of the mandarin. So the Bishop sang his Mass, feeling confident that he should not be interrupted. These are specimens of the uncertainty of their situation, even in those more happy times.

During these years the progress of religion was conspicuous. Churches sprung up, colleges were built, Christians, students, priests, all multiplied; and the lists of confessions and communions made plain how much steady work had been accomplished. Occasionally some grand ceremony was attempted, and one, the consecration of Mgr. Jeantet, January

1847, was especially famous. Mgr. Retort has given us the details, and that very minutely. 'It took three hours. There were two bishops besides the bishop elect, two European priests, twenty native priests, more than a hundred Latin scholars, all vested in surplices and officiating, with drums and other music, and a body of not less than ten thousand Christians, without counting the pagans.' It was a scene really to be remembered. It was at Ke-non, a college of the Bishop's own creation, deep in the retirement of a large Christian village, in the midst of extensive grounds, with beautiful flowers, and shrubs, and trees, sheltered by lofty hedges of bamboos. And when the ceremony was over there was a splendid entertainment; nineteen hundred tables, at which sat down eleven or twelve hundred guests. The fashion of the country takes from the expense of such repasts; for every one who comes contributes his quota in the shape of a present, and the missionary can venture on this scale of magnificence without being severely taxed.

There is another peculiarity prevalent in this part of the world which ought to be mentioned, that it may be better understood that proceedings of this sort are not so open to the public gaze as might be imagined. In Tonking, we are told, 'the houses are separated from one another by gardens more or less extensive, surrounded by large and thick-set bamboos. The meanest dwelling is as well enclosed as many of the convents in Spain.* It is this that

* This is from a letter of M. Marti, a Spanish Dominican.

affords the facility of our holding large meetings without being noticed from the outside. In the case of the churches and houses of the missionaries, they are still more secluded. The place selected for them is always the most safe and retired part of the village. The garden in which they stand is not only enclosed by a hedge of bamboos, it has its walls and ditch and counter-ditch, and no one is surprised at it, for all good houses are built in the same way. But what adds to the security is the fact of their being in the midst of a population of the most faithful Christians, whose dwellings are all around, and must be passed by all who would go in and out.'

At the end of ten years, when Mgr. Retort looked back on the past, he could behold a change that was most satisfactory. The three vicariates of 1839, when he was nominated bishop, had swelled out into six. The single consecrated bishop had amplified into ten, with the probability of two more. And when he contemplated his own vicariate, the thirty-eight native priests had mounted up to sixty-five; and instead of a reduced staff of catechists and students scattered in all directions, there were now in a large seminary and in five colleges thirty students already in their theology, and two hundred and fourteen younger scholars, with two hundred and seventy catechists, and six hundred pupils outside the colleges, in what they called the houses of God. And besides, the hundred thousands Christians of the earlier period had now become one hundred and thirty thousand.

Thien-Tri, as has been said, was never a persecutor. But it was fear that restrained him more than anything else. In 1847 his reign came to an end. He died, and was succeeded by Tudoc, his second son. The new reign was at first still more favourable to the Christians, and it was rumoured that the young king himself was well-inclined toward them. At any rate he did not seem to think much about them, and he had other matters to occupy his attention. His throne was not quite secure, for he had an elder brother who was not content to be put aside, and who more than once endeavoured to assert his claims. But the funeral of his father and the reception of the Chinese ambassadors were two matters of importance that occupied him for some time.

Funerals in this country are celebrated on a very grand scale, and in the case of a king with a profusion of expense and a strange elaborateness of detail.* And this requires time. So, though Thien-Tri died Nov. 4, it was not till June in the following year that his obsequies were performed. The day of burial must be settled by the rules of magic and sorcery. It is for the dealer in these arts to fix the day and the hour; and then, with great pomp, the corpse is borne to the grave. Up to the period of burial the body has been enclosed in its coffin, and this in Tonking is formed out of a single trunk of chiselled wood, hermetically sealed, so that for months, or even years, the remains of the dead may be kept in it, and no offensive smell exude. For months, then, the de-

* Letter of Mgr. Pellerin.

parted monarch lies in state, in a house of mourning that has been expressly raised for the occasion, where tapers are lit in his honour, incense is burnt, sacrifices of various animals are offered, and feasts are spread out, on which his spirit may regale; and on stated days those marks of honour and attention are multiplied. The new king, in mourning attire, is careful to present himself, and to adore the father whom he has lost. The formalities of these funerals are always a great boon to the professors of magic; for the decision of everything is left to their skill, and the slightest mistake is supposed to bring down incalculable mischief on the survivors. And of such fears these impostors dexterously take advantage; and it has happened that bodies have been exhumed and re-interred, simply because some clever old rogue, who has some reputation in his line, to gain a few sapecs has whispered his fears, and terrified a poor family. But it is not to the people generally that these vain terrors are confined; men of rank and learning are not exempt from them; and all the while the cheats will allow, when talking of these things with the Christians, that they have been lying. 'It is our calling,' they say in excuse. 'We should starve if we gave it up.' And the people cannot be persuaded to see the folly of these acts. 'The king does it,' they say; 'and what the king does we may do, for he cannot do wrong.'

The day of the funeral was really a grand day. First, the body had to be transferred to another house, also built on purpose, outside the gates of the city. It was close to the gates, by the river-side, where the junks, afterwards to receive the coffin, were lying prepared. All along the route rich silks and carpets and mats were hung out, and the banks of the river were decorated in the same way. Each village to be passed had its orders to erect altars, to provide incense and wax-candles; and, as the body was borne along, all were commanded to prostrate themselves. Soldiers lined the banks of the river.

The journey to be taken was only three miles, but it was one of three days; for the advance was slow, and there were to be three halts. At each halting-place there was a round of ceremonies; oxen and pigs were sacrificed, offerings were made of food, betel, and tobacco.

One whole day the coffin remained in a house built by the river-side, and thirty fine fat animals were sacrificed. In the evening the march was resumed. Soldiers raised and carried the body; the king followed on foot, clothed in a long wide-sleeved white-cotton garment, on his head a kind of straw cap, in his hand a bamboo cane. Next came the other children of Thien-Tri, and then his relatives, all in white garments and white turbans.

At the river the coffin was placed on a magnificent barge, built on purpose, and no one was permitted to remain on board. As they proceeded along the river, the first boat was the junk of the bonzes, who stood aloft on a platform, lifted on the shoulders of soldiers; there standing through the day they went on with their roaring and yelling, it being their office to proclaim the praises of the dead, and even to the pagans the sight was ridiculous. Then came another junk with another platform, and on this all you saw was a piece of damask on a wooden frame marked with sundry characters and devices. This, as they said, was the seat of the soul of the departed. A third junk bore also a platform, loaded with rice and fruit and bread and other food. A fourth followed, with a platform more curiously filled than any—a body of jugglers, painted grotesquely and variously, with strange dresses, with sabres, spears, flaming torches in their hands, grinning, weeping, howling, striking about with their weapons, and all this, as was said, to frighten the demons. After these, towed by other junks, came the barge of the deceased, followed by that of the new king, multitudes of little boats crowding in behind, scattering sheets of gold and silver paper as they moved forward.

The tomb was reached on the third day. It was a deep cavity in the mountain side, close to which was raised an edifice of beautiful stone, enclosed by walls, which was to serve as a prison for such wives of the late king as had been childless, whose duty it would be to spread before him a daily repast, such as the dead are thought still to require. The cavern in which the body is placed is hollowed far into the rock; and in order to keep the exact spot where it is a secret, there is a variety of different passages and windings, and all is carefully covered in by a large stone. This secrecy is maintained from a dread lest, in case of war or revolution, any enemy might profane the remains of the dead.

A platform from the river to the tomb had been raised, covered with beautiful mats, and over this was borne the coffin, as well as the whole cavalcade that had proceeded up the river, the barges and their several contents. Taking care to observe the exact moment signified by the astrologers, the body was introduced into its cavern, and with it was enclosed a treasury of riches — gold and silver and precious stones, and various other articles of value. And this was not the only waste. High piles were erected in the courts of this palace of the dead : the barges, the scaffoldings, everything that had been used for the purposes of the funeral, everything the king had used in his lifetime — his chess-boards, his chess-men, his musical instruments, his fans, his parasols, his mats, his carriages, his wooden horse, his great pasteboard elephant, his magnificent gilded state barge, with its gold and precious stones—all were recklessly consumed ; and as the flames were crackling, around were dancing those same jugglers who were before mounted on the platform, brandishing their swords and firebrands, and making their uncouth movements and noises, and with the same purpose of intimidating the demons, and hindering them from forcing a passage into the tomb and troubling the dead. And woe to those poor culprits who, during these long ceremonies, should fall into a mistake ! There is no mercy for such offences : down comes the bamboo for a very slight deviation from the outline prescribed.

But the work of destruction has not yet been completed. Those giant palaces also, elaborately fitted up as temporal resting-places for the dead, as he passed on to the tomb, with all their costly decorations, were, after their brief occupation, ruthlessly consigned to the flames; and all this was done under the vain fancy that the dead would be benefited.

Such were the earliest occupations of Tudoc on his ascending the throne. His next were the preparations for the reception of the ambassadors from China. And this, too, was the business of months. Although the monarchs of Cochin China and Tonking are entirely independent of China, yet the solemn investiture by the delegates of the Chinese emperor, performed at the commencement of each reign, is regarded as a matter of much consequence. It is of very old date. The ancient kings who reigned at Keeho had observed it through long generations; and so Gialaong and his immediate successors had gone from Huè to Keeho, that there, as had been the use, they might be invested. But Tudoc did not like the journey, and he had demanded that the ambassadors should come on to Huè; and this was done. But Chinese ambassadors travelled in great state, and expected extraordinary attention. They looked down with arrogance on the people amongst whom they came; and whatever cost and labour was employed for their reception, it hardly satisfied their haughty minds. The mandarin commissioned in this instance was only a mandarin of the second class. His retinue amounted to one hundred and forty persons. It took a month for this cavalcade to journey through the Annamite territory before it reached Huè; for Cochin-Chinese vanity prolonged it by short stages and indirect roads, that so the extent of the empire might be increased in the imagination of the travellers. After every twelve or fifteen miles there was a halt, and there a palace suitable to the dignity of these high visitors was erected. Crowds of persons had been pressed in for these labours, large wealth had been expended, and roads as well as palaces had to be prepared.

At length the investiture came off. The king met the ambassadors at the gate of the inner city, where he resided, and all entered together; then the imperial charter having been placed on an altar, in the midst of perfumes, Tudoc, on a sign from the ambassadors, advanced, knelt, and prostrated himself five times. While he still knelt, the ambassador read the paper, and handed it to the king, who, holding it on high, made another prostration, when the charter was given to one of the princes, and the king having saluted it with five fresh prostrations, the ceremony was terminated.*

Scarcely was this business concluded when there was a terrible visitation of cholera. It created a universal alarm. It suspended all business. The number of the dead was enormous. Two millions, in Tonking alone, are computed to have fallen. The Christians were not tried so severely as others; but Mgr. Retort considered that over nine thousand were

* Letter of Mgr. Pellerin.

victims within his own jurisdiction, and of these twelve were priests. The Christians, then, had a freedom which had been long denied them. Their processions appeared in public, as they bore their dead to the grave, chanting aloud their prayers, with the cross in front—so long proscribed, so often insulted in this country. There was now none to oppose them. Every one was shutting himself up, to get away from the plague. Satellites, mandarins, every one in authority, were withdrawn from observation. The king had secluded himself in his palace, and would allow no one to approach him; not even a mandarin could obtain an audience. And amidst this general dread and selfishness Christian charity shone out. The Christians did not bury their own dead only, but those of the poor neglected pagans; and they were at the bedside of the sick affording consolation and help; but their great work was the charge they took of the poor orphans, whose fathers and mothers were removed by the disease, and who were left friendless.

During the early years of Tudoc, then, the condition of the Christians was ameliorated. A general amnesty at the beginning of his reign brought out of prison all who had been captives. Amongst these was one remarkable for his sufferings and his firmness, whom Mgr. Retort thought fit to reward with the priesthood. He had before his arrest been tonsured, and had been also a student in theology. He had been in chains for eight years, and during his imprisonment he had been five times sentenced to death. The cangue had almost for the whole period been on his shoulders, and many a time he had felt the smart of the rattan. He was well worthy of the promotion which the Bishop awarded him; his name was Father Paul Tinh, and his name will appear again in this history.

The progress of religion on the year after the cholera was especially noticeable. Mgr. Retort was particularly struck by it. It was the year of the jubilee. The missionaries were very active, and their labours met with ample reward. Everywhere the confessionals were crowded, and the signs of amendment were very visible. At Ke-vinh, where the Christian population was very large, there were ten confessors at work, and they were not enough. From Hoang-guyen M. Castex writes to the Bishop and says: 'The abundance of the grace of this jubilee is beyond calculation. Such crowds! Such earnestness! And then the fervour with which they approach the tribunal of penance! And the patience with which for four or five days they will wait till their turn comes!' And the Bishop felt just the same. He saw such proofs of sincere conversion, and that in bold apostates, in hardened sinners, on whom previous appeals had been in vain; and again in pagans coming in numerously and asking for instruction.

But it was in the midst of these happy events that a change startled them. In this very year, 1851, of surprising success, a missionary was arrested. It was M. Shœfer, a young priest, who had been only three years in Tonking. Once before, shortly after his arrival, he had had a narrow escape. He was with the Bishop at Ke-vinh, and a troublesome mandarin, in the hope of a bribe, had shown a disposition to disturb them. In the flight the young missionary had difficulty in hiding, and very nearly fell into the hands of his enemies. But this time he was less fortunate; nor could he be afterwards extricated. The old hatred of the European was found to be still strong, and at the end of three months the orders arrived from Huè that he should be put to death. The king's mind had been turned against the Christians. There was by his side a mandarin who detested them, and his influence was powerful. And Tudoc had an idea that the Christians were ill-disposed towards him, and favoured his brother, who at this time had been trying to gain partisans, and had been worsted in an attempt to raise a rebellion. So a decree had been issued which spurred the mandarins to fresh activity, and it was in consequence of this that M. Shœfer was taken and put to death. Yet even this act of violence did not stop the great missionary work that signalised this year; it went on more silently and cautiously, but it was not interrupted. The next year, however, a new alarm occurred. Another priest, M. Bonnard, was taken. He also was young and new to the country. He had been there but two years, and the last year he had been stationed at Ke-banh, a large and important Christian village, where if he had staid he would have been safe. But his zeal carried him out into the neighbouring small village of Boi-kuen, and there he was suddenly set upon by a petty mandarin and arrested. M. Bonnard was giving baptism at the time to a number of children, and the mandarin was at the gate of the village before he had any notice; he could not complete the work begun. Stole and surplice were thrown off at once, and he started off to make his escape, if possible. The soldiers were already in view, and barred his progress in the direction he first sought. He waded through a pond, ran across some rice-fields, his catechist Kim by his side. They could not get on for the mud, and he knew not what way to take; the village of Dongdai, it is true, was not far off, and could it only have been reached, they might have been safe. But the soldiers were too quick, they came up and surrounded them; and with their hands tightly bound, the two fugitives were led away to prison. M. Bonnard was not at all dejected; he thought of Jesus Christ bound and before His judges, and he made the offering of his life to God. He was more troubled about his catechist and a young boy called Bao, one of his scholars, who by too eagerly pressing forward had been captured. M. Bonnard's imprisonment was not a long one, nor was he treated with any severity; soldiers and mandarins seemed to look kindly on him. He addressed himself to them with freedom, and never entertained the least fear; he spoke with such remarkable ease before his judges that he could not help calling to mind, and very vividly, our Lord's words to His disciples not to be careful as to their speech, for the Holy Ghost would teach them what to say. Though he would not answer many questions put to him, nor disclose matters on which the mandarins wanted information, they did not press him, nor did they ever strike him or even threaten him with the rattan. The young priest was cheerful and radiant; martyrdom was to him a prize; it was what he had long and earnestly desired; his feelings are very plain, and he speaks about them most naturally. The Bishop had sent Father Tinh, himself a confessor of the faith, into the prison, to hear his confession, and to carry him communion, and he wrote back to thank the Bishop. 'Yesterday,' he says, 'I had the happiness of receiving Holy Communion. It is long since I was so consoled in receiving the King of Angels. One must be in prison with the chain and cangue round the neck to tell the delight felt in suffering for Him who loved us so much. . . . My cangue and chain are heavy. Do you think that they grieve me? No! I rather rejoice in them; for I know that the cross of Jesus Christ was still heavier than my cangue; that His chains were less endurable than mine; and I feel happy to be able with St. Paul to call myself *vinctus in Christo*. This is a happiness for which I have sighed even from childhood. Now it seems that the Lord has heard my prayers.'

A letter which M. Bonnard wrote to his parents unfolds his sentiments more fully, and they are so noble and generous that we may well preserve the record of them.

'My dear parents,' he writes, 'within a short time my whole destiny has changed. But take courage; if the Lord strikes with one hand He heals with the other; if God be for us, in vain will hell be let loose upon us. . . . When you receive this letter you may be sure that my head has fallen under the sword, for it is not to be forwarded to you till after my martyrdom. I shall die for the love of Jesus Christ; the wicked will put me to death out of hatred for that holy religion which you taught me in lessons so wise and practical, and which I came out to preach in these distant lands—out of hatred of that religion which holy apostles and millions of martyrs have sealed with their blood. I shall die a martyr. Yes, my dear parents, I shall be sacrificed like Jesus Christ on Calvary. I hope to ascend to Him in the country of the blessed. Thus, then, my dear father, my dear mother, my dear brothers, rejoice, one and all; for already my soul will have ascended to the abode of the elect. If I can do anything for you before the throne of the Sovereign Majesty, I shall certainly not forget you who have loved me so sincerely, who have done so much for me. Do not weep for me; I feel happy in dying thus; I am happy in having to bear this cangue and this chain. From my early youth I have desired such an end; now that the Lord has heard my prayer, I kiss my chains with respect, and my heart throbs with joy at seeing myself so adorned. What more shall I say to you, my father and mother? I should like to console you; I should like to dry your tears. I should like also to pour forth my heart into yours once more in this world. But what other consolations can I give you than those afforded by our holy religion? If your parental tenderness should be moved in reading this letter, reflect that my sufferings, which I think myself so happy in bearing for the love of Jesus, will all be over long before you read these lines, and that my soul will have been transported into the heavenly kingdom. Endeavour, all of you, to save your souls by constantly turning your thoughts to the happiness of heaven. It is above, in that blessed home, that I hope to meet you. There I await you all; do not fail to come. The hour has struck; I cannot finish.

'Most affectionately yours,
'BONNARD.'

His execution took place on the 1st of May. A single blow severed his head from his body. The body and the head were recovered by the Christians, but with difficulty. A boat had been made ready, and the remains were placed on board, and were carried off to be sunk in some unknown spot, that the Christians might never get possession of them. But the Christians were on the alert. Another small boat was waiting, and when the pagan vessel moved forward it was anxiously watched: it was never lost sight of, and when the precious relics were dropped into the sea, the spot was well noticed, and soon one of the Christians dived down to the bottom, and successfully, for he brought back with him the prized treasure, and quickly conveyed it to the Bishop.

'At one in the morning,' says Mgr. Retort, 'our fishermen arrived with this sacred burden at the door of our college. It was at once dressed in all the sacerdotal ornaments, and placed in a handsome coffin, the gift of a Christian family. Up to the evening of the next day it remained exposed in the middle of the college church, with torches by the side. It was then buried with the ceremonies of the ritual. I was myself the celebrant, assisted by M. Legrand, two Annamite priests, and all the scholars. Very few others were allowed to be present, and all was done almost in whispers. His body therefore reposes entire within our college. O, how holy he looked stretched in his coffin, dressed in his priestly garb! One might have thought it an ivory statue of finest workmanship. His head well placed upon his neck, he seemed to be enjoying the sleep of peace, or rather it was the appearance of one in an ecstasy.'

But these two martyrdoms were not simple outbursts of bad feeling or mere chance occurrences, although there was a good deal of accident in them; they were indicative of a steady increasing dislike of the Christians, and a result of earnest conferences that had been going on in the palace of the king. At Huè, at this time, there had been much discussion on the subject of the treatment of the Christians. Some of the king's advisers urged him strongly to root them altogether out of the land; these counsellors were for no half measures, but for doing the thing completely, and amongst them was one of the most powerful mandarins, a bitter enemy of the Christians. But there was another party to whom such projects seemed harsh and unjust. They did not profess any friendliness towards the Christians, and they allowed that their religion was bad; but they said that the Christians were good subjects, that their conduct was quiet and orderly, that they paid their taxes and fulfilled their civil duties like others, and that in many respects they might be compared with their neighbours advantageously, for they were more free from crime, and showed a charity that could be seen no where else. This religion also, they urged, had been now for a long time established in the country, and those who professed it had received it from their ancestors; they were very much attached to it, and it would be useless to try to persuade them to give it up; and as for rooting out the religion entirely, the Christians were too numerous for such an attempt, and it would be as injurious to the kingdom as it would be cruel. At the head of this party was a man of great weight, a grand mandarin of Tonking, governor of extensive provinces, whose services had gained him much reputation. His name was Thuong-giei. He had had some kind relations with Mgr. Retort, and in different ways had shown his considerateness towards the Christians. The king's hand was thus restrained; and all that the Christians had to bear were occasional annoyances and injuries. One of these, a little later, in 1855, was an irruption into Ke-non. Ke-non was a principal college, the residence of M. Jeantet, the coadjutor, where he taught the young students preparing for the ecclesiastical state. It was a beautiful spot. 'It stands,' we are told, 'within three enclosures, with a circuit of tall bamboos, and through it runs a small river by which a boat may glide down to the sea. In the grounds is a succession of fine lakes, in which are an abundance of excellent fish; scattered about is a variety of fruit trees, pomegranates, oranges, bananas, mangoes, and others; and numerous little paths as well as broad terraces afford walks where the inmates may converse, meditate, or pray, away from the world and without a sound to distract, except it be the sweet warble of the birds; and then, by mounting the hill close by, as the sun sets, you may look out on a magnificent prospect, an immense plain that yields its two harvests a year, furrowed with rivers, and dotted all over with villages that are seen peeping out of bamboos and groves of verdant trees, closed in on the west by the lofty peaks of grand mountains.' Mgr. Jeantet had notice of the approach of the soldiers, and had just time to make his way to a cavern in the mountains. Although the danger was transient, and his absence from the college was not long, in the interval a chance occurrence very nearly proved fatal to him. One of the pupils thoughtlessly stopped up the entrance of the cave where they were hiding, and the fumes of a charcoal fire nearly suffocated them. One of the party dropped down senseless, and before it was too late the peril of their situation was discovered. The college itself on this occasion was not injured, but there was much depredation and loss of property.

The year 1856 was a memorable year in these annals. The missionaries were very busy. They moved about, and the work went on as if there was nothing to fear. It seems, as we look back on this year, that the missionaries were then taking their last farewell of each other and of their flocks. Stormy days were fast approaching, when they would have to separate, to wander on the mountains, to lie in caves, to be hunted like wild beasts, to stand before cruel judges, to have their bodies tortured, and to give up their lives. But this year they were still permitted to work, and to be happy for a short time in enlivenments, such as were seldom granted to them. Early in the year Mgr. Retort had a retreat at Vinh-tri, and afterwards an ordination; then, in the beginning of Lent, he set out on a tour, and spent some days amongst the large Christian populations of Kien-khe and of But-son. Then he went to Hoàng-guyen. Here was a college, and the place was dear to him, for it was his first station in Tonking. When he approached he was quickly surrounded by friends, who crowded anxiously to behold their old pastor. Twenty-four years had passed since it had been his residence. On his arrival the neighbouring villages poured out their congregations, eager to visit him; they came in quick succession, first in large bodies, then single visitors, men and women and children. 'Some of them,' says M. Galy, who recites the story, 'were over fifty when the

Bishop was amongst them, and now their children were advancing to old age, and their grandchildren, whom the Bishop had baptised, were men and women with families. A word from his lips suited to their age, some question as to the state of their family, some reference to past times, was to old and young alike a subject of pleasure. You could see their faces beaming with delight; and the Bishop, too, it was plain, was no indifferent observer. One very old woman, the mother of the chief of a canton, on the very first day had been brought to Hoang-guyen, and made happy by her interview with the Bishop, who had treated her with marked kindness. On her return she said to her children, 'God has granted me the favour of living till I could once more see the *Din-they-hien*. Now He may call me to Himself when He will. I die content.' And a memorable Easter closed this busy Lent. The solemnities of the Holy Week having been duly observed, Easter-day was celebrated with unwonted magnificence. The church was decorated. There was Pontifical Mass with music, and a sermon. There were numerous communions, and a privilege not common in this land was allowed, the Exposition of the Blessed Sacrament for adoration. The Bishop has told us how happy those days were. They were 'one of the most pleasant epochs of my life,' he says. He was in good health, and in the midst of friends, and in the seclusion of one of his loved colleges. For 'Hoang-guyen is a dependency of Vinh-tri, where we have eighty scholars, where there are buildings and gardens surrounded by ponds and bamboos, forming a little oasis, a residence to be contemned by no one.'

There was in the same summer, on the Feast of St. Peter's, at Vinh-tri, a gathering of the missionaries of the vicariate. The Bishop and M. Galy* arrived first. Mgr. Jeantet, with a band of students from Kenon, candidates for ordination, was the next; MM. Castex and Titaut and Venard came together from Hoang-guyen; afterwards MM. Charbonnier and Saiget, and last MM. Theurel and Mathevon. One party came down the great river Song-cai, another by a smaller stream, others on foot. Altogether there were two bishops and eight missionaries, and they remained in each other's company for weeks. The first object was their spiritual retreats. Then there was another retreat for the students, and then the ordination. The grand celebration of the Festival of St. Peter's closed the business of the season. But the work over which had brought them together, the friends did not at once separate; they lingered still in their beautiful retreat, and July had nearly drawn to an end before they retired from the cool and happy shelter and the enjoyable intercourse, soon alone to confront a storm of danger such as even this land had never seen before. The murmurs of its approach were very shortly heard. It was rumoured that Tudoc was irritated by the recent appearance of a French vessel on the coasts of Cochin China, that there had been some hostilities, and that the Christians were regarded as implicated in the business.

* M. Galy had returned from France for some years.

What had passed was this. The Catinat, a French ship of war, had appeared off Touron with letters and presents from the French ambassador, M. Montigny, for the Annamite monarch, but these advances had met with a rebuff. Tudoc refused alike letter and present. Some hostilities followed, and subsequently more serious complications; and instead of this visit of the French mending the condition of the Christians and the missionaries as was desired, the result was to stir up a fury of hatred that completely stopped the missionary work, desolated the Christian villages, and spread ruin and misery over the whole land.

It was towards the end of February 1857 that the storm first broke upon Vinh-tri. All through the month the mandarins had been busy. They had been searching for proscribed objects and persons. One large village, the centre of a Christian population of eight thousand, had been invaded, and eight prisoners, amongst whom were two catechists and the mayor of the village, had been led away by the soldiers. An old woman, bearing letters to M. Galy, had been stopped, and she had been tortured to force her to give information. At length, on the morning of the 27th of February, it was known that a mandarin and soldiers were approaching Vinh-tri with the intention of commencing operations there. MM. Charbonnier and Venard were at that time at the college with the Bishop. All hurried off to their hiding-places. The Bishop went down into an underground cell, hardly better than a grave; the two priests retired into a hollow space prepared between two walls. The mandarin in this instance was friendly, and did not conduct the search very strictly. No discovery was made, no great injury was done. The college, hidden under its trees, was not even noticed. But the mandarin did not leave the village without some prisoners. One of these was Father Paul Tinh, whose name has been already introduced, whom the Bishop calls a remarkable man, and who really was so. He was now an old man, being sixty-five years of age, and was a principal man at the college, being alike professor of Latin and director. When he was very young he had conceived the desire of imitating the old hermits of the desert. At the time he was a Latin scholar in one of the colleges, and had successfully completed his course, but, urged by this strong wish, he stealthily made off to the mountains, and for a time sustained himself on the roots and fruits of the forest. But coming down one day for confession to M. Eyot, he was persuaded to return to his college, and, having completed his course of theology, he received the tonsure from the Bishop of Gortyna. After that he filled various positions of trust. He taught the Annamite language to M. Rouge; he was sent to Laos by Mgr. Havart, to learn something of the dispositions of the people, and to ascertain the readiest access into those regions; he was employed as a courier to introduce missionaries into Tonking; and Mgr. Retort, when he was going to Manilla for consecration, chose him as his companion. On his return Paul brought back with him M. Tailliander, and then he fell into the hands of his enemies. Seven years he was in prison, with the cangue on his neck, and in chains; and seven times he had been sentenced to death, and as often respited. Then he was ordered into banishment, but owing to the amnesty at the beginning of the reign of Tudoc he obtained his freedom. He was thought worthy, after the proofs he had given of his great qualities, of instant promotion to the priesthood, and as quickly as possible he passed through the previous orders to the service of the altar. Vinh-tri then became his residence, and there he so approved himself as to be highly valued by the Bishop. His present capture was a consequence of his heroism. For the safety of the Bishop and the missionaries he presented himself at the entrance as the master of the house, and, being recognised as a priest, was captured and thrown into prison. At first it was supposed that a release might be managed, and that a sum of money would restore him to liberty. The chief mandarin was quite willing to grant the favour, but he found himself unable; the commands from Huè were imperative, and they were that this priest should be instantly executed.

So on the 6th of April, twenty-nine days after his arrest, he terminated his life as a martyr. The following letter, written twelve days before his death to his brethren and pupils in the college, shows what was the state of his mind:

'Paul Tinh, in prison and loaded with chains for

Jesus Christ, to all his dear brethren, the masters and pupils of our College of St. Peter, greeting.

'From the day when, by a special providence of God, I was removed from amongst you, you have ever been in my thoughts; and it is to give you proof of this that I now open my mind to you. Praise God for His goodness in all He has done for me. In an instant He has done what neither I nor any other could conceive. Praise the Lord, O my soul! My spirit hath rejoiced in the God of my salvation, because He hath looked on the humility of His servant. Praise the Lord, for He is good, and His mercy is without end. We are now in the field of battle. We want help. Assist us, then, with your fervent prayers, that the Lord may finish what He has begun. Brother Luong, your fellow pupil, though weak in health, has not failed in courage before the mandarin; he has done his part by word and act to animate the mayor and the other arrested with us, to be firm in their purpose, to die rather than to apostatise. But though the spirit is willing, the flesh is weak! Pray, then, much for me and them, that none of us may have the shame of being overcome.

'My three companions, besides the cangue with which they are loaded, are in chains during the night. I have only the cangue. This prison-life is truly painful to human nature; our dungeon is so dark that we can scarcely see anything at mid-day. Add to this darkness the stench, the mosquitoes, the heat and smoke of the fire, and you may have a conception of the misery of our abode. But I give God thanks that in the silence in which I am I can meditate at my ease. I have the happy confidence that nothing will be able to separate me from the charity of Jesus Christ: neither prison, nor hunger, nor the sword, nor death, for Christ alone is my life.

'Do not think that what has befallen us is for our loss or misfortune. It is only a wholesome correction, which at the moment seems painful, but in the end will work for us an exceeding weight of glory. When Jesus Christ slept in the boat, and His disciples, in the fear of shipwreck, cried out to Him, "Lord, save us, we perish!" He awoke, and commanded the wind and sea, and there came a great calm. So just now, Jesus seems to sleep while we are in tribulation, but his sleep is not an abandonment. He will soon awake, and change our afflictions into joy. The wisdom of God is infinite; He tempts us but to try us; He strikes but to heal us; the wounds that come from His fatherly hand are for our salvation.

'The martyrdom of blood, we know, is only occasional. God grants it to a few as a pure favour, not from a consideration of their merits; but the martyrdom of the will and the heart may be the lot of all. The new Jerusalem, the Scripture says, has twelve gates. It is not given to you to enter by the red gate of the scaffold; other ways will be opened to you; and, however different they may be, they all lead to the same centre, they all conduct to the same end, which is the possession of God. No; it is no chance by which I have fallen into the hands of the wicked; it is by the disposition of the Divine will.

I thank Him with my whole heart, and I earnestly pray to Him for our Bishop, our missionaries, our priests, and for the whole Tonkinese Church. May the Lord guard and protect them, and you also, my dear friends; and may He make you grow more and more in virtue! I may with truth say that the hour of my dissolution is at hand. I have kept the faith, I have finished my course, and I hope that the just Judge will give the crown of justice not only to me, but also to all who love His coming. On the point of suffering martyrdom, I write you these few lines as a testimony of my love for you. Love one another, obey your superiors, observe the rules of the community; by faithfulness in small things you may gain heaven. After my death, if I should have any power with God, I promise never to forget you. Adieu.

'P. TINH, Priest.'

Brother Luong mentioned in this letter was a catechist, who, with the mayor of the village and another Christian, was taken at the same time as Father Paul. These three were all sent to distant exile.

Although on that visit of the mandarin the Bishop was allowed to get off so easily, he was not allowed to remain long at peace. A few days after, another attack was made, and this time it was in great force. A military mandarin, at the head of a thousand soldiers, conducted it; but the mandarin who had before proved their friend was with him, and again very considerably averted the evil consequences of the visit. He got the management of the affair in his own hands, and a second time the village and college were saved. But some of the college buildings were pulled down, and the wreck began that would soon destroy altogether college and village, so long distinguished as the chief residence of the bishops of this vicariate. On this occasion the Bishop and the two priests did not stay for the mandarin's visit. They made off betimes in their boat, silently and unnoticed gliding down the river that runs by the college. Through Lent, Mgr. Retort lived with M. Charbonnier on the mountains, in a hut, at the foot of a gigantic rock, not far away from a small Christian village. They seldom ventured out of the dwelling, night or day; for there was a double danger to deter them—their persecutors and the tigers, which were numerous: 'And that very year,' says Mgr. Retort, 'they had devoured fifty Christians and many more pagans. 'In our hermitage,' the Bishop says, 'we spent some truly happy days, constantly occupied in reading, study, corresponding with our brethren, or praying to God with all our hearts. The time passed with astonishing rapidity.' On Holy Thursday they went down from the hills to the large Christian village of Kien-chi, in order to bless the holy oils. All was done in the night—the service and the journey. The Bishop was ill at the time, and fainted during the ceremony. The paschal solemnities of this year were a contrast with the glorious scene of the year before. In the darkness of the night, in their little cabin, both the Bishop and

M. Charbonnier said their Easter Mass in solitariness. They were called away from this retirement by the news of the illness of M. Castex, the pro-vicar-general: they remained at Hoang-guyen till he died. Afterwards Mgr. Retort ventured to return to Vinh-tri, and even to hold an ordination. For a time the suspended duties of the college were resumed. There was, indeed, a little interval in which missionary work could again partially go on, but it was short; and what hopes had been entertained soon faded away. The last days which the Bishop spent in that loved college were, indeed, sad ones. Nothing can be more sad than the language in which he has described them. 'We sat at home,' he says, 'like a bird upon a branch, ever harassed by fresh reports—that we had been seen by spies, that we had been already denounced, that the mandarins were coming to attack our village, and that so the village would be pillaged and many Christians killed.' They never felt themselves safe. They went from one hiding-place to another—to their boats on the river, to their dark subterranean cavern. It was a perpetual restlessness, and bad news was constantly coming. Fathers Dominic Dat, Peter Khang, Dominic Hien, all of Central Tonking, had been, one after the other, taken, imprisoned, and put to death. The large populous village of Ngoc-duong had been pillaged and destroyed. At last the destruction came more close. One of his own colleges, Song-nha, where Mgr. Jeantet then was, fell under suspicion. The church was destroyed, and the establishment broken up, and complete ruin only averted by payment of a heavy fine. The panic daily increased; and Mgr. Retort at length came to the conviction that Vinh-tri must be abandoned. It was a severe trial to himself and to the poor Christians; but there was no remedy. If he stayed, and was discovered in the village, its complete ruin would be inevitable. Unmoved by the fear of these consequences, the Christians asked him not to go. 'Stay with us,' they said; 'that if we must die, the fathers and the children may die together.' But the Bishop knew well that it was best to retire, and so he replied: 'If we must die, it is our wish to die alone, for God and for you, and without bringing you into trouble; we confide to Jesus and Mary your persons, your goods, and all we have here; we leave you under the care of the holy Guardian Angels; and for ourselves, we will go and seek in the mountains some secret retreat.' This was the final breaking-up of the college. In the deserted houses there remained a few old servants and five Annamite priests, lingering there to watch the progress of events, but hardly daring to trust themselves within the village, and passing the night in their boats on the river.

The mandarin, who was governor of Nam-dinh, was a cruel monster, who hated the Christians. He expressed his contempt for them in the most insulting language, posting notices on the gate of the city, of which the following is a specimen: 'Is it possible that people born in this great kingdom can give up the traditions of their ancestors to observe the bad practices of the religion of Europeans? What extreme folly! Have any of you ever been in Europe, so as to be able to form a conception of its customs? I once visited it in my youth, in the way of business, and what I learnt was this: there are no more than seventeen large villages, whose inhabitants are poor and barbarous; and the soldiers are not so many as there are in the single province of Nam-dinh. Can you hope for anything from them? So little are they able to help you, so powerless are they against our king, that should they appear on our coasts with their ships of war, I would, to show my scorn, without any fear, go down and open my theatre before their eyes. And what can you expect from the priests of Jesus and their followers, who are put to death, and sent into exile, and their God does not interfere to deliver them from our hands?' So he went on with his mockeries, urging the Christians to burn their books, to desist from concealing the priests, and to conform themselves to the customs of their country, which, he said, would insure their happiness. And when he had succeeded in making the poor Christians trample on the cross, he was not satisfied; he would then order them to take the rattan, and strike their brethren who refused to follow their example—to strike the crucifix, and insult it with blasphemous words. And that was not enough; they must also burn incense before the idols, bow the knee before them, and distinctly promise and give a written pledge that they abandoned their religion for ever, and agreed to forfeit their lives if false to their word. And, after that, he would keep them some months in bondage, employing them in the most degrading menial offices, that after such warnings they might sincerely abjure a religion that had brought them into such disgrace and trouble.

The series of sorrows of this year was truly calamitous. One of the first was the sacking of Ke-hanh, a large and flourishing Christian village, where there was a college and one of the homes of the priests. Spies had noticed the group of young Latin scholars and two Annamite priests, and had spoken of them as conspirators. So a large body of soldiers, with a crowd of what were named *heroes of the country*, came round the village, and commenced the work of desolation. The church was destroyed, and the home, the convent of the poor nuns, was over-run; the property of the church in large quantities was burnt in the public square, or carried off for profane uses; three students, a catechist, and fourteen of the principal inhabitants were arrested, and loaded with the cangue. The two priests and the rest of the pupils contrived to escape by forcing a passage through the bamboo fence, and making off over the fields. Those who were taken captives were very roughly used. A simple beating was not enough. Fifty blows of the rattan tore their flesh terribly; and they bore their suffering with courage. But when the red-hot pincers were produced, their hearts failed. All gave way but three: Chuphap, a lad of fifteen; the village chief, named Xa-tri, a man of fifty; and an old man upwards of seventy. The boy was firm throughout. He was flogged; he had to kneel on the nailed plank (a terrible punishment), and to continue kneeling a considerable time;

and he was burnt with hot pincers, and five large pieces of flesh were torn from his body; but he never yielded. It was not so with Xa-tri. The sight of the heated pincers had at first intimidated him, and with the others he had trampled on the cross. But afterwards his remorse was stronger than his fear; and in the prison he had met Father Khang, whose words encouraged him; so when his cangue was about to be removed, he boldly spoke his mind, and declared that the religion of Jesus was the only true religion, and that he would not abandon it; that he had been brought up in it, and that he would die in it. The old man, either from his great age or through a bribe, got off more easily; he received sixty strokes of the rattan, and was then dismissed.

Bishop Retort's last days were melancholy indeed, and sometimes he seemed almost to sink under the weight of his heavy burden of sorrow. One day, he tells us, when he was unusually sad, the many trials of his past life in Tonking coming before his mind, he could not help exclaiming in the presence of MM. Charbonnier and Mathevon, who were with him, 'O, that before my death I could only have had a few years of complete freedom, just to know what it was! What happiness should I have thought it. Yes; what happiness not to be obliged to lie hid like a criminal, to be able to preach the Gospel openly to all—to the mandarins as well as others, to labour without hindrance, and to give my whole energy to the good cause! But it is useless to expect it.' On this his two faithful friends interposed:

'What, my lord,' said they, 'are you not happy in suffering the many bitternesses of persecution? Ought you not to be content with the many and glorious crosses that the Lord has been pleased to send you? Recollect that on the day of your consecration you took as the arms of your episcopal dignity the two crosses of St. Peter and of St. Andrew, your glorious patrons, and that your motto was "Fac me cruce inebriari."' 'Say no more,' replied the Bishop; 'I know what you mean, and you say well. The will of God be done. May Jesus and His cross triumph! We will accept whatever tribulations His Divine Providence may send us.'

The Bishop's life was fast drawing to a close. Six months more of wandering, of risks, of escapes, flying from place to place as he was hunted by his enemies, and all was over. A fortnight before his death he concluded his last letter, and from that letter we can well understand the bitter trial which he had to bear. He does not say much of himself, where he has been, or what he has undergone; but one after another in full detail he repeats the subjects of his sorrow in the heavy calamities that have fallen on his mission. Villages, colleges, churches disappearing under the terrible hatred that has broken out against the Christians, Christians driven out from their homes, captives thrown into prison, catechists and pupils and priests hurried away to death and to exile. It is a melancholy picture. Good Friday was the date of his previous letter. From that time he takes up his story.

'A few days after Easter Nam-huan was blockaded. A bribe arranged that difficulty.'

'Father Kuang arrested.' He, too, was freed by a sum of money.

'Sixty principal Christians of Vi-hoang arrested.' Some of these escaped, some were let off for money, and some apostatised. Ten were sent into exile, and one, the most wealthy of the Christians of Vi-hoang, died for his faith. In the beginning of May came out fresh stringent orders to compel the Christians to trample on the cross. Then followed the blockade of Cangia, and much misery and loss of property, some apostasies, and some additional exiles.

This month also some very disastrous circumstances occurred. Letters were intercepted, which made revelations very mischievous to the missionaries. Their names and their homes were made known. Mgr. Retort and several missionaries and Annamite priests were in consequence denounced by name, and spies and informers were more busy than ever, eager to obtain the reward promised for their capture. Towards the end of the month one of the Annamite priests was arrested.

But it was in June that the flood of troubles set in. It was a month full of misery. One tale of sorrow after another reached the ears of the harassed Bishop, and has been marked down by him in his journal. 'On the 11th of June,' he writes, 'the mandarin of Kecho blockaded the villages of Hoang-guyen, Bai-do, Bai-vang, Dong-tee, Cham-theiong,

Cham-ba, and Con-biesi; they arrested a deacon and six other inmates of our college, three Christians, a pagan, and their wives, principal inhabitants of the place; our college, the refuge, and the churches of these villages were pulled down and burnt; and of those who were arrested, one was sentenced to death, three to penal servitude for a year and a half, three were ransomed, and the rest sent into exile.' Hoang-guyen was one of his loved colleges. It was the spot in which he had spent his earliest missionary days; it was there that two years before he had passed that happy Easter, and only the previous year there he had sat by the death-bed of M. Castex; and now Hoang-guyen, with the cluster of villages of which it was the centre, was desolated.

And next come Ke-non. 'On the 15th of June blockade of Ke-non for the first time, and then again the second time a few days after; the arrest of one of the pupils, and some ten others, Christians and pagans, the destruction of our establishment, and the confiscation of our gardens and fields.' Ke-non was the home of Mgr. Jeantet, and the theological college. What a pang went through his heart when he learnt this new destruction! 'It is an immense loss to the mission,' he says.

But worse news follows. 'On the 19th of June the blockade of Ke-vinh, the arrest of five pupils and thirty-three principal inhabitants, nineteen of whom are said to be condemned to death, the complete destruction of our community, and the pillage of our effects. The village is now being destroyed, the

Christians are being expelled, and their houses are given over to pagans. It is a frightful desolation. A military post has been formed at the head of the village, our garden has been completely trenched, and so have the sites of our houses. Many things we had buried have been found, and amongst them what was left of our wine for Mass. The convent of our nuns, the house of our tailors, and that too of our printers are quite destroyed. Buried in the ground there was still a considerable sum of money; we do not know whether it remains, but should it be so, it is out of our reach, and we have nothing left to provide for our wants. We are now living on borrowed money, and we owe more than a thousand taels.'

Ke-vinh is of all names the dearest to the missionary in Western Tonking. For nearly a century it had been the episcopal residence; it was the earliest college and seminary, the resort of each new missionary as he entered the country. Mgr. Reydellet had formed it. Ke-vinh was then a small Christian village. It was now a large one, and all around were many more villages, and all of them thronged with Christians. In the days of Minh-Menh it had been desolated, but Mgr. Retort had restored it and brought it to its glory. His community was that Vinh-tri, of which we have so often spoken, with its spacious church and ample accommodations for priests and catechists and scholars, its gardens and walks and trees. All was now gone.

But there are more sorrows yet before this fatal

month closes. 'About the same time the blockade of Kenguoi, the destruction of the convent, the dispersion of the nuns, the pillage of the rice, theirs and ours, and of all their effects; the sale of their gardens and fields, and of ours too, all confiscated to the public exchequer.'

At Kin-son, the arrest of one of our Latin professors and two pupils; at Vi-hoang, the arrest of a female of rank, named Cohai-nham, and her daughter; at Traingo, of another pupil and two principal Christians. The Cohai-nham here named was a person of much repute, very wealthy, and a great friend of the Christians, whom she had served in many ways, and so drawn on herself the particular hatred of the grand mandarin.

'On the 21st of June the blockade of Kien-khi, the arrest of the chief of the canton and of three others, the destruction of the splendid church.' Further loss was averted by the payment of a heavy fine.

'On the 27th of June the blockade of Ke-dua.'

It is needless to go on with this recital of woes. The Bishop, in his letter, prolongs them; they are continued through July and August into September, but there is no month like that unhappy June. Towards the close of the letter Mgr. Retort lets us see something of his own desolate condition, and how completely isolated it is. He is cut off from his old associates, and knows nothing of them except that they are in misery like himself. Here is his own picture: 'For six months I have had no news of M. Neron, and I do not know where he is, or if he is alive. M. Galy started in an Annamite vessel to seek aid from the Spaniards of Manilla, but what has become of him I do not know. My fear is that, like F. Salgot, he has been murdered at sea. MM. Titaut, Theurel, and Venard at first secreted themselves in the mountains of Dong-chien, living in a bamboo cabin, but spies found them out, so they went away and separated, and for the last two months I have heard nothing of them. Mgr. Jeantet, after wandering in the mountains of Lan-mot, found a temporary home with some peasants. One night he fell into the water and was nearly drowned. Now, I think, he is with the Christians of Bai-vang. I have heard nothing at all of F. Saiget; it is thought that he is in a pagan village with F. Dong. As to MM. Charbonnier, Mathevon, and myself, since we left But-son, on the 13th of July, we have lived sometimes in a Christian cottage, sometimes in a bamboo hut, and, again, under the trees, or amongst the brushwood. After toiling over rugged roads, rocks, thickets, and mud, we would lie down in the open air in the rain, with scarcely anything to eat, with little clothes to cover us, worn out with fatigue and grief, not knowing what to do or where to lay our heads, our sorrows have been and are still really beyond belief. Our whole party, besides our three selves, were three Annamite priests and six catechists. We have all been ill, and one of my men has died. We have not said Mass for the last four months; we have neither the furniture nor the place. Scarcely an Annamite priest is better off, so the sick

x

mostly die without the sacraments. Everything is dispersed, burnt, or some way destroyed. Few know where I am. I have no one to take my letters; those that are sent to me do not reach me, no one dares to bring them, so they are burnt. We are indeed at the last extremity.' This was the last communication of the worn-out Bishop with his friends in the outer world. In a day or two more he was prostrated by sickness, and the next tidings heard of him were that he was dead. The accounts first transmitted to Europe respecting the fate of this Bishop were truly sad. 'Mgr. Retort,' writes Mgr. Theurel, 'having been obliged to fly to the mountains, after wandering about nearly four months, constantly drenched with rain, sleeping in caves, suffering from hunger and occasionally from thirst, without having through the whole time the consolation of offering a single Mass, died on the 22d of October 1858. Attacked by a tertian fever, he had not strength to resist a third relapse, and he died in the midst of a forest, the haunt of tigers, in a cabin only six feet square, covered with the branches of trees.'

The details of these last six months of Mgr. Retort's life have been narrated for us by M. Charbonnier, his companion almost to the end. They left Vinh-tri together, and they were together at But-son. There they were joined by M. Mathevon. This missionary had very narrowly escaped being taken. While he was flying from his enemies he got unexpectedly into the midst of a new set of opponents; his guide and catechist were both taken; and it was only his own promptitude and presence of mind that saved him, for he broke away at once, and managing to conceal himself under some mats that were fortunately at hand, he avoided detection. But-son was not long a safe residence. Large bodies of soldiers were parading the country in search of the missionaries, and the Bishop thought it prudent to retire; nor was it at all too soon, for scarcely two days had passed before the mandarin and his men were in the village. But-son was close upon the mountains, and to them Mgr. Retort and his friends retreated. For days they wandered about, sleeping in caves or in the open air, as they could. Unfortunately it was the rainy season, and even in the caves where they found shelter the damp would ooze through and compel them to go out again. M. Charbonnier tells us of an escape of his own, which filled his heart with a sense of the kind providence of the Master in whose cause he was suffering. Wearied out with his fatigues he had lain down under a great pile of rocks, but the damp penetrated his mat, and he rose up and left the spot. Hardly had he moved away, when a large mass of rock came down just on the very place where he had laid his head. St. Peter's day is one of the days that M. Charbonnier notes. It was the great festival of the vicariate. How grand and happy had that feast been two years before, when so many missionaries met at Vinh-tri! This year it was a sad and weary one. In the hope of finding a cave, of which they had been told, at the top of a mountain, they set off on a toilsome march. They had to climb over steep rocks, and the Bishop, no longer strong, as he had been once, tired as he was, tripped and fell. M. Charbonnier, when he mentions this fact, tells us how it went to his heart to see his revered friend brought to this state. It was midnight when they reached the point they were seeking, but there was no cavern, only an empty well. Then they laid themselves down in the open air—the two missionaries on a flat stone, the Bishop on a clump of brambles.

On the top of that mountain they continued lying a whole day, exposed to a burning sun, parched with thirst, and with no more to eat than a little cold rice. The next day they changed their quarters. And now they found themselves deep in a forest, forcing their way through paths traversed only by tigers and wild animals. Once, at close of night, their situation was so perilous that the Tonkinese with them were in desperate alarm. They were in a deep gully of the mountain, shut in on all sides—a very lair of tigers. In such a place the attendants would not dare to sleep, so they lighted fires and kept watch through the night. All this while they were not far from But-son, and kept up their communication with it. A body of young men patrolled and brought them food. The mayor and two others kept their eye on the mandarin, that, should there be occasion, they might send timely warning. But the suspicions that had been aroused subsided, and the danger seeming to have passed, the fugitives returned to But-son. There they remained in close concealment, never venturing out of the house in which they were shut up; and to secure themselves from intrusive curiosity they hung up a sign which was understood to mean that there was a sick person lying within.

But again their stay in But-son was not a long one. The sub-prefect was not at ease. One day he sent for the mayor and angrily threatened him. He told him that there was a report abroad that there were two Europeans in his house, that the chief mandarin had an inkling of it, and that he would be down upon them some day and put them to confusion; that he himself should get into blame, but that the mayor would lose his head. So the poor man, when he appeared before the Bishop, was in terrible perturbation, and Mgr. Retort perceived that it was time to be off. Again, therefore, they sought refuge in the mountains. The country was inundated, so their journey commenced in boats; then they made their way into the forest, and for four or five days sheltered themselves in a hut. But tidings were brought which forced them to move. After a long day's journey they lay down in the open air; M. Charbonnier's bed was on an ants' nest, and of course he had no repose. On the next evening it was worse. The rain was pouring down, and their only protection was a tree. There was no spot where they could even sit down; so that they stood in the mud, with their breviaries and their little bundle of clothes—their sole remaining property—in their hands, with a mat held over their heads, a partial screen from the wet. They were making towards a point where there was a little body of friendly savages, and some of them here met them and became their guides. They moved onward through a succession of hills and valleys, and in the middle of the night were so exhausted that they could advance no farther; so, lying down under a tree, they got what repose they could. At break of day they were again on the march, and did not reach their destination till one in the afternoon; and a morsel of cold rice, the remnant of the evening meal, brought them by those kind savages, was all the food they had had for the day. In the little mountain hamlet they tarried a fortnight. They dared not remain any longer: the poor savages were afraid of the risk they ran, should such guests be discovered within their precincts. But they did not go far away. The savages built them a couple of huts in the neighbourhood, and there for the next six or seven weeks the Bishop and his little party had something like repose. They could not say Mass, but they could read their breviaries, and the New Testament, and an *Imitation*. They could walk about and converse together. But there was one disadvantage; the air was unwholesome, and they all fell sick; and one, a catechist very dear to the Bishop, died. Their sojourn here was in the end closed by the appearance of a party of hunters. The savages thought they were spies, and urged their visitors to go farther away, higher up on the mountains.

M. Charbonnier, soon after this, was separated from the Bishop, for Mgr. Retort sent him down to the plains to recruit his health, as he had been suffering from fever; so it is to M. Mathevon that we are indebted for the account of the last weeks of his life. 'In the beginning of October,' he writes, 'the savages again built us huts in the woods, and Mgr. Retort and I took up our residence in them. There were two huts, one for the Bishop and myself, and the other, which was much larger, for our catechists and three native priests. They were erected on an elevated spot, in the midst of trees, briers, and long grass, with morasses around, which made the place unhealthy. But we had no choice, and resigned ourselves to our fate, and here as always Mgr. Retort gave full evidence of his noble courage and piety. He was not to be said ill, but his many journeys had weakened him, and he suffered, though without any special symptoms.

'We had just received letters, telling us of the arrival of the French vessels at Touron, and we were cheering ourselves with the prospect of speedy peace. Bad news had been long wearying us, and now this glimpse of hope buoyed us up. A savage was ever on the watch. Savages daily, or nearly so, brought us rice that they had prepared for us. One old woman, a devoted creature, ought to be mentioned. She came almost every day with some companion or other, bringing provisions not obtained without trouble, running the risk of falling in with tigers, whose ravages are fearful, and toiling through the mud in order to reach us. "Is it that you do not fear the tigers that you come to us so often?" said Mgr. Retort to her one day, on seeing her arrive. "Venerable father," she replied, "if it were for any other errand I should not indeed stir from home; but as it is in care for you, I confide in the Lord and the Blessed Virgin that they will not permit harm to happen to me." And her faith always preserved her, though seventeen persons fell victims to the tigers during our sojourn in those parts.

'Things went on in even tenor till October was half over. Then, on the 16th Oct., Monsignor had an attack of fever that weakened him very much; on the 18th a second crisis left him altogether prostrate, and to fever was added dysentery of a most alarming character. A native priest, who understood something of medicine, tried some remedies, but without any success. On the 20th the fever increased, and when its crisis had passed the Bishop was so exhausted that he could no longer rise from his bed. On the 21st, a little after noon, he seemed to sleep, but this repose was disturbed by convulsive movements and an extraordinary snoring.' A day or two before, at the Bishop's order, a small hut, only six feet square, had been constructed for him. There he chose to lie alone that he might not be a trouble to others. The snoring and convulsive movements increased, and soon it became evident that the Bishop's last hour was approaching. M. Mathevon then proposed to him that he should receive the last sacraments, which he did with the greatest fervour. He could only speak in low whispers, and Jesus and Mary were the names he murmured. He was unable to receive Viaticum from the state of his tongue and throat. His agony lasted till nine o'clock Friday, October 22d, and then all was over. Vested in his episcopal dress the body was placed in a coffin, and the next day, amidst tears and sorrow, was borne away by the Christian natives, and interred in their village.

CHAPTER XI.

THE SPANISH DOMINICANS.

TONKING was at this time divided into four vicariates. Two of these, Western and Southern Tonking, were placed under the care of Mgr. Retort and Mgr. Gauthier, the other two, severally named Eastern and Central Tonking, were in the charge of the Spanish Dominicans. Central Tonking was from the first in the very front of the persecution. Some civil commotions that had prevailed there had drawn out a special animosity, and the governor of the province regarded the Christians with a marked abhorrence. Amongst the first victims was the vicar-apostolic, Mgr. Diaz, who, on the 21st of May 1857, was arrested in the village of Bai-chu, with two or three principal persons of this place. They were hurried away to Vi-hoang, the chief town of the province, there to await their sentence. For a short time there was an idea that the Bishop would not be executed, but it was erroneous; for after a detention in prison of a couple of months, on the 20th of July the sentence of his death arrived. The sentence, as it was presented to the king, was as follows:

'I, Nguyen-ton, together with the grand mandarins of justice and finance, in the consideration that the false religion of him who is called Jesus is forbidden by our laws under the strictest penalties; that, notwithstanding this prohibition, this European master of religion has dared to steal into this kingdom, with the bad purpose of representing falsehood as truth, and of making converts amongst the imprudent subjects of your Majesty; that, on being seized by the troops, he openly confessed his guilt; that he persists steadily in his error, and prefers to die rather than trample on the cross; that, moreover, had he a hundred mouths, he would not be induced to deny so execrable a crime;—

'Having thoroughly examined into the matters, we decree that this culprit be beheaded on an eminence, so that it may be in sight of all; that his body be thrown into the river; that thus all may be convinced that the orders of your majesty are in force, and that obedience will be compelled.'

Which sentence the king confirmed in these words:

'The European, Joseph An, chief master of the religion of Jesus, having dared, in spite of our laws, which strictly forbid this religion, to come into our empire and seduce our subjects by enticing them to embrace his worship, which crime he has confessed, and acknowledged himself guilty, we ordain and command that on receipt of these presents he be beheaded, and that his head be thrown into the air to intimidate others, and that afterwards he be thrown into the river, that so the cause of all this evil may be rooted out.'

A narrative of the proceedings at the execution was drawn up by a bystander, a Christian officer, and has been preserved for us by Mgr. Melchior, the coadjutor and successor of Mgr. Diaz. It runs thus:

'I, Nicholas Ky, now an officer of the army, obey my orders in declaring what I witnessed at the execution of Bishop An.

'I was on duty outside the walls of the town when I heard that Bishop An was to be put to death. I ran to the prison, and went to see the rev. father. I found the soldiers under arms, and Father An in prayer with his face turned towards the wall. The cangue was brought and placed round the neck of the victim, and he was led to the place of execution. The commander of the escort rode on an elephant, the colonel likewise, the inferior officers were on foot. The procession passed through the north gate, in the direction of the Seven Games, the usual place of execution. Although I was not one of the escort, I was able to accompany the prelate and keep quite close to him. There was a smile on his face; with one hand he supported his cangue, with the other he held up his chains; but he walked with difficulty, either from the weight of these things, or from the shortness of the chain, falling from his neck and attached to his feet, embarrassing him, and causing him to stoop. Being ordered to move faster, and saying that he was not able, he was told to let go the cangue, and take the chain in both hands, and he did as he was told. On arriving at the place of execution the troop formed a square round the martyr, the principal officer remaining outside the ranks, the colonel being close to the Bishop, as I was also. The Bishop was then asked in what direction he wished to look, to which he replied that he had no choice. Then a few rush mats were spread, and the Bishop's red carpet, with three garments which he wore in prison, and a cushion was placed, on which he was told to sit while they tied his hands behind his back. The executioner offered to strip off his clothes, but the Bishop said that it would suffice to bare his neck; and that was done. Next a smith with a hammer broke the chains from his neck and feet, and the cangue was removed. The officer cautioned the smith not to hurt the Bishop, who said he felt no pain. On uncovering the neck the executioner took away the rosary which was round it, but handed it to the officer, when I requested him to take charge of it.

'A stake was driven behind the back of the martyr, and he was tied with ropes passed over his breast and body. Bound in this way, for a time he remained on his knees in prayer. Then being asked if he was ready he said that he was, and the orders went out through the speaking trumpet that at the third sound of the tam-tam the executioner should strike. But he struck at the second, and almost severed the head from the body; another blow and the work was done, and the head rolled on the cushion. The commander, still aloft on his elephant, ordered the head to be thrown into the air, which was done. It was then placed in the basket. The body was then rolled up in the mats, and tied up tightly, with the soil saturated with blood, to be thrown into the river, that no one might possess themselves of the slightest relic. Two pagan soldiers, who had steeped pieces of linen in the blood of the martyr, were sent to prison by order of the commander.'

Such is the document signed with the narrator's name, Nicholas Ky.

Notwithstanding the earnest endeavours made to deprive the Christians of the honoured remains of their Bishop, his enemies were disappointed. The head in the basket was in the end discovered. It was not, however, till after a long interval and many an ineffectual search, for much pains had been taken to make the search in vain. A boat with ten rowers, all looking forward, and having strict orders not to look back, bore away the relics. Nothing could be seen, for the body and the head alike were both underneath the water, dragged on after the boat. An officer seated at the stern had the charge of cuting the ropes, and it could be done so secretly that when and where these treasures sank it would be impossible to know. But months afterwards, as if by chance, the head, deep in the mud, with the basket and the stones weighing it down, was drawn up unexpectedly by some fishermen, and Mgr. Melchior had the consolation of identifying it very shortly before his own turn came to suffer similarly from the same foe. But the sufferings of this latter Bishop were even worse.

It was less than a year after the death of Mgr.

Diaz when Bishop Melchior fell into the hands of his enemies. It was a sad year to the poor Bishop; he saw around him nothing but misery, and his heart was heavy under his many griefs. His own words alike reveal to us his unhappiness and some of the subjects of his affliction. 'My cheeks were still wan with the tears that I shed on witnessing the ruin of my mission,' thus he writes, February 22, 1858, 'and at the thought that if I should follow in the path of my predecessors, I should leave behind me nothing but the wreck of a vineyard once so flourishing and well-cultivated, when a new disaster came to increase my misery; it was the destruction of the town and Christian colony of Ngoe-duong, put into the hands of the mandarins by a traitor. And this wretch's villany knew no measure. The flames of the town, the death of several innocent persons, the arrest of many others, the complete ruin of the inhabitants, was not enough for his hatred; for he had conceived a bitter animosity against the young priest of the village, F. Dominic Huon, and only because this zealous priest would not listen to him when he opposed his purpose of building a church in the place; and because he had brought back to the fold some who had strayed from it, obliging this unhappy man himself to break off a scandalous connection.' We learn from the Bishop that this persevering renegade accomplished the death of the priest. The mandarin was willing to hush up the matter, and let him off, but the vindictive fellow opposed it; so the priest went to prison, and shortly after joyfully gave up his life for the faith. The same day four more Christians were beheaded, then eleven, then ten others, at intervals of two days.

The Bishop mentions also some instances of the bravery of the Christians under their trials. One was the hearty vigorous faith of an old soldier, a captain, who, standing by and beholding some Christian soldiers yielding to intimidation and denying their religion, boldly expressed his indignation, and who, though he thus brought down upon himself a most merciless beating, readily submitted to it. Another was the fortitude of some of the young boys brought up in the refuge; they would not be false to their faith, and although punishment followed on punishment they acted like little heroes. It was not simply that blows were to no purpose; but when their flesh was torn with the pincers, when they were ordered to kneel on the nailed planks, their resolution was equally firm; and at last when they were dismissed, they bore away as scars of honour the loved name they had refused to deny, stamped with a savage cruelty on their cheeks, and, loaded with chains, went away into exile.

One more letter came from this suffering Bishop; it was dated May 13. Three months had passed, and things had become worse. 'In the month of March,' these are his own words, ' the coming storm gave symptoms of its approach. April came in *furiis invectus*; complete ruin seemed to be threatened. The governor, who had already made himself so famous, now issued a decree that every Christian,

without distinction of age or sex, men and women,
old and young, should trample on the cross; and
every chief man in each district should in writing
make a public abjuration of his religion; that in
every house the family idol should be raised on its
altar, and that in every village it should have its
temple; and to make things worse, the execution of
this order was committed to persons only too eager
to avenge what they would call the wrongs of their
ancestors.' These harsh measures spread fresh desolation. The college of Ninh-cuong, before deserted,
and the village too were now completely ruined; the
college had been left in charge of two lay persons,
its sole occupants. One day two or three busy spies
came in with an officer, laid hands on one of these
persons, and were leading him off, together with a
little boy who happened to be there; but the people
of the village interfered, and the officer deserted by
his companions, was compelled to give back his
prisoners. But the poor people only made matters
worse, and brought down on themselves a double
weight of indignation. Next time came a troop of
soldiers with orders to destroy the town, a large one
with ten thousand souls. All was then confusion and
sorrow; but the chief of the village boldly came forward and surrendered himself. His name was Vonghuong-huy, and he deserves to have his name recorded. The Bishop knew him well, and held him
in much respect. He was no less distinguished for
his learning than for his virtue; and in this hour of
perplexity his constancy was a stay to the poor

Y

people who were so hardly used. He stood firm under the trial; no threats were of any avail with him; he would not trample on the cross. He had no fear, nor could they offer him anything that would allure him from his faith. He could speak up for it too. And in the prison his words and his example were a great encouragement, consoling and strengthening his companions.

The college became a complete wreck; it was torn down, and its materials either burnt or carried off by the pagans—even the trees surrounding it were not allowed to stand. All this while the Bishop was close by; he was in the neighbouring village of Kien-lai, the very village where some years before his predecessor, Mgr. Delgado, had been captured. It was the Holy Week, and in the middle of the night he had been consecrating the holy oils. The priests who had been assisting in the ceremony had gone away, and he and Father Estevez who remained with him were seeking some repose, when the report was brought that the soldiers who had desolated Ninh-cuong were approaching Kien-lai. It was a false alarm, but the anxiety of the panic was the same. There was the hurried attempt to hide every suspicious article that would indicate the presence of a priest; there was the careful search for some secure hiding-place for themselves. Just at the moment of this embarrassment, news of another kind reached the ears of the Bishop. Three additional fathers had just arrived in the country from Macao. Whether to regard the news as sad or joyful the Bishop did not know; 'but our situation,' he says, 'was so deplorable, we knew not where to conceal ourselves. Father Estevez, finding no other retreat, had come to join the poor sinner who is now writing to you; and the arrival of these three fathers, whatever joy it afforded us, greatly added to our embarrassment. But the Lord who sent these workmen into His vineyard did not abandon them. The Virgin who consoles the sorrowful shielded them, and on the 15th of last month, between twelve and one in the morning, we gave each other the fraternal kiss in the cabin occupied by F. Estevez. Two days we remained together, and then, not without regret, we were compelled to separate; our Christians were in a state of fear, and not without reason. Next day, in dread lest the mandarin might come, they destroyed the cabin. Then F. Valentin Berrio Ochoa with F. Riagno took up their abode in a house that had once served as a retreat for Mgr. Dalgado, afterwards for Mgr. Marti, and again for the Venerable Mgr. Diaz; and there F. Estevez and myself had found refuge in days of greatest danger.'

How worn and harassed the Bishop was is plain throughout his letter. He was surrounded with embarrassments, and he was almost alone. And when he wrote it was but a few weeks before he would be found out in his retreat, and fall into the hands of his enemies, to meet with a treatment which, amidst all the victims of cruel hatred of the Christian faith, with the exception, perhaps, of M. Marchand, is distinguished by a barbarity unmatched. We will return to his letter.

'The officers,' he says, 'went on enforcing the erection of pagodas; but happily, by means of the money brought us by F. Riagno, the vexations were evaded in most of the villages. A report has prevailed of late that an order has been issued for my arrest. I took the advice of my brethren on the propriety of giving myself up, but they were all against it; so I remain in my purgatory. The mandarin made his attack on our village of Kien-lai; but before he came he received a present of a hundred taels. Then he gave out that he had proposed to seize the European, but had received information that he had, several days before, gone away by sea; so he should leave.' Then the Bishop speaks of danger threatening one of the fathers, and of a bribe he had given to free a native priest from arrest.

'This father,' he says, 'had gone to visit a sick person, and had been surprised in the house by an officer. It was necessary to have recourse to a bribe, and this is done in other places. We feel the protection of the Holy Mother, whom we specially honour this month. To-morrow, *deo dante*, I hope to arrange for the election of a coadjutor. I am more than ever alarmed. F. Salgot, who was generally thought worthy of the dignity, left us in January to establish a college at Macao, and we have heard nothing of him since. The Chinese have spread a report that he was thrown into the sea. You will perceive, then, dear father, the painful position of your unworthy son. I am at present almost alone, with the responsibility of the whole weight of the vicariate on myself. I say almost alone; for Fathers Riagno and Estevez, who might have given me assistance, are both laid up with tertian fever. I am now quite tired, and will soon write at greater length. Do not in your prayers forget this vicariate, and especially its unworthy pastor. Should you go to Rome, and see the Holy Father, ask him to give us his blessing, and kiss his feet in the name of his prodigal son.'

The next tidings we have of this Bishop is that which is noted down in Mgr. Retort's melancholy journal of events. Thus it stands: 'July 8th. The arrest of Mgr. Melchior and two of his servants. July 28th. That prelate was literally hacked to pieces: his head, exposed for three days on the top of a pole, was afterwards crushed and cast into the river. His two servants were beheaded for the faith the same day.'

Mgr. Melchior was, indeed, arrested in the beginning of July, and led at once to Kecho, and was there massacred in the barbarous manner stated. His two servants suffered previously before his eyes. Then came the Bishop's turn. His hands and feet were tied to stakes. A sort of plank was then pressed down upon his breast. Five executioners, each ready with his axe, stood by. Then followed the bloody work. His head and hands and feet were cut off separately; his hands and feet first, and last his head. It was a prolonged torture, and the more so as the executioners did their work clumsily, and unnecessarily multiplied their blows. And there was the subsequent barbarity of crushing the head, and throwing it into the river.

But fierce as was the hatred indicated in these acts, what was done must not be understood as a mere wanton burst of irregular fury; it was but the merciless application to Mgr. Melchior of a law in force against rebels. The Bishop was treated as a rebel, and he was made to feel the weight of the angry feelings stirred up by the interposition of foreigners. The visit of the French to the coasts of Tonking, and the demands and threats of the French ambassador, had irritated the minds of Tudoc; and the Christians were regarded as the causes of this interference, and were made responsible for it; and additional local disturbances in Tonking had brought down all the violence of the hatred then felt on this Bishop, and it was not simply as a Christian, but as a political offender, that he was punished with that peculiar atrocity.

CHAPTER XII.

COCHIN CHINA DURING THE PERSECUTION.

THE great change which had taken place in the condition of the Christians, and the severity of this new persecution, had originated in a visit made by some French ships and a French ambassador to the kingdom of Tudoc. This visit was not at all relished by the haughty monarch, who, puffed up by the abject homage he received from his own subjects, was indignant that a stranger should dare to intrude upon him, and make suggestions he had no mind to hear. Throughout, the welcome that Tudoc gave to his guests was a cold one. First came the Catinat; it lay unnoticed off Touron—it could obtain no consideration at Huè,—and when, on his return to Touron, the French captain found his endeavours to open a conference ineffectual, provoked by a treatment so uncourteous, he battered down the forts at the entrance of the river. Soon after came the Capricieuse, and it met with a little more show of respect; but there was no alteration in the feelings of Tudoc; and whatever he might pretend, he was resolved not to treat at all. At last the ambassador himself, M. de Montigny, made his appearance. But it was a tardy one, and he came unattended by a force that might have induced a deferential hearing. Tudoc had been already provoked, and had been employing the interval in preparing himself for the visit. He had collected a considerable body of his best troops; he had laid in stores of ammunition; he had erected batteries, and had obstructed the entrance of the river, and was in a condition to despise demands which were not supported by anything beyond what the French ambassador could show—the small Chinese vessel in which he came, and the French ship which had preceded him. M. de Montigny very soon understood that Tudoc did not intend to listen to him; for the king never deputed any one to confer with him except a mandarin of low grade, who came, too, without any powers; so the ambassador retired; but in doing so he augmented the irritation already raised, for he left with a threat that he would return again, and would severely retaliate for any injury done to the missionaries or the Christians. So the cause of the missionaries and the Christians was mixed up with that of the invaders; and though they were far from intending it, the French by this visit, and by the mode in which it was conducted, were the means of drawing down upon the Christians a series of miseries of which we have yet only contemplated the beginning.

The Catinat's visit to Touron was in September, 1856. On February 7, 1857, M. de Montigny went away, disappointed in the object of his mission. From the very first the Christians had been made to feel the serious consequences that would revert on themselves. There was in Huè at this time a Christian mandarin of rank named Ho-dinh-hy. This man became at once an object of suspicion to his brother mandarins. A direct accusation was brought against him and laid before the king, and by the king's orders he was degraded and thrown into prison. The poor man under the torture of the rattan made some admissions that compromised several persons; and some things he said, and which caused a great deal of mischief, were not true. For he allowed that there had been intrigues with the French, and named a priest, F. Oai, who, he said, was implicated in them. He also gave the names of different Christian mandarins, and supplied other information that led to several arrests. But, although under the terrors of his punishment he showed some weakness, this mandarin was never false to his religion; he rejected offers of pardon which the king sent to him on the condition of apostasy, and besides, as far as he could, he endeavoured to repair his first faults. He was ready, indeed, to retract what he had said falsely, and he promised the Bishop that he would do so, though it was with a shudder that he thought of the terrible tortures that such an act would involve; but he was spared the trial, for he never had the opportunity. He bore several beatings afterwards when subject to his examinations, and when the day of his death came he confronted it manfully. He was kept in prison several months, from September till May, when the king confirmed the sentence of death. The terms of the sentence were as follows:

'Ho-dinh-hy, at one time a simple recorder, has gradually risen to the rank of a grand mandarin. He has dared to despise the laws of the kingdom, and to follow a perverse religion, and that without manifesting the least signs of repentance; and, what is worse, he has secretly sent his son to study at Singapore; he has visited the priest Oai, and consulted with him respecting the French ships. He is plainly a wretch with two hearts; he deserves death a thousand times; let him be beheaded at once to serve as an example to others. We further order that on three days successively five mandarins and fifteen soldiers lead Ho-dinh-hy three times round the interior of the town, through the markets and all the squares, and in each place the public crier read out the following proclamation: " Ho-dinh-hy is guilty of having practised a perverse religion. He is a rebel. He has no pity for his relatives, for he involves them in his condemnation; he has transgressed the laws of the country in not obeying the edict." Then he is to say, " The Christians declare that all who die in this way go to Paradise. Is it true? We know nothing about it. Where is Jesus, while Ho-dinh-hy is suffering? Why does he not come to release him?" This proclamation is to be published as widely as possible, that all may know that there is no help for those who are Christians. Further, let the criminal receive thirty strokes at each cross road, and when he shall have been thus led about three times, let him be publicly beheaded, that the Christians may be confounded at the sight, and may correct their errors. Let all men respect this command.'

Accordingly, on the 15th of May, five mandarins

and fifteen soldiers led out Ho-dinh-hy, or Michael, as the Christians called him, and in two different places he received thirty strokes. But he had now learnt to rejoice in his sufferings for Jesus Christ, and went back to his prison happy. The same process was twice repeated, on the 18th and on the 21st of May. Once, when they were about to flog him by a temple of idols, they told him to turn his face towards the idol, but he would not comply. The day of his death was May 22d. Early in the morning he was removed from his prison, and led out into the street but there, for some cause, he had to wait hours, which he spent in prayer. After a long delay the procession was formed; a mandarin on horseback in front of the prisoner, the four other mandarins following, lines of soldiers on each side. On the first mournful sounds of the tam-tam, the signal for moving, 'Michael,' says Bp. Sohier, who gives us the account, 'turned pale, and the sweat poured down his face. But soon he recovered, and afterwards there was no show of weakness.' Loaded as he was with the cangue he walked on rapidly, and with a firm step, so as to quite outstrip his escort. A crowd of pagans, with Christians mingled amongst them, were around. The man was loved and respected, and they wished to show him honour. Two priests were near him, unnoticed in the multitude, and more than once at a concerted signal they gave him absolution. He was dressed in poor simple clothes, which in a spirit of humility and penance he had adopted from his first arrest. Mats and carpets were spread at the place of execution, where, having arrived, he washed his hands, smoked his last pipe, arranged his hair and clothes, and then knelt down; and, on a signal from the mandarin, his head, with two strokes of the sabre, was severed from his body. His pagan servants, who throughout had shown their grateful feelings to a master who had been kind to them, took it up and conveyed it to his Christian friends. More than once while he was in prison, he had been visited by a priest, who heard his confession, and ten days before his execution brought him Holy Communion.

Active search was made for the priest Oai, whom Ho-dinh-hy had declared to have been in communication with the French, but the search was in vain. The soldiers were busy in An-van and Da-mon, two villages which were suspected as his resorts, and they arrested several persons, amongst them his sister Madeleine Ho, and Anthony Con, the mayor of An-van. In all there were twenty-four persons arrested. Six of them failed when ordered to trample on the cross, and amongst them were the four mandarins and the mayor of An-van; but this last made an effort to recover himself, and withdrew his recantation; but under the pains of the rattan he again yielded, and a second time denied his religion. Some others gave way under punishment, but the majority stood firm, and of the number was the girl Madeleine Ho.

The false statement about the priest Oai was a cause of further trouble to the Christians, for it was the occasion of the disgrace of the sub-prefect of the district in which Oai resided. The sub-prefect was a pagan, and by reason of his disgrace he conceived a most malevolent hatred towards the Christians, and out of revenge endeavoured to work them all the harm he could. And he soon had an opportunity of gratifying his feelings, for within his district there was some land, the property of Mgr. Sohier, which had been held for him by the mandarin Ho-dinh-hy. This property the sub-prefect got hold of, and would not give it up, and, soon after, he gained over a confederate, who helped in his mischievous designs. This partner was a Christian, a lawyer, who had been so much in the Bishop's confidence that he employed him to manage the business with the sub-prefect. But the man was false, and consented to sacrifice his friends, and unite himself with the pagan in all his bad purposes. And the malice which he afterwards showed was extraordinary. He wantonly forged a letter purporting to be from some catechists of the village of Kim-Long to a missionary, most damaging in its character, and implicating the Christians in projects of revolt; then he caused this letter to fall into the hands of the sub-prefect, and a number of persons were arrested. But Lay, so the lawyer was named, got himself into trouble as well as the Christians, for he could not prove his case, and was obliged to acknowledge his own treachery; but still the Christians were the sufferers; the catechists accused, as well as others, were imprisoned and beaten, and five of them died. Although the arts of their enemies were in a degree frustrated, the trouble that they caused went on for months, and, besides the arrests actually made, there was a widespread panic, there were inbreaks of soldiers, and Bishop Sohier in his retreat at Diloam only narrowly escaped.

In September 1858 the persecution received a fresh stimulus. On the first day of the month there appeared off Touron more French vessels, but this time it was a fleet, large and small vessels, with an army of French and Spanish troops, come with the purpose of redressing the wrongs of the Christians, and of freeing them from their miseries. There was no doubt at all in the minds of those who composed this expedition that with very little difficulty they should force the Annamite monarch to listen to terms; and the Christians were full of hope, and their hearts revived in the assurance that very soon their deliverance would be accomplished; and it might have been easily. Tudoc could not have resisted this force if there had been as much promptness and vigour as there was excess of caution. Touron was mastered as soon as it was attacked, a few shots were sufficient to reduce it, and it was in the hands of the French within an hour after their ships had taken up their stations. But when this was done, the army did not move; it stayed where it was, close by Touron. If Huè* had been at once the object of attack, if the ships without delay had steamed up the river to the capital, Tudoc could not have withstood them. He had not made his preparations, the batteries proposed to be raised were not built, the troops were not assembled, and he had not the means

* Letter of Bishop Sohier, who was living close by the capital.

of effectually resisting a power such as the united French and Spanish troops. The delay was ruin. The river was quickly barred, an army was brought together, the first awe of the Europeans subsided, and the opportunity once lost was never recovered. The French had some conflicts with the Annamites and worsted them, but they never advanced to Huè; they loitered on for months by Touron, and at length retired even from thence, and went away to Saigon. In this way the poor Christians were brought to an extreme degree of suffering. The whole fury and hatred which the invasion had stirred up fell upon them; and from this date the ardour of the persecution went on increasing till there seemed a prospect of Christianity being blotted out altogether from the land. Tudoc did not hesitate; up to this time he had held back the hands that wanted to act more vigorously against the Christians, but now he urged them on. He gave orders that crosses should be placed at the gates of Huè, and that every one who passed should trample on them; he required that every one who resided within the Inner City should show the same sign of hatred of the proscribed religion; he commanded crosses to be laid on the public roads, and that the passengers should put their foot on them; and there was a special scrutiny amongst the soldiers. Some thirty soldiers, who had been discovered to be Christians, and had refused to abandon their faith, had already been imprisoned and exiled; but much more stringent measures were now adopted. They were now called forward by hundreds, and ordered to give proof of the abandonment of their religion; many shrank from it, but very many bravely stood the test, and were willing to be beaten and to be thrown into prison, and sent off into exile, if not to sacrifice their lives, rather than be false to the name of Jesus. One stout soldier very early became conspicuous. He was a captain named Francis Trung, and refusing to trample on the cross, and declaring that he would never apostatise, he was put in irons and conveyed to prison. Reiterating his refusal on a fresh demand, he was cruelly beaten, and that a second and third time, receiving as many as a hundred and fifty strokes of the rattan; but, as he could not be moved, he was reported to the king, who ordered him to be executed. He bore his blows and the privations of his prison with courage, and said that he would readily give his body to be cut in pieces, and that he did not fear at all the cutting off of his head. In his love for the cross he asked that a cross might be formed with chalk on his neck, and this done, he presented it to the executioner. He was very earnest in his request for prayer, that his courage might be so sustained, and to gain the grace of perseverance he asked that a votive Mass might be said in honour of the Blessed Virgin. He died October 6th, rather more than a month after the French landing.

The severities of the persecution went on constantly increasing, and were sharpened by a succession of decrees, growing more and more stringent, and exacting heavier penalties from the Christians.

They were hauled up before the tribunals in large batches and thrust into prison; pressed to surrender their religion, and not trusted when they consented. The persecution was gradually conducted on a more systematic plan, and with the aim of stamping out the religion of the Christians. Every person of influence became a marked man, and no mercy was shown to him. Christian mandarins were carefully sought out and degraded, even though they abjured their faith; and if they would not, exile was their punishment or in the case of those of higher rank death. The influential men in the villages, the *daumucs* as they were called, *i.e.* those who had attained the age of fifty, were no longer allowed to remain in their villages, but were put under custody. The soldiers, too, were jealously examined, and strict endeavours were made to discover every Christian. The exactness and rigour of the decrees issued by the king may be perceived from the following specimen bearing date January 17, 1860:

'It is now a long time since the false religion of the Christians made its way into this kingdom. It has spread everywhere and seduced the people. Severe edicts prohibit it. Whenever they are denounced the Christians are punished; but so blind are those people, that still a great many adhere to that foolish religion. When without any cause foreign vessels came here, spreading alarm through the provinces of Quang-Nam and Gia-dinh, they made futile attempts to enter into an alliance with us, and wanted us to grant freedom of religious worship. This showed plainly what was the purpose of these barbarians in coming here. The followers of this perverse religion imagine that we will revoke our decrees at the desire of these savages. . . . They must be chastised then once for all; the wheat must be separated from the tare, the faithful from the refuse, that thus we may put an end to delusive hopes. The provincial mandarins know very well how many of these vile fellows there are, where they are living, and what they do. We have published an edict, ordering them to search out and imprison the most obstinate who are the chiefs of the sect. As for the old people, the women, and the children, we are not speaking of them; but all those who retain hostile feelings must be separated and dispersed in the neighbouring villages, and put under strict superintendence. Thus we clearly mark out who are to be imprisoned, who are to be dispersed, and who may be let alone. All the mandarins of the provinces must study this decree and strictly execute it. There are villages composed entirely of this low rabble; there are others in which the good and bad are equally mixed; and there are some in which there are only a few bad. The chiefs must be imprisoned, and so must those forward women who carry letters. Such as remain quiet, and such as apostatise sincerely, and all the simple and unlearned, as well as women and children, may be left in their own villages with guards to watch them. All the men who appear hostile must be dispersed in the adjoining villages, and put under the superintendence of the mayor and the chiefs of the district. But when there are only a few of these raff the good people of the village will suffice to keep them in order, and it is not necessary to choose officers for the purpose; but the leaders, and all who excite suspicion, must, notwithstanding, be arrested and put in prison. This is the business of the prefects and sub-prefects. Besides, all the youth over fifteen must be registered, and reviewed on fixed days, that it may be ascertained that all are present; and should any be missed, those who have the charge of them must be at once arrested and punished, and be obliged to find them, and failing to do so, must be severely punished. Similarly, all negligence of the prefects and sub-prefects must not be overlooked. In this way honest people will be separated from cheats, the good from the bad; and if there are any who maintain their bad feelings, they will by degrees be forced to give them up, and in the end they will become honest.'

This decree was supplemented by another, published in the following August, in which it was added: 'It is not long since we issued a decree dividing these sectarians into three classes: first, those who have apostatised, but are not sincerely converted; second, those who have refused to apostatise, but remain quiet; third, such wretches as are obstinate in their refusal to give up their religion. The first may be set at liberty, and may go back to their homes; the second must be imprisoned; the third, besides imprisonment, must be ignominiously punished. Those who are sent back to their homes must be placed under the charge of the pagans of the neighbourhood. We command the mandarins of the provinces, from the highest to the lowest, to see that these sectarians —men, women, and children—do not absent themselves. Further, the prefects and sub-prefects shall visit their villages, and review them and give them instructions. Lastly, every two months, all mandarins must send in an official report, stating how many have apostatised. These commands are clear. Our wish is this alone: to make our people perfect. This decree must be communicated to every mandarin of every grade, so that it may be obeyed, and the Christians may be obliged to abandon their religion, and in such a manner that there be no fear of their returning to it again.'

Such was the elaborate plan for breaking up the Christian villages, and eradicating the faith from the country; and gradually this plan was more and more worked out, and towards the end of the persecution even this plan was too mild for the vehemence of the hatred that had been aroused.

One of the first efforts was to lay hold of all the Christian mandarins, and as many as thirty-three were arrested. As they were mostly of inferior rank, exile or imprisonment was, with three exceptions, accounted sufficient punishment. Of these three, however, one died in prison, and another was let off because he was blind; only one therefore of the number was a martyr. This man's name was Captain Thi. He was in prison several months before he died, and anticipated his death with desire. 'I wish for one thing only,' he said; 'that is to be a martyr.' Of the thirty-three mandarins only three failed; all the others witnessed boldly for their religion.

Many Christians who were not martyred died under their sufferings in prison; amongst them was a principal man of Diloam, whose name was Peter Shuan, and who is highly eulogised by Bishop Sohier, who lived there. 'He was the king, so to speak, of the Christians in Diloam, and full of kindness to the European missionaries. It is to him that Mgr. Pellerin and myself are indebted for our safety in Diloam during fifteen years of persecution, and also for the building of our college only lately destroyed.'

The sufferings of a man named Cao may be narrated as a specimen of the deplorable condition of the poor Christians who were torn from their villages and placed under pagan custody. Cao with some other Christians had been transported to a pagan village, with the purpose of forcing them to abandon their religion. The heads of six families apostatised. Cao, however, would not follow their example. But he was awed by his enemies, and he fled away. His apostate brethren were employed to fetch him back. They went after him and found him; to move their pity he threw himself at their feet, and entreated them to let him go. But they would not listen to him. After he was brought back he again escaped, when he was a second time seized and bound, and lodged in the house of the mayor of the village. Hitherto the man had seemed timid and without any resolution, but under prolonged and severe trial he displayed an indomitable spirit. He was beaten, he was threatened, he was almost starved; but in vain. Day after day the same efforts were repeated, but his strength seemed to increase with the duration of the cruelties he had to bear. 'Do you suffer pain?' he was asked. 'I am a man like others,' he replied. 'Are my bones brass, or my flesh iron, that I should not feel pain? It is God's grace that sustains me.' 'Why,' he was then asked, 'has your Master, Jesus Christ, if He assists you, allowed your brethren to apostatise?' To which he said, 'The Lord Jesus assists those who are willing to receive His grace, not those who reject it.' Another time, when they saw him persist in refusing to give up his religion, notwithstanding their violent beatings, they searched him all over, to see if they could find the grace of God that gave him such strength. But he told them that God's grace was something that could not be seen. They then thought that the beating that they gave him was not hard enough. So they summoned another man for the work. 'Call Narn,' they said, 'and let him use the rattan.' Narn was an old soldier well drilled in the office, and he had compelled many a hardened villain to make his confession. So Narn came, and was told to strike two or three blows, and then to pause, and to draw blood at each blow. He went on up to sixteen, pausing at each second blow. After each two the cross was brought, and Cao was asked to trample on it, but he would not. It was dreadful agony, and the poor man cried out in his pain: 'O Jesus, O Mary, help me!' His body was as it were on fire; he was almost fainting away. 'Trample on the cross!' cried the mayor. 'No!' said Cao. The mayor would have had Narn go on, but the other chiefs interfered, and the victim was for the time released.

Then it was tried to force him to place his foot on the cross. One foot was tied to a post and the other seized by two soldiers, who, using all their strength, were still unable to compel him to comply with their wishes. Next, his thumb was placed in a vice, and crushed, but he bore the pain resolutely. From the beginning of September 1860 to almost the end of October these barbarities went on; and then he was released. Afterwards he moved about freely, and he was no longer anxious to hide himself, boldly confessing his religion, and strengthening and encouraging others by his word and example.

In the beginning of 1861, January 3d, one of the native priests was made prisoner. He was the principal one of the vicariate, and his name was Father John Hoan. He was on a visit to the little Christian district of Sao-Bim, that he might administer the sacraments, and was there arrested, with eight other Christians, and carried off to Dong-Hoi, the district town. He tried to escape, but ineffectually; he got aboard a little vessel, but was speedily chased, and had to return; landing, he concealed himself amidst some reeds, but a soldier espied him, and led him away. Of the Christians taken with him the most important was Matthew Phuong, who had received him into his house. The two were examined and beaten as usual, and several times, but their faith and courage were not to be shaken. They were detained in prison some months, and then led out for execution. Father Hoan had conciliated his keepers, and had been treated by them with kindness and respect. There were several Christians in prison, and he was allowed to go amongst them freely, so as to be able to exhort them, and to hear their confessions. A priest went in at times to visit him, and was able to take him Holy Communion. He was well aware that he should die, and the thought made him glad. When it was announced to him that the next day was to be his last, he received the tidings with the words: 'I thank God, who makes me know the hour when my blood shall be shed for His glory.' The hearing of the news had at first given him a thrill, a short passing fear, but he was happy again in a minute, and composed as usual. All the evening he was busy hearing the confessions of his fellow prisoners; and rising after a short rest to pray, again on the morning of his death he heard more confessions. As he went forth from his prison he met his old friend Matthew Phuong, from whom he had been separated during their confinement. They recognised each other with pleasure. Matthew Phuong till that morning had not known that his death was so nigh. When the messenger came in to summon him to execution he was engaged in cooking his meal of rice. But the man was ready. His whole imprisonment had been a preparation; he had borne all his sufferings patiently and cheerfully, and to die the death of a martyr had been regarded as an honour and a triumph. As they walked to the place of execution a placard was borne in front of them; that before F. Hoan was marked thus: 'This is the man Hoan. He is a priest of the Christians; he teaches a perverse religion and seduces good people,' &c. The other was: 'This is the man Nguen-Nan-Dai, surnamed Phuong. He is a Christian; he dared to conceal the priest Hoan; he is a breaker of the law and a great criminal,' &c. Father Hoan's death was a painful one. The executioner was inexpert, and made terrible gashes again and again before he was able to cut off his head; but Phuong's head was severed at a single blow. Father Hoan was sixty-four years of age; Matthew Phuong was seventy. The day of their martyrdom was May 26th, 1861.

Mgr. Sohier, through the early years of the persecution, had been able to live at peace and unknown in the Christian village in which he was harboured. It was but two or three days' journey from the capital; and the tyrant who was raging against the Christians little suspected that he had so near him one of its chiefs. But the villany of a busy-body, who afterwards became an apostate, betrayed the Bishop, and drove him out from his asylum. The traitor was called Nhieu-Han. He was a Christian of southern Tonking; and when the French had appeared at Touron he had gone down to them, and got into favour. But his bad character brought him to disgrace, and then he went away to the mandarins, and became an informer. He told them that a Christian Bishop was lying hid close to Huè, though he could not name the village. But his story was the cause of an active search for the Bishop, who was obliged to fly. At first he did not go away very far from Ke-sen, the village in which he had been lodged, only to the neighbouring mountains, and he came back again after a short absence; but the danger increasing, at last he was under the necessity of leaving altogether. For the mayor of Ke-sen was taken, and carried off to Huè; and although he bravely bore the torture to which he was subject, there was the constant risk of some information being extorted that would be prejudicial; and however true he might be, two men of the village, out of a private enmity, had gone and corroborated Nhieu-Han's statement, and declared that the Bishop was concealed there. There were very few places to which Mgr. Sohier could now retire, except to the mountains, which he dreaded; for the unwholesome atmosphere was sure to lay low in fever all who dwelt long in their dense recesses. Fortunately he secured a refuge in a Christian house, in a little nest of Christians in the midst of a large pagan population. The small number of the Christians in such a vicinity was the means of their safety; and the pagan prefect was a humane man, willing to shut his eyes, and not notice too strictly what was going on. Here the Bishop lived during the last months of the persecution. But there were moments of extreme danger, there were times when he was so pressed that he was obliged to run the hazards of the deadly mountains. He was on the mountains at one time for a month. But one of his party died; all were visited by fever, and he was ill himself.

But sickness was not the only danger of the mountains; there were the tigers prowling about, and there were chance parties of their enemies occasionally coming on their track. More than once they were so brought into imminent risk. When he was at Ke-sen there were two Europeans with the Bishop—M. Barlier and M. Choulex—and besides, a number of youths, students of the college. M. Choulex had been on a sick-bed for four years; he was perfectly helpless, and wherever he went it was necessary that he should be carried. A permanent home in the sickly mountains was in those days of flight the only resting-place to be found for him. There he had to linger on till the peace came. And sick as he was, and hard as was the condition in which he was placed, he survived. Once, for a week, with no covering but the coverlet of his bed and the branches of the trees, he was hanging in his cot between two trees, the rain of a tempest pouring down and drenching him, his attendants unable to prepare him a better place because of the fury of the storm; and often his only fare was a little cold rice. The Bishop kept with himself two deacons and some of the youth of the college. They went with him into the mountains, and he got them homes in Ke-huc. There were one or two moments of extreme peril when the Bishop was lying concealed in that friendly village. Amongst the inhabitants there were some who would have betrayed him if they had known of his presence, and some of these one day most inopportunely obtruded themselves. It was late in the evening, and they broke into the house and asked for Duong, the master of the house. He was out, and they would not believe it, and they wanted to push into another room to see if he was not there. But there was the Bishop in bed. It was only the clever management and presence of mind of a young girl, a cousin of Duong's, who was there, that saved the Bishop from a discovery. Duong was terribly alarmed when he heard of the matter, and declared stoutly that it should be the last time that he would meddle in such matters. But after all the good fellow was too faithful to keep his word. The Bishop, however, when the intruders took their leave, could not lie quietly in bed; he got up, and sought another hiding-place. It was from emergencies like these that he was driven to the mountains. It was hard to say in which place was the greatest peril.

That last year was one of horrible misery to every one. Bad as things had been before, in August 1861 they reached a degree of wretchedness that was more shocking than ever. Then came out a fresh decree, so exacting that there was no evading it. Then almost universally the Christian villages were completely ruined. The Christians were torn from their homes with merciless severity, and sent away in parties to live in pagan villages. There they were crammed in any place that came to hand; in out-houses, stables, or some sort of pen hastily raised for the occasion. There they were left almost to starve, little food was given to them, and they had no means of getting any. Their property was gone; it had all fallen into the hands of the pagans. Numbers of them were in the open air, day and night, and there they had to lie, often without clothes, in the rain and in the sun, exposed to all the casualties of weather, and all the time with cangues on their neck and fetters on their feet; and small children, some hardly seven, were of the number. After a while they were taken from these temporary resting-places, and thrust into prisons purposely raised for their reception, not within the pagan villages, but outside, and generally in places least favourable, and where the air was most unwholesome. There they were shut in, with no way of going out but a single door, before which lay a cross; and whoever would go out must first tread on it. Very little food was provided for them; they had to get it as they could, by work, by begging; and what they gained was very insufficient, and it was little better than starvation. Indeed, if they were starved, the end desired was obtained; for what was wanted was their extermination. Under hardships like these it is not surprising that some Christians gave way, and that they sought relief in the abandonment of their religion; but even so relief was not to be had; they had something more to do before they could come forth from that foul pestilential home; to purchase this favour they were required to use their efforts to induce others to give up their faith too. From time to time the pagan mayors and chiefs of the cantons would come into the prisons; and then, to intimidate the poor Christians, and to oblige them to submit; blows were showered down upon them most pitilessly; it was as if they were no more than beasts. The horrors of the scene are really only imperfectly told. And there was little to mitigate their sufferings. Now and then, perhaps, a priest might penetrate within the enclosure, and his visit might bring a short happiness. And all this weight of sorrow a great number bore with heroic patience—their separation from their homes, the loss of their property, their loathsome dwellings, their want of food, the contempt, the blows, the threats which their cruel masters bestowed on them. There were, indeed, in some places mitigations of these evils; the same rigour was not practised everywhere. All the pagan guardians had not the same harsh feelings; there was mercy in some of them, and a feeling of sympathy towards the Christian was widely extended through the country. But the government had no pity at all; the sternness of their purpose was not to be shaken. It was resolved that, rather than allow the escape of the Christians, there should be a general massacre. Should the French arms prevail, plans were laid for the destruction of the poor Christians herded together in the prisons—the wooden buildings were to be fired. Combustibles were to be prepared and everything arranged, that at a short notice the tragic work might be accomplished.

It was in the month of August 1861 that these cruel plans for the destruction of the Christians began to be systematically and generally carried out.

There were some happy spots which had hitherto been comparatively exempt from the hard trials felt elsewhere. The provinces in the centre of Cochin China were, through the early years of the persecution, favoured beyond all others. These provinces formed the vicariate of Mgr. Cuenot, who for a long number of years had been vicar-apostolic of all Cochin China, though lately he had severed off from his jurisdiction the provinces alike north and south, forming with them two fresh vicariates, which he committed to younger and more vigorous hands. He himself was a very old man, not only failing in his strength but also much enfeebled in mind, and, though unwilling to leave his post, hardly equal to the weighty and difficult duties of the present time. But fortunately the persecution had not touched the Christians in the provinces where he was sheltered, as it had almost everywhere else. He was living all the time in quiet at Go-thi. His college was not broken up, but scholars and students in theology went on pursuing their studies under the care of M. Herrengt, experiencing no interruption. The Christians were more numerous there than in other parts of Cochin China. The mandarins were not inclined to trouble them, and did no more than they could help in execution of the decrees which issued from Huè. Some of the *dau-mucs*, or leading men of the villages, were removed and put in prison, but the Christians generally were let alone. But after the fatal decree of August this state of things could not last. The king was not satisfied, and new mandarins were sent into these provinces to see that the laws were enforced. Two mandarins well practised in the abominable theories then in vogue came down to Binh-Dinh, to spread confusion and misery. The Christians were ordered up before the tribunals to have their faces scored with the words of disgrace, *te-dao* (perverse religion), cut with sharpened fragments of porcelain; women and children were marked as well as others, and as their cries were heard, and the blood was seen streaming down their countenances, even the pagans crowding round the tribunals were moved to pity. The next step was expatriation; torn away from their homes, these poor people were dispersed in the pagan villages. It was no longer safe for Europeans to remain in their ordinary retreats. So the college was broken up. M. Herrengt with his pupils got aboard a Christian vessel, and sailed away to Saigon, where the French were. Mgr. Cuenot could not make up his mind to retire. He sought an asylum in the house of a pagan, but it became suspected. A body of soldiers surrounded the house, and active search was commenced. A deacon was apprehended and another Christian; books were discovered and articles of the Bishop, indicative of his presence, and it seemed certain that he could not be far away. The Bishop was in one of those hiding-places the priests frequently used in this country, a little narrow space, jammed in between two walls. On the third day the old man was wearied out with his confinement, he was parched with thirst, and he could not bear the pains of his situation. So he came out of his own accord and delivered himself up. He was then thrust into a narrow cage and carried off to the chief district town. He met with no ill-usage, and was allowed a certain amount of liberty. But his prison life was short; soon an attack of dysentery came on, and he sank under it. Hardly was he dead than the orders arrived from Huè that he should be beheaded. But it was too late. A ruthless mandarin proposed that the sentence should be executed on the corpse, but his colleagues were more merciful and would not consent to the barbarous act. He died November 14th, when he had been in the hands of his enemies little more than a fortnight.

Mgr. Cuenot was the veteran Bishop of the country. He had first come out to Cochin China in 1828, and for nearly thirty years he had been a bishop. His administration had in many respects been a successful one. It had commenced in a time of trouble, when the Church in Cochin China had suffered great calamities from Minh-Menh's persecution. There was then hardly a missionary, and few native priests. He had seen a happy revival, the multiplication of priests, and a considerable increase of Christians; and the three separate Christian populations of Cochin China—in the north, the centre, and the south—had received each their own bishop to govern them. But in his old age and at the hour of his death fast were disappearing the fruits of the labours of those many years.

The troubles of Binh-Dinh increased with the

death of Mgr. Cuenot. The discovery of the Bishop secreted within this province drew down on the Christian population immediate severities. No more indulgence was allowed them; but they now felt, as others had done before, the rigours of the persecution. Now those great enclosures which had been raised in other provinces were raised up here, and even little children in fetters and with the cangue on their necks were forced into them. The village census was carefully examined and any errors rectified, that no Christian might be overlooked. Houses were torn down, plantations were destroyed; cocoa-nut trees, mulberry trees, bamboo hedges, all ruthlessly desolated. On the roads travellers were stopped and questioned, and even the houses of pagans were entered to see whether they were harbouring Christians; and at times deeds of reckless violence were committed. Any barbarity was preferable rather than that these Christians should be rescued by the detestable stranger who had invaded the country. So that fell purpose was really executed of burning the Christians in their prison. In the town of Bien-Hoa there were three hundred and seven Christians imprisoned. The French troops attacked this town, and were on the point of taking it, and then fire was set to the four corners of the prison, and soldiers standing around with their lances and sabres drove back into the flames the unhappy captives who tried to make their escape. Every one perished except eight, and one of them was a girl of sixteen, who contrived to fly in the midst of the tumult, and then hid herself in a tree, where, three days after, she was discovered and rescued by the French soldiers.

The wretched state of this province, so long spared, and the ruin that had fallen on the Christians, is thus described by M. Herrengt:

'On my departure from the mission I left there twenty-two native priests; thirteen of them have fallen into the hands of the mandarins, two have disappeared no one can say where, six are wandering in the mountains, one only, after numerous escapes, has managed to reach this place of safety. Half the clerical students, all the pupils of the junior college, all the nuns, as many as two hundred and fifty, besides the thirteen thousand Christians remaining in the province of Binh-Dinh, are now in the hands of the persecutors. They are branded on the face with the letters of infamy, *te-dao*; they have either a cangue or a chain round their necks, some have both; they are divided into small parties, and dispersed in the different villages in number proportioned to the size of the place; they are crowded into miserable dwellings surrounded on all sides with combustibles, as the persecutors are expecting to receive the orders to blow them up in these homes.'

This was the work of a few months. It was August when these fatal measures began to be executed in Binh-Dinh, and by the end of the year such was the result.

The French armament maintained their position

in the neighbourhood of Touron for a year and a half; then, in the beginning of March 1860, they decamped and fixed themselves at Saigon. Here they made arrangements for a permanent occupation, and offered protection to the little body of Christians that were in that part of the vicariate of Mgr. Lefebvre. This vicariate was the only one that was in any way shielded from the desolating persecution that was prevailing.

Towards the end of 1858, when the persecution received its new impulse from the French invasion, the alarm and the trouble had been felt down here. The college near Saigon was broken up, the scholars were dispersed, and Mgr. Lefebvre retired to the hills. One of the missionaries, lying in concealment in a Christian's house, has in a pleasant way sketched for us the anxieties of his situation.

His poor host, he tells us, was in a constant quiver; in dread lest he should be found out harbouring a Christian missionary, yet too faithful to dismiss his guest. 'Missionaries, native priests, nuns, Christians of all ranks, are hunted like beasts. The very man who is offering me a refuge is ever in a tremor, and the tidings which are constantly reaching me are enough to excite alarm. We are told of the destruction of a Christian village, of some night attack, of the arrest of a priest, of a party of Christians led off with the cangue round their necks, or of a convent desecrated by soldiers. How my poor host's countenance falls as he listens to the news! Should I be obliged to sit up at night to get through my correspondence, off he goes at once to mount guard outside with several of his most trusted friends, that no spy of the mandarins may get a glimpse of the light that may gleam through a chink of my hiding-place, and so arouse suspicions. But when the light is put out, and they are all resting on their mats, he feels no more secure; then the slightest noise outside the cabin, the fall of a cocoa-nut, the barking of a dog, no matter what the sound may be, to him it is as if a troop of soldiers were approaching, coming to seize me.'

And the danger was real. Great activity was shown here as elsewhere in detecting Christians. 'Crosses were placed in all the ports, in front of the custom-houses, inland as well as by the sea, and all travellers were required to put their foot on them if they would be allowed to pass on.'

In a village called Cai-mung there was a convent; into this, one morning in December 1858, just as Mass was concluded, there suddenly intruded a captain with a body of soldiers. It was only chance that brought him there, for he was out on other business, and he was willing to go away and be silent for a sum of money that was offered him. But a bad Christian of the village, who had a grudge against the village chiefs and wished to get them into trouble, opposed himself to the plan, and the indulgence that had been intended became impossible. The nuns had mostly fled; but two, the Superioress, Martha Lanh, and another named Elizabeth Ngo, were taken, and led away with five other persons to Long-ho, the district town. The governor was a man of harsh temper, who delighted in cruelty, and he satisfied himself on the present occasion. John Hoa, was first called up; he was the village chief. All he had done to get himself into blame was that he had secreted some of the church articles. Stretched on the ground, with his arms and legs extended and tied to stakes, he was questioned. Long and tedious these questionings are, and throughout there is the constant dread of the rattan. This time twenty strokes were his award, and he bore them patiently and without a single cry.

The next summoned was Martha Lanh, the Superioress. She had twenty-nine strokes; she cried out, but her cries were the names of Jesus and Mary.

Elizabeth Ngo the nun, as she was led into the court, gave an evidence of her firm spirit. The satellite who held her traced a cross on the ground and tried to drag her over it; but she resisted, and would not be compelled to dishonour the sacred emblem. She had twenty-five lashes; twenty she received in silence, and when forced by her sufferings to utter a cry it was only to call upon Jesus and Mary. 'Very well,' said the mandarin in irony; 'call on your Jesus, and let Him endure the torture for you.'

The last brought up on that occasion was Peter Ngoan. He was a young man not in the least daunted, but if anything proud of the honour of confessing his faith. As he walked up to the hall of judgment, he seemed not to feel the weight of his cangue; he ran on in front of the others, as if eager to present himself. 'Here is one,' said the mandarin, 'who has no fear;' and throughout he showed none. When he was asked to trample on the cross, he said, 'The grand mandarin may spare me or he may condemn me to suffer—that is for him to decide; but for me I would rather die than deny my religion.' Eighteen lashes were his portion; and he too with a loud voice called upon Jesus and Mary.

The next day they were brought up again before the mandarin, and the beatings were renewed. John Hoa's beating was a very severe one. The governor seemed determined that he would conquer him and force him to tread upon the cross. The blows went on to fifty, when the poor man's courage was shaken, and he could bear up no longer. He asked to be let off, and gave what was understood as a promise that he would obey. But, when relieved, he could not bring himself to do a thing so shocking to his feelings, and God gave him strength to say that he would not be an apostate. But the impression of that scene had a sad influence. There were three prisoners standing by, whose turns would come next; and the unhappy men, rather than endure such agonies, gave the fatal consent, and abjured their religion.

The two nuns, however, and Peter Ngoan showed no signs of being intimidated. Martha Lauh on this occasion received eighteen stripes, afterwards fourteen, and lastly thirty-eight. The successive beatings much enfeebled her, and, out of commiseration for her weak state, she was, on the last turn, brought into court lying on a mat. But the governor had no pity, and was angry that any such indulgence should have been allowed her, and ordered her at once to trample on the cross or submit to another beating; and so they went on beating her till she swooned, and she was borne away on the shoulders of one of the Christians as if dead. Elizabeth Ngo was treated even worse than this. The brutal governor seemed resolved to bend her energetic spirit. The second time he contented himself with thirty blows. On the third trial, however, it seemed that he would never stop. The blows were counted to over a hundred, and still they were repeated. The poor woman was lying on the ground silent; she had lost her power of speech. Then the blows ceased. The governor, determined to have his way, as she was carried out, ordered that she should be dragged over the cross. But the heroic nun, conscious of their purpose, opposed with all the earnestness of her strong faith, and while she resolutely drew back her legs, with one of her hands she seized the loved sign of redemption, and, raising it on high, exclaimed, 'God be praised!'

Peter Ngoan's courage also stood out to the end. Twice he received forty lashes. 'You must be a master of religion,' said the governor, vexed at his perseverance, 'or you would not thus refuse to trample on the cross.' 'No,' he replied; 'I am only a poor day labourer; but I will not renounce my religion.'

This same year, on the 21st of December, Paul

Loc, a young native priest, was made prisoner. This young man was very dear to Mgr. Lefebvre, who, noticing his intelligence and good disposition, kept him much with himself. Not long before they had been talking together, and the Bishop was quite astonished at the burst of enthusiasm with which he spoke when the conversation turned upon martyrdom. 'His voice,' said the Bishop, 'became animated, his countenance beamed with joy, his features expanded, and I really felt some confusion, for I perceived that he had an appreciation of the signal favour that God confers on all on whom He bestows it beyond what I had myself.' Paul, when a child, had been left an orphan, and a priest, his countryman, had taken him and carefully brought him up. He was then sent to the college of Pulo-penang, and came away from the college in 1850 with very considerable commendation. For some time he remained a catechist, then he was admitted to orders, and in 1857 he was raised to the priesthood; when the persecution broke out he was presiding over the college at Saigon. After the dispersion of the college students, he was one day in the house of a Christian near Saigon, where he chanced to meet a pagan woman. This woman talked of what she had seen, and the mandarin heard of it, and soldiers were sent out to arrest the priest. So he was taken and put in prison; but there was no harsh usage in this case. He was not beaten at all. His stay in prison was short, for orders came down from Huè that he should be executed, and they were at once obeyed.

Very early one morning, when he was not at all expecting it, the soldiers came in to lead him out to execution. He was at prayer when they entered. Without delay they hurried him away, and he had not even time to send, as had been before agreed, for a priest, who might attend him and give him the last absolution. Two strokes of the sabre sufficed to cut off his head. 'Where are you, dear Paul?' asks the Bishop, as he concludes his letter. 'I am now in the house where we were once together; my eyes in vain search for you in the place where you used to be; how glad should I be to speak to you as of old! There lie your clothes and sandals; there is the seat on which you sat beside me. But why do I lament? You are much better off; the house in which you now dwell is much more beautiful, and your companions are the saints and angels. Live and reign through all eternity with Jesus Christ, and aid us with your prayers, that one day we may share in your happiness.'

Three days after Paul Loc died, about the middle of February 1859, the French occupied Saigon; and although the whole fleet and army did not yet retire in this direction, still there was now a retreat provided for the missionaries, and a certain amount of relief.

Another young priest before this, early in the January of this year, had fallen into the hands of the mandarins. This priest, whose name was Peter Kee, was the very priest who had said Mass at the Convent of the Immaculate Conception on the day on which it was visited by the soldiers. He had been ordained priest only three months before, and had been stationed in the village of Cai-mung. On that morning he had showed no fear of danger, but had come forward and done his best to extricate the nuns, and would have succeeded if it had not been for the untimely interruption. Much against his will he was removed by his superior from this spot, under the idea that he was there exposed to danger. But in the college of Pulo-Penang he had acquired the same eager desire of martyrdom that was noticeable in F. Paul Loc. Having heard that M. Borelle wished him to leave, he thus wrote to him: 'I wish the father would send me a formal order when he desires me to quit this post; for, till such express order comes, your son will remain where he is.' Then, unable to control his feelings, he burst out—'Shall I not have the happiness of fighting and dying for the glory of God? A chain would be a precious necklace, and handcuffs costly bracelets. Alas, my companions bear away the palm, and I am left like some disregarded sentinel. O my God, grant to me also that I may suffer martyrdom!' And these words the young man had written in Latin and in rhythm, and had set them to music, in which he had remarkable taste and proficiency. It was a genuine burst of feeling; and the wish of his heart was granted. What M. Borelle directed for his safety turned out to be the very means of conducting him into the hands of his enemies. He went, as he was told, from Cai-mung to Dau-Nuoc. This last place was a flourishing Christian village, where there was a church and a college and a convent. The principal Christian, named Emmanuel Phung, was a great man in the neighbourhood. He had built the church, and it was the finest one to be seen in the country. He was the great stay of the mission and of the Christians all around. He was not only rich, but he was bold and fearless, tall and grand in his appearance, and exercising very large influence. The sub-prefect and the district chief were both his friends, and they did not interfere when he did a number of things that were not permissible by the law. The church which he built had no disguise about it so as to conceal its character; it showed plainly enough what it was; and it stood in a conspicuous spot, and invited persons' attention; and persons complained about it to the governor; but the sub-prefect, being deputed to investigate the matter, could see no church at all, nothing more than an ordinary house, and he reported accordingly. But what was done in more smooth times could not be safely continued in these days of peril. Fresh representations were made to the governor by persevering foes bent on carrying out their ends; and it was positively stated that within the dwelling of Emmanuel Phung there was harboured a European priest. The consequence was, that a body of three hundred soldiers, with the judge of the province at their head, surprised the village. There was a priest really living in the house of Emmanuel, but that very morning he had left it, and had been guided away to a place of security. But

Emmanuel Phung himself was no longer safe. The rumours about him were confirmed, and there were too many proofs of his complicity to allow him a chance of escape. Only a few days before Father Peter Kee had come to this village, and he was found in the house of Emmanuel Phung, and made prisoner. Possibly he might have escaped if he had made the attempt; or, if it was not for a chance, it might never have been known that he was a priest, being so very young; but the words of a little boy revealed him, and then the fact was not to be denied. Thirty Christians or more were led away to prison with the priest and his host, but they were not all brave enough to suffer for their faith; considerably more than half faltered, and some of them were the children of this valiant confessor. Nine of the number, however, went into exile, and Emmanuel and the priest had to forfeit their lives. They were kept in prison several months, and it was July when the order came from Huè that they were to be executed. There was for a moment some show of irresolution in Emmanuel, but it passed off. When the question was finally proposed to him whether he would apostatise, he replied, 'If the grand mandarin pleases to send me away acquitted, well; if he wills to take my life, well also. But for my religion I cannot renounce it.' Father Peter Kee walked by his side to the place of execution. 'This is the hour,' he said to Emmanuel, 'that God has reserved for our last combat; let us suffer with courage.' On which the other smiled, saying he was happy to die. Then the priest became lost in prayer, but the joy he felt was visible in his countenance. As he knelt before the executioner his constancy was remarkable, for the man was nervous and his hand shook, and previous to striking the fatal blow he passed the sword across the martyr's neck; but Father Kee remained unmoved on his knees, and he continued erect till the third blow had quite severed the head from the body. In his hand was found a statuette of the Blessed Virgin, to whom he had a marked devotion, which was attached to his finger by a silver thread. He loved to sing of her, and one day, in a letter to M. Borelle, his fervour breaks out in the words, 'Mary, my mother! O, how I love her!'

Emmanuel Phung was strangled. The death of the two martyrs was almost simultaneous.

CHAPTER XIII.

PERSECUTION IN TONKING.

ON the death of Mgr. Retort the charge of the vicariate of Western Tonking fell into the hands of Mgr. Jeantet, the coadjutor. This prelate was, and had been for some time, the senior missionary in the country; that is, he had been living in Annam longer than any of his brethren. Even Mgr. Cuenot, who had reached Cochin China in 1828, had here to yield precedence to Mgr. Jeantet, who began his residence in Tonking as early as 1821. He was one of the first batch of missionaries that came to fill the gap made by the dying off of those honoured men who toiled on so many years, at the beginning of the century, without having their ranks replenished from Europe. He had come out when the name of Gia-laong was fresh in the minds of persons, and before any of the cruelties of Minh-Menh had been felt. He had enjoyed a short intercourse with the Venerable Bishop Guerard, and had been edified by his words and example. He had lived through the persecution of Minh-Menh, and, again, into the midst of that of Tudoc, and not without many narrow escapes. In the early part of Minh-Menh's persecution he was on the point of being captured. Bitten in the leg by a dog, he was unable to walk. So having been lifted on the shoulders of some faithful Christians, he was being borne away to a place of safety, but the fatigues of the painful journey were too much for him, and although his enemies were on his track, he ordered the Christians to put him down and leave him to his fate. The providence of God, however, protected him, and he was not discovered. At that time, like other missionaries, he lived in caves and on the mountains, and where many perished he was preserved; only lately he was all but smothered in a cave where he had sought refuge on an inroad of soldiers into Ke-non; and since that, while wandering in the mountains, he had in the night fallen into the water and been nearly drowned. For several years he had been coadjutor, and the day of his consecration was famous as one of the grand days of the mission. His residence since then had been generally at Ke-non, where it was his business to instruct and train the students in theology for their missionary duties. Mgr. Retort in his pleasant way used to style him the *Mortar Bishop*, for he it was, he said, who had to shape and polish the stones which would be the principal ones of the spiritual edifice to be raised in this pagan country.

Mgr. Jeantet, in a letter written nearly two years after the death of Mgr. Retort, takes up the thread of the sad story of ruin which that prelate has narrated. 'During the two last years,' he says, 'five priests have been removed by sickness, but much more fatal has been the executioner's axe. From September 1858 up to the present time (August

1860), nineteen of our priests have been arrested.' Then follow their names, names which to us sound strange, and convey no meaning, but to Mgr. Jeantet they would be names familiar and dear, many of them being the very pupils he had himself trained, and with whom he had lived in kind intercourse at Kenon: 'Kwei, Cân, Loo, Kwei, Tri, Ngôn, Ngân, Dieû, Thinh, Too, Thuyêt, Chân, Cân, Khoan, Xuyen, Phu, Ly, Honh, Thu. The twelve first have already been beheaded, the others are still awaiting their sentence in prison. Within the same period five of our Christians have been strangled for the faith, viz. Soa, the doctor; Thi and Huinh, mayors; and Soo and Nho, assistant mayors; the four last all of Kevinh. And Kevinh is now wholly razed, and its site is under cultivation by the pagans. Phuong, a soldier of Kebang, died after three days' suffering, the effects of torture; and Conh, another Christian, died in prison. One of our scholars named Bôt, having first yielded under the anguish of the pincers, after his release went back of his own accord, and was then mercilessly thrown to the elephants, and crushed under their feet. . . . Too, a deacon, and Mau, a catechist, died in prison; eighty-five of our principal Christians are witnessing to their faith in exile; thirty-five more confessors are in prison, waiting their sentence; fifty of our religious catechists and pupils have been already sent away into distant provinces, and fifty more are in chains expecting the same doom. Three Annamite nuns, lovers of the cross, have given a noble testimony of their faith before an immense assembly of persons. The youngest of the three was dragged forcibly over two crosses laid on the ground; she then took them up in her arms, and pressed them to her lips, heedless of the rattan strokes that came showering down on her back. "What can be done with such fanaticism?" said the mandarins one to the other; and then the two other nuns followed her example. All were led back to prison, and there they are still. Our youth of the refuge have also shown admirable courage under torture; several received hundreds of lashes with the rattan, a great number had to bear the trial of the pincers, cold and hot also, and, thanks to God, they have never failed in resolution. One of our priests has had to submit to that most cruel of tortures, the table, with its six large nails driven through it, on which he was forced to kneel, two soldiers pressing with all their weight on his shoulders, so that the nails should penetrate more deeply. This was what Father Ngôn had to endure, because, when arrested on the highway, he would not give the name of the village in which he had lodged.'

Then we have a summary of the ruin of the mission: 'Since June 1858 we have seen our three colleges, with their thirty-five theologians, and their two hundred and eighty Latin students, one after the other, invested by the mandarins, and reduced to ashes, all our churches and presbyteries pulled down, and not less than a hundred of our most flourishing parishes sacked, or only saved by a sum of money.'

In such dangerous times Mgr. Jeantet did not like

to be without a coadjutor; so he summoned to his side M. Theurel, and in the secrecy of the night, with two Annamite priests as his assistants, he consecrated him. The new Bishop had neither stockings nor gloves, and for a crozier he had a bamboo cane with a crook of straw at the head covered over with some gilt paper.

Up to August 1860, when Mgr. Jeantet's letter was written, no missionary in Western Tonking had fallen into the hands of their enemies. Mgr. Retort had died on the mountains, and M. Titaut had died of privation and sickness. So close was the seclusion in which this last priest had kept himself that, writing to M. Venard, he dates his letter from the 'land of moles,' and says that for eighteen months he had not seen the sun. And in the unendurable misery of such a situation he soon after succumbed. But towards the end of 1860 two missionaries were captured, first M. Neron and then M. Venard. M. Neron had for a long time been living in a very solitary way. His mission was remote, and he was separated from all his brethren, and for a time they were altogether ignorant of his fate. About August, however, a little before his arrest, letters came from him to Mgr. Jeantet and Mgr. Theurel, setting forth his difficulties. He had been living, up to the end of 1859, in the Christian village of Taxa, but had been obliged to fly to the mountains; and there his hardships had been such, that one day after a long search he was found by some Christians, stretched on the ground, worn out with hunger and fatigue, and only just conscious. His last home was a lonely cottage outside the Christian village of Yen-top. Very few persons knew where he was, for a strict concealment was urgent. How necessary his own case proved, for he was found out; and those who came to deliver him to the mandarins were persons whom he might have supposed to have been his friends, for they had previously given proofs of friendship. One of them was the mayor of Taxa, a Christian, in whose house he had been living concealed, now turned into a traitor, either from some unworthy hope or fear; and the other, though a pagan chief, had two years before, when M. Neron had been taken prisoner, for a very slight ransom restored him to freedom. And now these two came against him as enemies. They came together in the night to the house where M. Neron lodged, and called on him by name. M. Neron recognised the mayor's voice as the voice of a friend, and imagining that he had come to warn him of some fresh danger, without the least distrust came out at once. He was immediately beset and knocked down, bound, and dragged away. Then, loaded with the cangue and in a cage, he was carried off to the chief town of Son-Tay. On September 2d he was brought up before the mandarins. Then followed the usual long process of questionings. M. Neron, refusing to give the information which was sought, had to lie down on the ground and submit to forty strokes of the rattan. But neither word nor sound proceeded from his lips; so they gave up beating him, perceiving it to be useless; and after that they made no further attempt to torture him. In the early part of his imprisonment, for three whole weeks M. Neron abstained from all food; he would take nothing but a little cold water; his motive for so doing is not explained; and Mgr. Theurel, who tells us the fact, was not able to account for it. During the whole time of his imprisonment, which lasted nearly three months, he held no communication with his brethren. Mgr. Jeantet and Mgr. Theurel wrote to him many times, but could obtain no reply. Why he maintained this silence no one could tell; but Mgr. Theurel considered that it was in the wish to die entirely detached from the world, and without a record of himself. November 3d he was led out to execution. He had become very thin, as the deacon who witnessed the scene reported to Mgr. Theurel. Perfectly abstracted, with his eyes cast on the ground, praying as he walked, M. Neron proceeded to the place where he was to suffer; he noticed nothing, not even his deacon, nor a priest, who were both standing very near to him. Two strokes of the sabre were sufficient to sever his head from the body. The executioner did not like the task, and tried and tried in vain to get another to take it in his stead. A pagan, at the request of the priest of this place, asked permission to bury the body, and it was granted. The head, by the terms of the sentence, was to be exposed three days. And when the three days were expired, the priest was not able to obtain it, for it was ordered to be thrown into the river. Three officers had this business committed to them. The head had been put into a case, and on opening it to throw the head into the river, these men reported that they had seen issue from the case a red ball, which rose up into the air. It might be true or it might be false, but this is what they said. The head, nevertheless, they threw into the river, and it was not recovered. M. Neron died in the twelfth year of his residence in Tonking. He had been arrested twice before; once he was rescued by the Christians, and the other time he was bought off.

November had not closed before a second captive was in the hands of the persecutors. And this captive is one that in a singular way arrests our attention. It was M. Venard. His name has not, indeed, been hitherto often mentioned in this history, and as a missionary, though six years resident in the country, he was never conspicuous; but, when notice is drawn to him, there is about him an attractiveness that rivets the attention. The one grand desire on which his soul seems to be set was to be a martyr. It was the object of his ambition, and had been so for a long series of years. And although, in the minds of all the missionaries of this land, martyrdom is always regarded as an honour, and as a thing to be desired, there is no other person whose whole heart seemed so absorbed with the wish as is very apparent in this holy young man. There are two or three letters of his, written to different persons, just at the time of his receiving his appointment to Tonking, and the enthusiastic glow that runs through them, arising simply out of the idea that there is now a chance of his attaining that grand distinction on which his heart is set, is something marvellous. 'Well, my dear people,' he writes home to his family, 'I am going to Tonking. There the venerable Charles Cornay died a martyr. I do not say that the same fate is reserved for me; but if you will only pray ardently, perhaps God may grant me the same grace..... I am not going to China,' which he had been expecting; 'but I must guide my boat to another shore—a shore on which MM. Schœffer and Bonnard, one on the 1st of May 1851, the other on the 1st of May 1852, obtained the martyr's palm. It is in the Annamite country, which includes Tonking and Cochin China, that the spirit of persecution is most active. A price is set upon the head of every missionary, and when one is found, they put him to death without hesitation. But God knows His own, and only to those whom He chooses is the grace of martyrdom given. The one is taken and the other left, and there, as everywhere, His holy will is done.' Here he is unveiling his inmost thoughts in familiar confidence to those whom he loves. How he has treasured the names of the martyrs and the days of their martyrdom! The venerable Charles Cornay from the days of his early childhood has been on his thoughts. When he was a little boy, tending his goat on the hills by his father's home in France, he read over with avidity the account of the sufferings and death of this missionary, and the impression never left him. It was many years after that his own destination to the foreign missions became a possibility, and at the time there was no prospect or purpose of his being led into the ecclesiastical state. But the dream of his childhood ever lived vividly in his mind. He had the privilege of a holy home, and amongst his first companions was a sister who shared his sentiments; and, as the two talked together, they fostered and stimulated the earnest feelings and desires which each had of giving themselves wholly to God. Happy as was his home, and dear to him as were all in it—father and sister and brothers—yet there was no tie that held him so fast that the ardent wish he had to go out into foreign missions, and preach the Gospel to the heathen, and sacrifice his life for the love of Jesus, was not more strong. And the words of that letter only reveal the feelings that were ever ruling within him. But this letter is not yet finished: as an additional subject of pleasing thought, he goes on to tell them the chances there are of suffering and danger, even before he reaches Tonking. With him that is counted as a privilege which is usually only matter of dread. 'We run the risk, too, of being cut off by pirates in the passage from Hong-Kong to Tonking; but that must be as God permits.' Then, again, after an enthusiastic picture of the glorious duties in which he is about to engage under the holy Bishop Retort, his mind runs back to the old subject. 'And, then, think of the martyrs—those real glories of Tonking, those immortal flowers gathered by our Lord's own hand in the garden of His choice. These martyrs are the patrons and protectors of the mission; their blood, shed in the cause, is always pleading for us before God, and the remembrance of their triumph gives fresh courage to those who are still in the strife. Only think what an honour and what a happiness it would be for your poor Theophane if God should deign— You understand. "Te Deum laudamus. Te martyrum candidatus exercitus."'

It is in language precisely similar that he writes to his old friend, Father Dallet, to whom he can also speak out his thoughts with freedom. 'Only a few years ago MM. Galy and Berneux were seized as soon as they arrived in Tonking. Should but the same good fortune befall us! O dear old friend, every time the thought of martyrdom comes across me, I thrill all over with joy and hope. But this better part is not given to all. "Exultent in Domino sancti. Alleluia." I dare not aspire to so brilliant a crown. "Domine non sum dignus;" but I cannot help feeling a longing and sighing for such a grace. "Domine, qui dixisti majorem charitatem nemo habet ut animam suam ponat quis pro amicis suis." You do not forget our mutual prayer; it has for me an inexpressible charm. "Sancta Maria, regina martyrum, ora pro nobis." Pray, pray for your poor little friend, who never forgets you for a single day.' There is no mistaking words like these—they are words that come from the heart with an easy naturalness which makes us sure of their truth.

It is this man that, after a residence of six years in Tonking, has now become a prisoner. And his mind is no way changed. A few days after he was taken, he wrote with a paint-brush for a pen from his cage to his family in France. The letter is dated Dec. 3d, 1860: 'My dearest people,' he begins, 'God has permitted me to fall into the hands of the wicked. On the Feast of St. Andrew I was put into a square cage, and carried to the prefecture, from whence I trace these few lines for you with some difficulty with a paint-brush. To-morrow, Dec. 4th, I am to appear before the judge. God knows what awaits me, but I do not fear. The grace of the Most High will be with me, and my Mother Mary will protect her poor little servant. . . . Well, here I am in the arena of the confessors of the faith. Certainly God chooses the poor and weak things of the world to confound the mighty! I have confidence that the story of my fight will be the story of my victory; for it is not on my own strength that I lean, but on the strength of Him who has overcome the powers of death and hell. I think of you all, my dearest father, my beloved sister and brothers; and if I obtain the grace of martyrdom, O, then still more shall I have you in remembrance! *A Dieu*, my best-loved ones, to our meeting in heaven! In a moment I shall be adorned with the confessor's chains. Once more, adieu.'

The six years that intervened between these letters were six years of suffering. 'Suffering,' said Mgr. Retort of this missionary, 'is M. Venard's specialty.' Up to the end of 1856, or for about two years and a half, he was constantly ill, and sometimes his sickness was so severe that there were little hopes of his recovery. 'I am dying out like a candle, and hold to life by a mere thread,' he says in one of his letters. 'I think the doctors have given me up.' Afterwards, again he writes: 'I fell sick of a violent fever, with an attack of asthma.... Just as I was beginning to rejoice in a kind of convalescence, I caught the typhoid fever, which brought me to the very gates of death.' When every one thought him dying, he was restored by a Chinese remedy, a kind of cauterisation, little balls of a certain herb being burnt on various parts of his body. 'They burnt me in five hundred different places, about two hundred of which were round or near the lungs. At the end of a few days these cauterisations or inoculations produced a little yellow pustule full of matter; that is a sign that the operation has been successful, as the system is supposed in this way to reject what is noxious. The result has been that I am wonderfully better.'

But as health was restored came other sufferings —the persecution. He was at Vinh-tri on that fatal day when the soldiers burst into the village of Kevinh to begin their work of desolation. It was February 1857. 'One Monday, at eight o'clock,' says M. Venard, 'one of the villagers came in hot haste to tell us that the mandarin of the southern province had surrounded the village, and was coming to seize us. Mgr. Retort was forced by the students into a subterranean hiding-place; M. Charbonnier and I were stuffed into a place between two walls, where we remained for four hours without seeing the light of day. . . . But this was but the beginning of a series of misfortunes.'

Before the full dangers of the persecution, however, were understood, there was a short season of comparative repose; and during that interval M. Venard had sufficient health to do a little real missionary work. M. Castex, with whom he had lived at Hoang-Ngueyen, died this summer, and M. Venard was installed in his post; and in a letter to his sister he has given us some insight into his situation and his labours.

'I have upwards of 12,000 Christians here, divided into four large parishes, with six or seven native priests under me. My duty is to go from parish to parish to see that all is in good order, to make peace if there are disputes, to give the necessary dispensations, to confirm in cases where the Bishop or Vicar-apostolic is not able to fulfil the office, to give retreats and missions; in fact, to do all I can to increase in all hearts the love of God and zeal for His Church. As to the pagans, I have not counted them, but there must be 250,000 or 300,000. It needs ten St. Francis Xaviers to bring all these people to the knowlege of the Gospel. At this moment it is difficult for us to do much in the way of conversion, in consequence of the rigour of the persecution. But still occasionally souls are brought in. When children are ill the mothers bring them for baptism. A young widow the other day brought me her dying child. She was in the greatest distress, and had not eaten above five times in twelve days. I baptised her child, and intrusted her to the care of a Christian woman, who is preparing her for the same sacrament. After the Feast of the Assumption I went to a district almost entirely pagan. There were not above two hundred Christians scattered here and there amongst them. It was close to the residence of the mandarin. No European had ever before been seen there, so I had to keep myself as much as possible out of view. But the children whom I had confirmed chattered about "the little European who had come into their village, very small, but very white and pretty;" and so unintentionally betrayed me. . . . But I resolved not to lose courage; so, putting my trust in God, I worked day and night in this neglected vineyard for one whole week; all the while the Christians, who were in a terrible fright, acting as sentinels, and not allowing any curious visitor to have a look at the European.

'This work done, I moved off quietly in the night, protected by the darkness, and visited another place, where there was a Christian population of four or five thousand, and where the pagans around where favourable to Christianity. It was easy to go about from the inundations, which continue four or five months, the country becoming an immense sea, the green villages peering out of it. Every one travels in his boat, and boats there are in abundance, of all shapes and sizes. I have one that just holds one person, very light, woven of bamboo, and here I sit each evening, paddling myself about to my different penitents, meeting sometimes one or other by the way, and then racing with them to make a trial of speed, but always coming off second best. Visiting my flock in their own homes is a great point with me, and they have much pleasure in it. And than these poor Annamites there is not a better-disposed people, nor anywhere more fervent pious souls. The inundations of this year have been extraordinary, and the water rose above a foot in my house. Fishes, frogs, toads, crabs, and serpents were swimming about my room very happily, while I was perched on some plank not more than three or four inches above them. But the least pleasant were the rats, that would come and compose themselves on my mat; and one night I crushed one in sleep. But worse than this, on waking, there was a venomous viper, striped black and white, coiled up also upon my poor bed—a claimant for hospitality —and hissing when I stretched out my feet. Under such circumstances it was necessary to raise my house. So the Christians set to work, brought a quantity of earth, and lifted it up four or five feet. For the house, like others, is but two or three wooden posts, twined with bamboos, and plastered outside with a little mud, and if it is to be very smart, coated with lime. Ten or fifteen feet is the utmost height, and the roofing is of dry leaves.'

But work like this was not possible very long. For a few months, from the summer or autumn of 1857 to the spring of 1858 it might be continued, but very early in 1858 the persecutors were busy. Mgr. Retort had left Vinh-tri in April, and was in flight.

But still M. Venard, with his friend M. Theurel, remained undisturbed at Hoang-Ngueyen. These two, who were now permitted to be together, were old friends; they had been together at the Seminary of Foreign Missions, and they had met again at Tonking, and they were able to keep a good deal together during the dark days of sorrow that were coming. It was in that terrible June of which.Mgr. Retort has given so dark a picture that their flight commenced.

'On the 10th of June, in the middle of the night, a Christian woke us hurriedly.' This is M. Venard's own account in a letter to his brother Eusebius. 'The troops were on the march to surround our house and to make us prisoners. Pack up our traps and fly we must; and this was not easy. We were two Europeans, three Annamite fathers, ten or fifteen catechists, above a hundred students, and there was all the mission furniture to be disposed of. But sudden flights are common affairs here, and two hours were enough to put away every thing. On the morning of St. Barnabas's day the mandarin and troops arrived. There were 2000 soldiers and 1500 young pagans of the neighbourhood posted so as to watch all the approaches to the college. In a few minutes not only the college, but three neighbouring villages, almost wholly Christian, were also surrounded. Escape might seem impossible. But our warning had been in time. Our students had been sent off to distant villages; two only, who had delayed their departure and were seeking their way out, were caught, and treated at once with the cangue. The soldiers, who had been promised a rich plunder, finding nothing but bare walls, and houses looking as if they had been long deserted, in their rage spread themselves over the country, and came upon the very village in which the larger number of our students had sought shelter; but again they had been in time, and just managed their escape. Only ten, less prompt than the others, as they were flying across the fields were overtaken by the soldiers, and carried back to share the torture with their companions. Of the number was a deacon, over seventy years old. Several others were afterwards taken, three Annamite priests, and some fifty others; the three priests were beheaded; the two catechists and the poor old deacon died under their tortures; and the rest were exiled to an unwholesome and wild mountainous district.'

The full fury of the storm was then pouring down. M. Venard's own situation at the time has been pictured for us by himself. 'Our Christians keep guard round my cabin; all I have to do is to sit quiet in my corner, without a word or the slightest noise. Even a sneeze or a cough might betray me. In these retreats we consider it good fortune if we have a little hole for light, so as to be able to read our office or some word of consolation. In this weary though self-imposed imprisonment we learn patience, and to surrender our lives wholly to God's providence. Should a mandarin seem disposed to search the house, as soon as darkness allows there is a speedy flight to another hiding-place, just like the one that has been left. On a temporary lull or some favourable moment we may get a stretch of our legs or a breath of fresh air. But our greatest trouble is that we cannot administer the sacraments, and that large numbers of our converts die without any spiritual help. And another grief is the danger of the poor Christians who give us hospitality, so that we often choose rather to trust ourselves to the good faith of pagans, for these last are less suspected. M. Theurel and I stayed two days and two nights in one of their houses, but we did not see the master; he kept himself hid, that he might not see a European face. In the night we received a sudden notice to leave, and we had not gone a quarter of an hour before the mandarin was there to seize us. Mgr. Retord, knowing how we were hunted from place to place, advised us to try the mountains, as he and Mgr. Jeantet had done. We did; but an apostate, who had caused much mischief, got a clue to the matter, and the cave where the Bishop had been lying was surrounded and all the mountain passes beset. All our little property was taken, but there were no prisoners. . . . M. Theurel, M. Titaut, and I ascended the mountains; we walked with bleeding feet over the cats' ears, and were alone in the forests. We were in perfect peace for a fortnight; things daily became better; rain-water served us for drink and for cooking; we made a little straight path to walk and recite our office; the inhabitants of the village of Dong-Chiem every morning brought us provisions; we were beginning to dig up the ground to plant some vegetables, when one morning we had a visit from six pagans, fully armed, out on pretence of tiger-hunting. We received them with great civility; but presently we were off to the forest close by, and down we went as quick as we could to our boat on the river, which was there against emergencies. These hunters were only so in pretence; they were really spies sent by the mandarins in search of us. We then determined to keep to our boats amidst the reeds, now in one place, now in another. A devoted young Christian, quite trustworthy, brought us food daily, as if he had gone to fish. This wandering life went on for weeks, when we perceived that we were noticed, and were forced to separate and seek shelter in houses as we could. I went back to my old district, and for three weeks lived in the house of one of my catechists, but amidst constant alarms; then I lodged myself at But-Son, in a convent, and there I am now,' *i.e.* in December 1858. 'This village is half Christian, half pagan; and in case of alarm I have promised not to leave the place, but to take refuge in a cavern that has been prepared for me. M. Saiget, who has been for three months in a dark place, escaped through a hole in the roof, and has been able to come and join me. Now we enjoy a certain tranquillity. The nuns have given us up their own room, which is large enough for us to walk six or seven steps; and two of our catechists are with us, so that we study Chinese together to fill up our time. But the spies of the mandarin surround us, and the poor nuns are in a continual terror. There are sixteen of them, and they take it by turns to watch day and night. But still it is a great happiness to them to have the administration of the sacraments, confession, and communion, while we do our best to strengthen and console them.'

In this convent he was afterwards joined by his friend Mgr. Theurel, for he had now become the Bishop Coadjutor, and here together they remained, till one day the mayor, at the head of a party of persecutors, broke] in upon them. M. Venard and the Bishop contrived to hide themselves between the double walls prepared for such occasions, and through the chinks they could see the ill-usage of the poor nuns who had been their friends. They could see the intruders laying their hands on every article of any use, and making it their prey, and could hear their savage cries and threats. For several hours this went on; M. Venard and his companion close to their enemies, and not daring to move, and hardly to breathe, lest the sound should penetrate and discover them. But in the end the party broke up, and went away to regale themselves, and in the darkness of the night the fugitives got away and sought another refuge; and this next refuge was what M. Venard calls 'a smoky hole belonging to a pious woman;' and there, he adds, 'we were joined by another missionary, who had equal difficulty in making good his retreat.' Here they were, three missionaries, one of them a bishop, 'lying side by side, day and night, in a space of about a yard and a half square,' their 'only light and means of breathing being three holes, the size of a little finger, made in the mud wall, which the poor old woman was obliged to conceal by some fagots thrown down outside.' 'Under our feet,' says M. Venard, 'was a brick cellar, constructed in the dead of the night with great skill by one of our catechists; in this cellar were three bamboo tubes, cleverly contrived so as to have their openings to the fresh air on the borders of a neighbouring lake. This same catechist has built two other hiding-places of the same sort in this village, with several double partition walls.'

Here the three remained together for three weeks, and, wretched as the confinement was, they were cheerful and gay. 'When our three holes gave no more light, we had a little lamp, with a shade to prevent its tiny rays from penetrating outside through the chinks of the prison. One day we found ourselves surrounded—in fact completely blocked up —by sentinels posted at every corner of the house where we were, so that there was no possibility of passing from one house to the other. An apostate had betrayed us, who knew that we were in the village ... From morning till night the pagans passed and repassed us, upset every thing in the houses, hunted in every corner. They broke in the outer walls, inside which we were concealed, and I thought our hour of martyrdom was come. But vain are the efforts of men when God opposes their designs!'

Life of this sort, prolonged for weeks and months,

was very trying, and even on a mind so elastic as M. Venard's made its impression, and it was most exhausting to the bodily frame. What is here narrated is taken from one of his letters written in the spring of 1860 : 'I write,' he says, 'from a little dark hole, of which the only light is through the crack of a half-opened door, which just enables me to trace these few lines, and now and then to read a few pages of a book. For one must be ever on the watch. If the dog barks or a stranger passes, the door must be at once closed, and I must be ready to go down into a still lower hole, hollowed out beneath in this temporary retreat.' And the painfulness and weariness of this situation his own words give us some idea of: 'To be always shut up between two walls, with a roof one can touch with one's hand, with spiders and rats and toads as our companions, to be obliged ever to speak in a low voice, "like the wind," as the Annamites say, and then to be continually hearing of the torture and death of brother priests, of the destruction of missions, of the exile of scholars, and worse again, as is sometimes the case, of their failing under torture—it is only a special grace, a grace fitted to our state, that saves us from being utterly discouraged and cast down. For our health, we are as poor plants in cellars, stretching out their lanky, sickly branches towards the light and air. When I put my mouth close to the door which guards our retreat, I own that I have sometimes a feeling of envy towards those who are free to enjoy God's fresh air and sunshine. A few days ago I made my way to a neighbouring house, and wondered to find myself tottering like a drunken man. In truth, with the habit the power of walking was also gone, and daylight made me giddy.'

All this while M. Venard was living in the midst of his faithful Christians. They were numerous in that district. But the mandarin was furious. Eager as he was, he could not lay his hands on a missionary. He exercised his cruelty and tyranny in various ways, but the Christians were too many for him, and they were all of one mind. One day, however, one of those secret hiding-places which the missionaries used was discovered, and it produced a great burst of activity. Spades and hoes were quickly at work, and it was threatened that every Christian house should be dug up till the Europeans were got hold of. This led to M. Venard's changing his residence. He went away and hid himself in the midst of a pagan population. 'They seem kind and friendly,' he says, 'but God only can read their hearts. They have a high sense of hospitality, and would rarely wrong a stranger who has come to seek it.' M. Venard's letter was to a friend in France.

'Dear old friend,' he writes at its close, 'when I think on all our sorrows I am almost overwhelmed, and I can scarcely restrain my tears. How flourishing was our mission before this terrible persecution! How many were the souls gathered in! And now I am as Jeremiah lamenting over the ruins of Jerusalem. Will these ruins ever be rebuilt? It is like Ezekiel's vision of the dry bones? Can they be brought back to life? I have given you an outline of our miseries, but there are a number of little circumstances adding to them, too many indeed to name. "Magna est velut mare contritio tua! Quis medebitur tui?" But for myself, dearest friend, I have a confidence in God that I shall complete my course, and not lose any of the deposit of faith, hope, and charity; and that, finally, by the merits of our Lord, I shall share with his friends in the crown of the just.'

M. Venard was not idle when he was living amongst the pagans. He preached and taught them with great success, and if it were not for the terrors of the persecution many would have avowed themselves Christians. But it was not safe, after having attracted notice, to stay there long, so he removed to the Christian village of Ke-Beo, where, again, he did not spare himself, and where there was much to be done. His active zeal produced a great change amongst them, and restored the fervour and courage which had been sadly dimmed. Thence he went to Ke-Bang, and there also strengthened and consoled the terrified Christians, and ministered to them the sacraments. After that he had some quiet at But-son. But-son was one of the most heroic of Christian villages. Its people had signalised themselves by their bravery, and it was the most safe and sure refuge which a missionary could seek. This people had been put to the proof and had stood it nobly. The mandarin, with a body of soldiers, had gone to the village and ordered the people to trample on the cross. He expected instant submission, or at least that some would comply. But one and all these inhabitants refused; and they stood out so resolutely that they prevailed. At But-son M. Venard met Mgr. Jeantet, but he did not stay long. He went back to Ke-Beo. And here it was that he fell into the hands of his enemies. He was living in a house outside the village where he could be easily surprised without a chance of escape; for the country was at the time inundated, and the spot was quite surrounded with water. The mandarin had learnt his presence, and, at nine o'clock on the morning of November 30, he came with several junks and a body of men, and surrounded the house. Then a party of them entered and found M. Venard between the double walls. In this instance the thin partition was no concealment. The mandarin kicked it down easily, and M. Venard was dragged out and carried away; and before the Christians knew anything of the matter he was gone. He was taken to the district town, and from thence to Kecho, and in both places he was treated with respect and consideration. The prefect of the district gave him a more comfortable cage and a lighter chain, and carried his condescension so far as to invite him to dine with him.

As he was journeying in his cage he was an object of much curiosity. Crowds assembled to witness his departure from the district town, and a young Christian in his fervour threw himself on his knees before the cage imploring the father's blessing; but he did it at the cost of his own liberty, for he was quickly made a prisoner. Large crowds thronged the way also, as he was borne into Kecho, making their remarks as he passed. 'What a pretty boy that European is!' 'He is gay and bright, as if he were going to a feast.' 'He does not look afraid at all.' 'He has come to our country to do us good, and for that they will put him to death.' M. Venard heard them, and has repeated their words to us. Without any delay he was led before the judge. His catechist Khang was with him. 'I prayed God's Holy Spirit,' he says, ' to strengthen us both, and to speak by our mouths, according to our Saviour's promise; and I invoked the Queen of Martyrs, and begged her to help her faithful child.'

He was asked various questions; but these questions are much of the usual character, and it is needless to repeat them. The judge, as a preliminary, gave him a cup of tea, and throughout he was dealt with very easily. He was asked to name the places and persons who had sheltered him, and to trample on the cross, which of course he refused; and he was let alone. They did not offer to touch him with the rattan, or to ill-use him in any way. Throughout his imprisonment he met with kindness and respect; the soldiers showed even signs of affection; they opened his cage and let him come out to walk, and continued to do so though they were rebuked for it; they checked themselves when he reproved them, as he did not fail to do when they used licentious language, which is a custom with them. And one of their number named Tien was conspicuous in his show of attention; and the delicacy and simplicity with which this excellent fellow, as M. Venard calls him, gave tokens of his high respect were quite touching. At Kecho M. Venard was near his old friend Mgr. Theurel. The Bishop was not more than a day's journey away, and kept up a constant intercourse with him. Little notes passed between them, and in many ways the Bishop was able to render kind offices. He provided him with food on the mandarin stopping his allowance; which could be easily managed by a Christian widow named Nghiên, who chanced to be sister of the great mandarin's cook. He sent in an Annamite priest to him, Father Thinh, the vicar of the parish of Kecho, as he calls him; and here he was helped by a Christian soldier named Huong Moi. This was one of those fine specimens of native character that from time to time appear in this history. The Bishop's own words about him ought not to be left out. He was 'the head of the patrol, a man true as steel, whose house had been my refuge for two months, and who mingled with the troop of servants of the prefecture, and obtained his present post out of devotion to our sufferer.' The contrast between Father Thinh, good but timid, and the brave Huong Moi is well brought out. 'Huong Moi,' says the Bishop, 'undertook to introduce him into the mandarin's palace, and even to the cage of M. Venard. The meeting took place on the 15th of January, in the presence of the guards and a whole crowd of people in the suite of the mandarins, who filled the hall. M. Venard, making a show of not recognising Father Thinh, asked the chief of the patrol who he was; to which Huong Moi replied that it was the *thây-câ*, an ambiguous word meaning priest as well as head of the family. Poor Father Thinh at this word felt his heart sink within him; but Huong Moi, careless of danger, went on with his fun, however, which served to divert the attention of the people around, and hide the confusion of the poor father. M. Venard, on this introduction, as if to a stranger, was suffered to leave his cage and walk in the garden, using the opportunity to make his confession. On his return the good Huong Moi again sought to amuse the audience, and Father Thinh, standing by the bars of his cage, spoke a few low words to M. Venard, and gave him absolution. Then in the evening, the widow before named brought him the blessed sacrament, which had been left with her by Father Thinh.'

M. Venard never lost his composure, and to whomsoever he speaks it is in the same tone of happy confidence.

'My heart is as tranquil as a lake that reflects the blue sky, and I have no fear,' he writes, December 28, 1860, to his friend Mgr. Theurel. 'I am waiting patiently for the day when God will allow me to offer the sacrifice of my blood.' So, January 2, 1861, to his father, brothers, and sister: 'I do not regret this world; my soul thirsts for the waters of eternal life. My exile is over; I touch the soil of my real country; earth vanishes, heaven opens; I go to God.'

And, January 3d, to Mgr. Theurel: 'I am now come to the hour so long desired by us all. It is no longer, as in the Hymn of Departure, "*Perhaps* some day," but "*Very soon* all the blood in my veins

> Will be shed for Thee. My feet (O, what joy!)
> *Are now* loaded with chains."

In the long weary hours of my cage I think of eternity. Time is, after all, so short when thus measured. You will repeat the words of St. Martin: "Domine si adhuc populo tuo sum necessarius, non recuso laborem;" but I may say with St. Paul: "Jam delibor, et tempus resolutionis meæ instat, (*tibi*) vivere Christus est, mihi mori lucrum. O quam gloriosum est regnum in quo cum Christo gaudent omnes sancti. . . Audivi vocem. . . Beati mortui." [He was repeating over words familiar with these missionaries, which they sang together with moved hearts on All Saints and All Souls day]. I do not know that I shall ever be allowed to write again; good-bye. I should have been very happy to have gone on working with you. I do so love this Tonking mission; but now in place of the sweat of my brow I give them my blood. The sword hangs over my head, but I have no fears. Our good God has taken pity on my weakness, and filled me with Himself, so that I am happy and even joyous. . . . When my head falls under the axe of the executioner, receive it, O loving Jesus! O Immaculate Mother! as the bunch of ripe grapes falls under the scissors, as the full-blown rose which has been gathered in your honor. Ave Maria! I will say this also for you. Ave Maria!' These last words refer to a request which Mgr. Theurel had made him, that on entering Paradise he would salute Mary for him.

To Mgr. Jeantet, January 20th, he writes: 'I have not received a single stroke of the rattan; I have met with very little insult and much sympathy; no one here wishes me to die. The people of the household of the great mandarin are kindness itself to me. I have suffered nothing in comparison to my brethren; I have only to lay my head quietly on the block, under the axe of the executioner, and at once I shall find myself in the presence of our Lord, saying, "Here am I, O Lord! Thy little martyr." I shall present my palm to our Lady and say, "Hail, Mary; my Mother and my Mistress, all hail!" I shall take my place in the ranks of the thousands slain for the holy name of Jesus; and I shall intone the eternal Hosanna. Amen.'

The day of his death was fast approaching. Ten or twelve days more, and the scene so strongly depicted in his mind would be realised. But there are other letters which must be given at length, the last letters which he wrote to his sister and brother, full of affection and faith. First to his sister:

'Now that my last hour is approaching I wish to send you, my darling sister and friend, a special word of love and farewell; for our hearts have been one from childhood. You have never had a secret from me nor I from you. When, as a schoolboy, I used to leave home for college, it was my little Melanie who prepared my box, and softened with her tender words the pain of parting. It was you who shared in the joys and sorrows of my college life; it was you who strengthened my vocation for the foreign missions; it was with you, dearest Melanie, that I passed that solemn night of the 26th of February 1851, which was our last meeting upon earth, and which we spent in a conversation so full of intimate thoughts, and feelings of sympathy and holy hope, that it brought to my mind the farewell of St. Benedict and St. Scholastica. And when I crossed the seas, and came to water with sweat and blood this Annamite country, your letters were my strength, my joy, and my consolation. It is, then, but fair that in this last hour your brother should think of you, and send you a few last words of love and never-dying remembrance. . . . . It is midnight. Round my wooden cage I see nothing but banners and sabres. In one corner of the hall where my cage is placed, a group of soldiers are playing cards; another group are at draughts. From time to time they strike the hours of the night on their drums or tam-tams. Two feet off from my cage a small oil-lamp throws a vacillating light on this sheet of Chinese paper, and enables me to trace these few lines. Each day I expect my sentence. To-morrow, perhaps, I shall be led to execution. Happy death, which conducts me to the gates of eternal life! As we may judge, I shall be beheaded; a glorious shame of which heaven will be the reward. When you hear it, dearest sister, you will shed tears, but they must be tears of joy. Think of your brother with the aureola of the martyrs, and bearing in his hand the palm of victory!

A few short hours more and my soul will quit this earth—will finish her exile—will have done with the fight. I shall mount upwards and reach our own true home. There, in that abode of God's elect, I shall behold what the eyes of man cannot see; hear harmonies such as have never reached his ears; enjoy a happiness beyond what his heart can conceive. But first the bunch of grapes must be trodden in the wine-press. May I become pure bread and wine, fit for the Master's use! I hope it, through the mercies of my Saviour and Redeemer, and through the protection of His Immaculate Mother. And so, though still in the arena and in the midst of the fight, I dare to intone the hymn of triumph, as if certain of victory .And you, dearest sister, I leave in the field of virtues and good works. Reap a great harvest of these for the eternal life that awaits us both; gather faith, hope, charity, patience, gentleness, sweetness, perseverance, and a holy death; and so shall we be together now and for evermore.'

To his brother Eusebius again : 'By the time you receive this your brother will be no longer in this bad world, *totus in maligno positus*. He will have left it for a better, where you must strive to join him some day. Your brother's head will have fallen, and every drop of his blood will have been poured out for God. He will have died a martyr! That was the dream of my youth. When, as a little man of nine years old, I used to take my pet goat to browse on the slopes of Bel-Ari, I used to devour the life and death of the venerable Charles Cornay, and say to myself, "And I too will go to Tonking, and I too will be a martyr!" O admirable thread of Divine Providence, which has guided me through the labyrinth of this life to this very mission of Tonking and to martyrdom. Bless and praise our good and merciful God with me, dearest Eusebius, who has taken so much care of His miserable little servant. *Attraxit me, miserans mei!*'

The writing of these letters is his occupation on the night of January 20th, and he only ceases writing because his feeble light fails him. 'My lamp gives no more light. Good-bye, dearest Eusebius, until the day when you come to rejoin me in heaven.'

On the 22d of February the death which he had been expecting came. He did not know it the day before; he would hardly believe it on that morning when, very early, the widow Nyhién stole in and told him that the sentence was arrived, and preparations were already being made for the execution. And soon after the soldiers crowded round his cage, so quickly as to deprive him of the opportunity just offered him of feeding himself once more on the Bread of life. An aged female, sent to him by Father Thinh, had brought him the sacred Host in a tiny box. It was already in his hands when it was snatched away by the soldiers; but though he lost the happiness, the widow Nyhién, terrified by the idea of the profanation, by her earnest boldness recovered the box, which was restored to Father Thinh.

M. Venard had prepared for himself a dress of honour for the occasion—a white vest and a robe of silk never worn before. After hearing his sentence he made a short address to the mandarins, but ending it with the words, 'One day we shall again meet, at the tribunal of God,' they were offended. 'I will have no insolence,' said the mandarin of justice, rising hastily; and the procession was ordered to move off. There were two elephants and two hundred soldiers. M. Venard sang psalms and hymns as they passed through the town. The death was not an easy one. The executioner was a brutal fellow, an old soldier, greedy of gain, and bent on possessing himself of the new clothes worn by M. Venard. He asked M. Venard what he would give him to do his work promptly; but M. Venard said, 'The longer it lasts, the better it will be.' And it was prolonged; for the first blow given was but a slight one, nor was the second sufficient to sever the head from the body, and the wretch went on hacking, so as to move the indignation of the bystanders. The head was recovered, but not without considerable delay and difficulty.

Towards the end of June of this same year, 1861, rumours reached Mgr. Theurel that two more priests were in the hands of the enemy, MM. Charbonnier and Mathevon. It was but a rumour, and for months it remained a matter of uncertainty, for he had no means of ascertaining the fact. He was able at length, but not before November, to send a nun, 'one of our most intrepid and clever couriers,' according to his own words, to gain the information he wanted. She came back, and brought a horrible tale of the cruelties to which the missionaries were subject; but the story was not true, for it had been told her only to make her more frightened, and to get money from her employers. Nevertheless, MM. Charbonnier and Mathevon were really prisoners. Their life, since the time of their parting with Mgr. Retort, had been a series of trials; and M. Charbonnier has himself written out an account which might read like a romance. On separating from the Bishop he made his way to the village of Bach-hat. The journey itself to one just risen from a sick-bed was hard enough. It was one of two days, it must be done at night, amidst heavy rains, and through woods thronged with tigers. However, Bach-hat was a Christian village in which there was a convent of nuns where he might have lodgings. And in this convent he stayed several months, up to January 1859. It was a quiet easy time after his roaming life on the mountains. But he was disturbed. Some soldiers one day appeared in the village, and all were in terror. M. Charbonnier for safety attempted a ruse. He made out as if he had effected his escape from the village, but his flight was only a pretence; for making a circuit of the village, he entered it again, and chose for his refuge the very place which of all others would seem the most insecure, that of the village chief, where the soldiers were constantly resorting, and where the missionary would seem to be exposing himself to certain capture. The boldness of the act, however, was its security. The chief himself was a firm friend, and could be trusted. But soon after suspicion fell on the chief, and he was made prisoner; and M. Charbonnier thought it prudent to hasten away. It was difficult to manage, for the soldiers were all round; nevertheless it was the only chance. So under cover of night he cautiously stole away through some gardens, and reached the outskirts of the village; then caution was over, the whole party set off at speed, running for life over the fields, to look for a fresh concealment. M. Charbonnier thought that he knew of one, but when they reached it, it was only to be disappointed, and no better shelter could be found than a solitary cottage in the midst of the fields, into which a poor widow allowed him entrance. After which a military chief admitted him into his house, but not to stay; for suspicions were excited almost immediately, and it was thought best to go away altogether, and seek safety in some other direction. There was a convent sixty miles off where M. Mathevon was lodged, of which he had been told, and there accordingly he went; and for nearly a year it afforded him shelter. It was a happy thing in those stern times to be able to live in such peaceful retirement, to be able to say Mass, to have the society of his friend. But in 1860 came out that fatal decree that made such havoc in the Christian villages, and ordered off to prison all the principal inhabitants. Then it became no longer safe to remain in the convent, and some other refuge had to be sought. First the mountains were tried, but as usual the bad atmosphere was too deadly in its influence; M. Charbonnier was soon prostrated, and at whatever cost it was necessary to remove. The next idea was to make for the coast, and to seek a refuge with the French at Touron. It was a long and difficult journey through the mountain forests, and M. Charbonnier was too ill to walk, and must be carried all the way; but it was the only safety they could think of. All the travelling had to be done at night, and they had to pass through dense woods, to traverse deep ravines, and to thread paths so intricate and dangerous that at times they had to turn and seek some new passage. The journey took them a fortnight. It was with more alarm than pleasure that they were received by the Christians whom they then encountered, who dreaded the terrible penalties they would suffer should a missionary be discovered in their house or village; and so the missionaries found them forward enough in helping them in their design to make the voyage to Touron. They soon got into a vessel, and set out on this object. But it was only for a disappointment. The voyage was one of nine days. They reached Touron March 31, 1860. It was a few days too late. The French were gone. The first thing that struck them on entering the bay was the remarkable silence. There was not a sound to be heard, there were no vessels to be seen. But it caused no suspicion of what had really happened; they thought the forces were away perhaps on some military expedition. On landing they noticed a little cabin where there was a light, and advancing towards it put a question in French, but looking in, and observing a soldier in the Annamite dress, it roused a doubt; and soon with dismay they learned from a catechist, who had been out to make inquiries, that six days ago the whole French armament had sailed away. Then they became aware not simply of the futility of their voyage, but of the perils of their present position. They were close upon a military station. There was the risk of immediate discovery. The tide was now setting into the bay, and whether they must wait till it turned, or whether they could make way against it, they could not tell. And for the nine days that it would take to go back from whence they came they had not enough provisions, hardly enough for half the time.

In their pull out of the bay they succeeded; and for two days the wind favoured them, but then they got into trouble. First a dead calm, then a strong and adverse wind, then a narrow escape from being driven on a rock and perishing. But after all they accomplished their voyage back, and as for food they managed to pick up some as they coasted along.

But on again landing there was the old difficulty where to find a lodging. The Christians, however, in this instance braved the danger, and gave shelter to the missionaries; and miserable as their state was, still for months, I may say a year, they were in safety. Till April 1861 they remained undisturbed in this Christian village: they could occasionally say Mass, they could breathe fresh air. But then the village fell under suspicion, and there was a visit from the soldiers, who searched about, and entered the very house where MM. Charbonnier and Mathevon were. The missionaries from their underground hiding-places heard them tramping about over their heads. After this there was perpetual moving about—now in one house, now in another, now in some cavern on the mountains. One day towards the end of August, with two Annamites as their companions, they were sheltering themselves in one of these caverns. They had just finished their morning meal of a little rice, when a man from the village was seen going out into the forests to cut wood. He stopped as he passed the cave, and gave a glance inward; he might have heard a sound of voices; it was but for a moment he paused, and quickly he went on as if he had noticed nothing. On his return in the evening he walked steadily by without turning his eyes in the direction of the cavern; and the little party, who had been troubled with fears that they had been observed, regained their spirits. But next day suddenly they were beset by six armed men, who overpowered them and made them prisoners. They had a little money, and offered it for their freedom; and if a fresh and larger body of men had not subsequently come up, their capturers would have let them off. They were carried in the first instance before the sub-prefect, who was no way harsh towards them, but they were invested as usual with the cangue, and then sent on the next day in palanquins to the chief town. There MM. Charbonnier and Mathevon were separated. M. Mathevon was taken to his prison, and M. Charbonnier was brought up for examination. On the first examination the mandarins were very lenient. They asked a number of questions, but were content that many of them should remain unanswered. M. Charbonnier's words and demeanour seemed to make an impression on them, and they asked him whether he did not feel shame at seeing himself treated like a criminal, and at the ignominy of being bound with a chain and having on a cangue. But M. Charbonnier said that as he had committed no crime, he felt no shame, that it was rather a glory to him, as it was suffered in his endeavours to preach to them the true religion. The mandarins let him go this time, warning him that if he continued obstinate in his silence he would be tortured.

The next day accordingly the examination was resumed; and to show M. Charbonnier that they were in earnest, there were conspicuous in view the preparations for the torture. There were the soldiers rattan in hand; there was the smith with his fire heating the pincers; there was the frame studded with nails, and a man sharpening them. M. Charbonnier was led in by two soldiers with drawn swords, and conducted before the judge. Again they commenced questioning in the same polite manner that had been observed the previous day; but when nothing could be got out of their prisoner—when he would not name a person or a village where he had been—the mandarin's patience would hold out no longer. 'Tie him to the stakes,' he said. Then the soldiers drove three stakes into the ground, and M. Charbonnier was placed on the ground, and tied to the middle one. His hands were then stretched out and tied to the two others. There he sat with naked legs forcibly stretched out like his hands, and pulled by cords to other stakes a short distance off. 'What a disgrace,' said the mandarin to him, 'to be thus exposed before this crowd of persons!' But M. Charbonnier was pleased at the shame he was suffering for God's sake. 'Press his fingers,' said the mandarin. Then a soldier, taking four small sticks about eighteen inches long tied at one end, inserted his fingers and began to press them. As he did not speak, the mandarin ordered another soldier to press his other hand in the same manner; but still it was of no use. Then the pincers were tried. A soldier pinched the fleshy part of his thigh, and as he did so the mandarin put his questions. But he could not get a word out of M. Charbonnier. After one more attempt, alike unsuccessful, he thought it useless to proceed, and gave up the torture. M. Charbonnier said that the pincers were less painful than the sticks; and the mandarin wondered much that his attempts to inflict pain made so little impression. One of the soldiers asked him why it was that he looked up to heaven when his fingers were being pressed with the sticks. 'Do you not know,' said M. Charbonnier, 'that the God of the Christians is in heaven? He it was that gave me strength to endure all the torments I suffered; and I have confidence that He will yet support me in whatever I shall have to bear.'

M. Mathevon's case was worse than that of his companion. In his first examination he fainted as his hands were pressed with the sticks. But he was tortured a second time. There were two applications of the pincers, and the pain made him vomit. Still, on the whole, the sufferings of these two missionaries were much less than that of many of their brethren. They had to undergo the tedium of many months' imprisonment, shut up in a narrow cage, ignorant of what would be their lot; sometimes imagining themselves on the eve of martyrdom, and then, after a short glow of expectation, brought back again to the dreary monotony of their prison life. Towards the end of the tenth month, as June was drawing to a close, there came a change. The mandarin's manner was quite altered. He offered them tea, inquired if they did not want clothes, permitted them to come out of their cages, and they did not know what to make of it; then they learned that they would certainly be restored to liberty, that a treaty of peace had been settled, and that the persecution was at an end. But it was by only a slow process that they realised these advantages. First they were transferred to Huè. During the journey to the coast they had to remain in their cages, and if they were let out on ship-board, it was only as a favour; nor were they perfectly free till they sailed up the river to Saigon, when in a moment their situation changed entirely. Then they found themselves in the midst of friends, and their sorrows were at an end. August had far advanced, and it was nearly a twelvemonth since the beginning of their captivity.

Heavy as the persecution had fallen on Western Tonking, it had fallen heavier on the Dominican vicariates. Mgr. Melchior's martyrdom in its circumstances was more horrible than any other. And two more bishops and a priest of those vicariates were taken and executed during the period of the imprisonment of the two French missionaries. Just before his arrest Mgr. Melchior had consecrated a successor. The person chosen was Mgr. Ochoa, one of those priests who only a month before had made their appearance in Tonking. Mgr. Ochoa was already a man of note. His learning and his piety had both made themselves felt. His previous life had been a succession of rises in holiness: he had first chosen the ecclesiastical state; then, to draw more close to God, he had taken the Dominican habit; then he came out to confront the dangers of a missionary life in Tonking, and had hardly reached the spot before he was singled out to fill the most prominent position. A few days after his consecration the whole weight of the vicariate of Central Tonking fell on his shoulders. Mgr. Melchior was taken, and hurried off to Kecho, and tragically slain, as has been already narrated. But the new Bishop was equal to the task imposed on him, hard as it was. He was not discouraged, but resigned himself to the will of God, and braced himself for his task. He was new to the place, he was a stranger to the language; so to learn the language and to gain experience he went for six months into Eastern Tonking, and sojourned with Mgr. Alcazar. Then he went back to his own vicariate; and though he was obliged to live in concealment, in caverns, and in subterranean passages, still his administration was vigorous and active; and the three years through which it was continued were fruitful in advantages to his flock. But the cruel edict of August 1861, which spread dismay and misery so widely in Cochin China and Tonking, brought a change in the situation of M. Ochoa. The hiding-places which he had hitherto used were no longer safe places of concealment, and from his cavern he transferred himself, with F. Almato as his companion, to a fishing-boat; and there, amidst the numerous boats that swarmed on the river, he hoped to pass unnoticed. Soon after he fell in with Mgr. Hermosilla, Vicar-apostolic of Eastern Tonking, who had also betaken himself to the river; and all three kept together. While they were at anchor off a town on the banks, one of their boats, that of Mgr. Hermosilla, was boarded by an officer and soldiers, and the venerable prelate was made prisoner. He was a grand old man, as M. Venard tells us, who enjoyed his hospitality on first landing in Tonking. He had been bishop just twenty years, having been consecrated by Mgr. Retort on his return from Manilla. He, like Mgr. Ochoa, had been the successor of martyrs, for he filled the place left vacant by the two bishops, Henares and Delgado, the victims of Minh-Menh. And now his own turn came. His capture was the result of treachery. The sons and nephews of the very men who were harbouring the missionaries in their boats were the guides who brought their enemies to take them. The boat in which Mgr. Ochoa and F. Almato were was at a little distance; and learning what was going on, they made off. They left their boat and went ashore; but the land was no more free from danger than was the sea; and again it was through false friends that their ruin came.

Some pagans spoke to them kindly, and promised to aid them in their efforts to escape; but they gave information to their enemies, and were the instruments of their capture. Loaded with the cangue and chains, the Bishop and his friend were led to the capital, near to which they were at the time. At the gates of the city they saw lying across the road the sacred emblem of their redemption. Immediately they fell on their knees with the most profound respect, and persisted that they would not move a step until the cross was taken away; nor did they advance till it was done. Without any delay they were taken before the governor and examined; and then, shut up in cages, they again found themselves by the side of Mgr. Hermosilla, who had preceded them. There was no cruelty displayed towards them; they were strictly watched, but treated with respect. But their execution was hastened. Orders from Huè were anticipated, and the mandarin on his own authority gave the sentence of death. November 1st was the day fixed. An immense crowd had assembled. There was the usual procession: two elephants, lines of soldiers, and the three martyrs, this time borne along in their cages. On descending from their cages their first act was to throw themselves on their knees; and on the request of Mgr. Hermosilla, a short space was allowed them for prayer. They were then bound and tied to stakes. When all was ready the voice of the trumpeter was heard giving orders to the soldiers to arrest any one who might show sympathy or compassion towards the sufferers. The poor trumpeter who gave out these words was a Christian; the tears streamed down his face as he spoke, for he could not command his sorrow. Then he spoke again through his trumpet, and this time it was to command the executioners to strike at the third sound of the bell. At the given signal the blows were struck, one head falling at the first stroke, and the other two at the second. The heads were then fixed on posts and exposed for three days. This time, however, no farther indignity was offered to the martyrs. The Christians, indeed, were allowed to possess themselves of them, though it was at a high price that they obtained the favour. This premature execution of the Spanish missionaries was of service to MM. Charbonnier and Mathevon; at least it kept the local mandarins from acting previous to receiving commands from Huè. For the king was not pleased with this haste, and was beginning to feel that it would be better not to too far aggravate the hostile feelings of his enemies. With his own subjects he had no intention of holding back his hand, but his policy with respect to the Europeans had become more cautious.

The calamities suffered by the Christians in this part of Tonking were at this period at their height, and, owing to local circumstances as well as to the character of the governor, were worse than anywhere else. Villages were depopulated and destroyed, and the Christians being too numerous to be tried and executed, all sorts of methods were devised to put them out of the way. Their unhappy state has been thus described by one of the missionaries: 'They were beaten pitilessly, loaded with heavy chains and the cangue, tormented with every instrument of cruelty their persecutors could devise; their limbs were dislocated by stretching them with cords; they were exposed bareheaded to the burning sun; they were bound and thrown down precipices, to live or die as chance might be. And all this was not enough to satisfy the bitter hatred that was growing stronger and stronger. They were teased with hot pincers; they were crushed under the feet of elephants, or tormented and mutilated by their trunks, striking them down just as heavy flails would thresh the corn.' So speaks a missionary who had lived in the midst of these sufferings, and had known all the anguish of the numerous sufferers. The decree of August was the culminating point of these severities; and the following summary, supplied by one of the priests, gives us a view of its extreme stringency:

Art. 1. All who bear the name of Christians—men, women, children, and old men—shall be dispersed amongst the pagan villages.

Art. 2. Every pagan village is responsible for the Christians sent there, and in the proportion of five pagans to a Christian is chargeable with their guardianship.

Art. 3. Every Christian village is to be destroyed.

Art. 4. All the Christian lands are to be divided amongst the pagans of the neighbouring villages.

Art. 5. Every Christian must be branded on the

face, with the words 'False religion' on one cheek and the name of his district on the other.

The universal misery occasioned by this decree is pictured for us by M. Fernandez: 'The Christians,' he says, 'on its publication were quite stupefied. The men might be seen, with their heads bowed down and their faces settled into deep melancholy, wandering up and down; the women were heard uttering loud cries of grief, while the children wept by their side simply at the tears of their mothers. And when the decree came to be executed their sorrows were increased. Then the men, with cangues round their necks, were handed over to the mayors of the pagan villages; then the women, with bitter lamentations had to leave their homes. After this came the work of destruction. The houses were pulled down, and everything the Christians had possessed became at once the prey of the invaders. The poor captives were reduced to the most wretched plight. Their whole property had been taken away from them. The little rice they were allowed to retain would furnish only a few meals. What clothes were left to them were soon sold to buy food; and it only staved off a little longer the misery that must come. Soon they were crowded in their prison, and were dying from extreme want. They were starving by hundreds, and it was wished that they should; to be rid of them was the one great object of the persecutors. Some scanty relief was brought to them by a few who had compassion; but what relief could equal the wants of the thousands who were shut up with no more to eat than the trifling dole of rice that was sometimes allowed?'

As the term of their sufferings approached they rose to their greatest height. That was in the months of May and June 1862. Civil war was then raging in Tonking, and passions were inflamed. One Pedro Phung had raised the standard of rebellion, and was followed by a large number of persons, and the rebellion had become formidable. He had collected an army of 200,000 men. He had engaged the royal troops, and had worsted them; he had mastered three whole provinces. His successes had created apprehension, and had excited more bitter hatred against the Christians. The mandarin who was governor had himself been defeated, and his rancour had been envenomed. The complete destruction of the Christians became an object of stirring interest with him. He presided at the executions, and urged them on. He ordered the Christians to be beheaded, to be burnt alive, to be coupled together and thrown into the river. In one place he collected together some five hundred, and daily ordered them out for execution. We have the numbers and the days. May 18th, twenty-one; May 22d, forty-three; May 26th, sixty-seven; as many more on the 27th, and a still larger number on the 28th. And then this brutal mandarin thought beheading too slow a process, and on the 30th, 112 more were ordered to be led out of their prison and tied together to be flung into the river; and the next day the same was done with the rest. None of these Christians, with the exception of three, flinched in their trial. They would not, though ordered, trample on the cross. Their faith was strong, and they animated each other. In their prisons the night before their death they made the Stations of the Cross, and as they went to their death they recited together the Rosary.

Scenes like this were taking place in other provinces in this disastrous month. On the 27th of May, at Sân, in the chief town, fifty-six Christians were beheaded; on the 29th, at Chânh-Dinh, ninety-six. At Quinh-Coi a number of Christians were shut up in prison, fire was set to it, and they all perished. Some broke off their cangues and tried to force their way out, but the soldiers pricked them back with their sabres, and they could not escape from the flames.

At Doi-Yen, again, one hundred and fifty were thrown into the river; and several of them, after gaining the bank, were pitilessly driven back into the stream and drowned.

This is only a glance at the cruel deeds then multiplied in all directions. How many really died it is impossible to say, but it is computed by the missionaries that in Central Tonking alone no less than sixteen thousand perished. In this list there were three bishops, a vicar-provincial, and thirty-six priests. The apostasies were not many. The colleges had been dreadfully thinned. The number of the scholars had been seven hundred, and almost all were lost; they were dead or in exile. Only six had failed in the great trial that had been made of their faith; and of these six more than one had repented and had made reparation for their fault.

An instance or two of the vigorous faith of these Christians may be adduced. A Christian named Khoa-Cuong, about thirty-five years of age, was arrested, and made a bold confession. He was beaten, and then, in chains and with the cangue lingered for months in the foul air and filth of a prison; then he was branded, and the words 'False religion of Jesus' were marked on his face. This indignity to his religion and to his Saviour he could not bear, and first with all his might he resisted the affront, and not succeeding, he afterwards got one of his companions to cut out all the other words, only leaving that of Jesus. Learning this, the mandarin ordered him to be branded again; but in this next instance, so vigorous was his resistance, that he was not overpowered. To force him to submit to the infliction he was beaten, and he was told that the only way of saving his life was to yield; but he said he would rather die, and was taken at his word.

Two women had got themselves into trouble by joining in an attempt to rescue a priest, and then, under the threat of torture, had renounced their religion; but, on a second demand made upon them to repeat their abjuration, moved with remorse, they refused. 'We have been unhappy enough,' they said, 'to deny the God of heaven and earth; our fears took away our senses, but we repent of what we have done, and we will not obey your commands for we cannot do so without sin.' The mandarin could not patiently hear of this rebellion on the part of women, and his anger was the more because they were joined in their disobedience by a young Christian girl who displayed remarkable resolution. Threats and promises alike had not the least influence on her; so all three were sentenced to be hanged. The sentence did not frighten them, but with cheerful ready mind they went away to suffer its execution.

The persecution in Tonking was prolonged even after the treaty of peace. A priest was executed, and several Christians were drowned and burnt days after the treaty had been signed, so loth were the persecutors to spare and to give up the prey of which they had once had possession.

The French arms were successful in relieving the Christians from the sufferings of this dreadful and prolonged persecution. On the 5th of June 1862 a treaty of peace was signed, followed the next month by a decree granting religious liberty, which, although it only slowly and imperfectly came into operation, yet brought the Christians out of prison, and restored them to their villages, and again allowed the missionaries to appear and minister amongst their flocks. There was still much to be borne; but the change was a very great one for the better.

CHAPTER XV.

A RETROSPECT OF THE PERSECUTION.

SOMETHING more than a year after the establishment of peace a missionary chanced to pass through central Cochin China, on his way from Laos to Saigon. During the persecution he had been living free and undisturbed amongst the savages of Laos, busy and successful in converting them to the Christian faith. What he saw on his journey made strong and vivid impressions, and he has recorded them in a letter to a friend; and they are interesting to us, because they supply certain details which well chime in with the story we have already related. They refer to that part of Cochin China where Mgr. Cuenot resided when the ravages of the persecution, though delayed, were so wide-spreading and overwhelming. 'First, I must say, that though France has imposed on the tyrant of Annam a treaty, according to which religion is to be quite free, there is much wanting as to the enjoyment of liberty. I could not show myself openly because I had not a passport, and though I was not afraid for myself if I had been taken, my Annamite companions would not have escaped torture; so I was obliged to hide. We hastened our journey in order to reach before daybreak a village in which were some hundreds of Christians. In the dark night we were travelling through a forest of grand old trees, when a cry of terror came from our guide in front. All of us shouted out as loud as we could. It was a tiger. God did not permit him to attack us, but I should not say the truth if I did not acknowledge that I had some fear; my heart sank within me. The alarm had scarcely passed away when before dawn we entered the village of Binh-Thuoc, where we rested with the patriarch of the Christians in this place—Huong. What a blessed family is this! Huong himself, his wife, his children, and his grandchildren were all assembled the evening before, having received a notice of our approach. The day, too, was a feast, the first of the year. My God, my dear friends, what a noble country! The terrible persecution which during these last years has been raging in Annam did not, in all this family of above forty persons, find a single apostate. How those countenances, scarred all over, brightened up at the sight of a priest about to offer up the Holy Sacrifice in their own house! Huong and his four sons were a little while ago in the prisons of this tyrant of Annam. Their bodies were lacerated with the rattan, but they were always constant in their faith, which makes them now so happy. Their lands and goods were under the care of Providence, and have not been lost. The family was so loved by all that the pagan chiefs themselves took care of their property, and have restored it to them; so that, after a persecution that has brought ruin to so many Christians, this family is in a state of affluence. After a short rest I prepared myself for Mass, they in the mean time making all ready in a large hall for the celebration of the sacred mysteries. From all sides numerous Christians poured in. They did not know of my arrival; but even when there is no priest to say Mass, every Sunday and holiday the faithful are accustomed to meet and pray, and then this venerable old man presides, who, by his virtues and lessons, stirs up their piety and fervour. The sun was rising when I finished Mass, and then for an hour more the Christians went on with their prayers and singing; and after that they came to pay their respects to the travelling missionary. This day was one of the happiest in my whole life; it was a prolonged festivity. Such kindness, such easy politeness, such profusion of hospitality, I shall never forget it. But we had to go. Borne along by the current, we proceeded down the river. . . . We were sailing rapidly onward when suddenly one of the boatmen, himself a confessor of the faith, interrupted me with the exclamation, "Father, we are now at the spot where the martyrs suffered." Close upon the river there was a sandy plain, and farther off a knoll level at the top. "There," said my companion, pointing to the more distant spot, "six Annamite priests were beheaded, and here, just by us, three others. I was present at their death. I dipped handkerchiefs in their blood; and I was also happy enough to steal some of their bodies, and to consign them to the ground." I was silent, for I could not reply; thoughts crowding on my mind that I am not able to express.

Alas, I said to myself, I am come too late. I looked on that holy ground intently. My God, if I had not the happiness of mingling my blood with Your martyrs, O may their blood draw down graces and blessings on this country and me!

'We continued our course down the stream, but not a word was spoken. From my abstracted manner and whole bearing it was easy to see that I did not wish to talk. But moving scenes were not yet over. A little farther on again my companion broke out, "This, father, is the spot where stood the house of that famous woman Leu." The name of this grand woman ought indeed to be retained in fondest recollection. When the persecution was at its height, Mgr. Cuenot came to her for shelter, and though she well knew she could not grant it except at the peril of her life, she was too faithful a Christian to refuse the hospitality asked. So in the house of this charitable woman the Bishop secreted himself. . . . . To have given him refuge made her a great criminal. She was put in chains, her house was razed to the ground, and her property confiscated and sold. The judge ordered her to trample on the cross; but it was to no purpose. This resolute woman excited the admiration of every one; it was not only courage and constancy that she showed, but a joyousness that communicated itself to the other confessors. Just before she laid her head on the block she had suckled her little infant, and then, the hour of her martyrdom being come, she placed the child in the arms of her aged mother, and she herself—mounted to glory.

She was a widow, and left four helpless children, once accustomed to every luxury, but now reduced to an abject poverty. May God have mercy on the orphans of the martyr!'

Such reminiscences of the persecution might constantly be excited. As late as 1866 Mgr. Theurel chances to make mention of one. 'Here we saw two living relics of the last persecution, a woman and a child. The woman's face is all covered with deep wounds made by leeches. The child, aged two only at the time of the persecution, had borne the cangue on its neck, and spent twenty days without any other nourishment than a betel-root leaf, which had been used to envelop a ball of rice. He chewed this bit by bit till he was let off.' It is but a scrap of the incidents of those days of terror that have been recorded, and by reading these we have proof of what fearful days they were.

CHAPTER XVI.

CONCLUSION.

It is not necessary to carry on this history any farther. The treaty with France brought a real end to the persecution. Slowly indeed and unwillingly was the cruel grasp of the persecutor relaxed; but compelled by superior force he finally gave up his prey. The prisons were emptied, the Christians returned to their homes, the missionaries resumed their labours, and travelled from village to village in safety. But the twelve years that have since passed, though years of progress, have not been without their serious hindrances. The government, at least ostensibly, has not been unfaithful to its engagements. The missionaries have at times thought that they had grounds of complaint, and that they were subjected to capricious restrictions, but whatever their suspicions of connivance they have not been able to bring home to the supreme authority the charge of open persecution. But though the government has refrained, the people have not. There has been a secret indignation widely felt at the intrusion of foreigners into the country, and at the submission which has been compelled, and at intervals the pent-up feelings have broken out, and brought considerable mischief on the Christians.

There is one special season when these excitements are roused, the time of the literates meeting together for their competitive examinations. Then, congregated in great numbers, they rouse the dormant hatred and prejudices latent in them all, and going back afterwards into their several districts and provinces, they stir up a flame that spreads wide destruction. They collect large bands, who go about the country armed, full of fury, bent on plunder, and these set on the Christian villages, rifle their houses, set fire to them, kill and drive out the inhabitants; and the misery and ruin that they cause is incalculable. Nobody opposes them. The mandarins, who are all themselves of this literary class, mostly sympathise with their fellows; the Christians appeal in vain, and find no redress; and it is not till the heat of the violence is worn out, or the government finds it dangerous to allow the continuance of the disorders, that the Christians are relieved from their calamities.

Very shortly after the treaty of peace had been signed troubles of this sort were felt. The malcontents formed a conspiracy, and meditated the deposition of Tudoc, if he would not fall in with their wishes, break with the French, and renew his persecutions of the Christians. They had commenced their attacks on the Christian villages, but the plot was discovered, and that danger was averted. Three years afterwards, for it is every three years that these examinations occur, there was a renewal of the same bitter feelings against the Christians. Mgr. Theurel, by the death of Mgr. Jeantet become the Vicar-Apostolic of Western Tonking, tells us of them and explains them. All had been quiet. He had completed a tour of his vicariate, in which everything had gone well. The Christians had crowded to meet him, the pagans had showed no unkindness, the mandarins had been civil; but immediately afterwards there was a violent outbreak of hatred. Christian villages were attacked and plundered, and the inhabitants driven out; the marauders had it all their own way, and nobody stopped them. Mgr. Gauthier tells a worse tale still. In Southern Tonking the violence and loss was greater, and many Christian villages were ruined by the inroads of the infuriated pagans.

But nothing that has happened since the days of actual persecution has equalled what has only lately reached our ears. In the last year letters came to hand which gave a picture of ruin and misery that was startling. Again the number of sufferers was told in thousands—seventy thousand exiles, five or six thousand slaughtered, more than a hundred villages burnt. Such was the last story of sorrow that came to us from Tonking. But it is to be hoped the trials are over. The government did, indeed, at the time make a show of opposition; the king's troops went against the rioters; there was at least the appearance of disapproval. But they are now bound by new engagements, and are aware that their French neighbours at Saigon will not patiently see a repetition of such violence.

The French in this instance have, indeed, interfered, and Tudoc has bound himself by a new treaty which promises a great amelioration of the condition of the Christians. On the 15th of March 1874 the treaty was concluded at Saigon, and on the 4th of August was ratified in the National Assembly in France.

The treaty, as we may see, promises much. By Article 9:

'His majesty the king of Annam, considering that the Catholic religion teaches men to do good, revokes and annuls all prohibitions directed against that religion, and grants to all his subjects permission to embrace it and freely practise its ordinances.

'Consequently the Christians of the kingdom of Annam may assemble without any hesitation in the churches for the exercise of worship. They shall not be obliged under any pretext to perform acts contrary to their religion, nor shall they be obliged to make any particular return to the authorities. They shall be admissible to all examinations and public employments without being required to perform any act contrary to their religion.

'His majesty promises to have all the registries of the Christian population made during the last fifteen years destroyed, and to treat the professors of that religion exactly like all his other subjects. He promises, moreover, to renew the prohibition so wisely enacted by him, and to forbid once more the use in common speech or written language of terms obnoxious to that religion, and to have corrections made in the articles of Ihap Dieu, in which such terms are employed.

'The bishops and missionaries shall have full power to enter the kingdom, and to travel whenever they wish to do so through their dioceses, provided with a passport from the governor of Cochin China, viséd by the minister of public worship or by the governor of the province. They may preach the Catholic religion in every part of the country; they shall not be subject to any particular supervision; and the villagers shall not be obliged to report to the mandarins their arrival, or their residence in the place, or their departure.

'The Annamist priests shall be free, like the missionaries, to exercise their ministry. If their conduct be reprehensible, and if, according to the terms of the law, the crimes committed by them should be punishable by the stick or the rattan, the penalty shall be commuted to an equivalent infliction.

'The bishops, missionaries, and Annamite priests shall have the right to purchase houses and lands; to build churches, hospitals, schools, orphanages, and all other edifices provided for religious purposes.

'The property taken from the Christians on account of their religion, and under penal sequestration, shall be restored to them.

'All the above regulations, without exception, shall apply to the Spanish missionaries as well as to the French.

'A royal edict, published immediately after the ratifications have been exchanged, shall announce the liberty granted by his majesty to his Christian subjects.'

It is well to be able thus to close our history. What the Christians have long been struggling to obtain they have now got—a freedom, a protection, that puts them on an equality with the other subjects of the empire, and exempts them from the liability of annoyances of which they have always complained. If the treaty is fairly carried out they may hope that not only shall they be delivered from direct persecution, but that they shall also no longer have to dread the evils that proceed from such bursts of hatred and violence as have lately caused them so much trouble.

THE END.

ALSO BY THE SAME AUTHOR.

THE COREAN MARTYRS:

A NARRATIVE.

New edition. Cloth, 2s.

A Narrative of Missions and Martyrdoms too little known in this Country.

'This is a notice of the martyrs who have fallen in this most interesting mission, and of the history of its rise and progress up to the present day.'—*Tablet.*

'No one can read this interesting volume without the most genuine admiration of and sympathy with such zeal and constancy.'—*Literary Churchman.*

ALSO EDITED BY THE SAME.

TRUE TO TRUST;

OR THE STORY OF A PORTRAIT.

A TALE OF THE TIME OF QUEEN ELIZABETH. Price 4s.

'A powerful and more than ordinarily well-written story of Catholic life at that eventful period so full of interest to Catholics. Several of the characters are admirably drawn. We are sure that it will prove a favourite amongst our young people.'—*Weekly Register.*

'The volume will be a welcome addition to the Catholic stories of days long gone by. The style is lucid, the plot very fairly shown, and the characters are natural. There is a religious and social tone about the book which makes it most acceptable. We are sure that amongst the young it will be a favourite.'—*Catholic Times.*

'A valuable addition to the narratives of the sufferings of our forefathers during that period.'—*Tablet.*

LONDON: BURNS AND OATES,
17 and 18 Portman Street, W., and 63 Paternoster Row, E.C.

www.ingramcontent.com/pod-product-compliance
Lightning Source LLC
Chambersburg PA
CBHW051722300426
44115CB00007B/421